To re

The British Olympics

Britain's Olympic heritage 1612 – 2012

The British Olympics
© English Heritage 2011

English Heritage is the
government's statutory
advisor on all aspects of the
historic environment

Fire Fly Avenue
Swindon SN2 2EH
www.english-heritage.org.uk

Design by Doug Cheeseman
Additional imaging by
Jörn Kröger

Series editor Simon Inglis

Production and additional
research by Jackie Spreckley
and Rachel Howard

Maps by Mark Fenton

Malavan Media is a creative
consultancy responsible
for the Played in Britain
series

www.playedinbritain.co.uk

Printed by Zrinski, Croatia

ISBN: 978 1 848020 58 0
Product code: 51538

The British Olympics
Britain's Olympic heritage 1612–2012

Martin Polley

Editor Simon Inglis

ENGLISH HERITAGE

From the Shropshire Archives, this whimsically worded poster from Oswestry in August 1834, advertising 'Ho-Limpyc Gaymes' and 'Ethennyun' or Athenian sports – with bear baiting clearly a prime attraction – is a reminder that the British embraced a form of Olympianism long before the modern Games began in 1896.

Page One Withy sticks at the ready, one for attack, one for defence, and with wicker hilts to protect their hands, participants at Robert Dover's Cotswold Olimpicks in 2009 put on a demonstration of cudgel fighting. Such contests have featured at the Games since the 17th century, the original object being to draw blood from one's opponent's head.

Page Two Runners gather at Windsor Castle before the start of the 1908 Olympic marathon, a race best remembered not for the victory of New Yorker Johnny Hayes (number 26, second from the left), but for the disqualification of the Italian Dorando Pietri.

Contents

Chapter One

Introduction

Medals await the victors at the 2009 Wenlock Olympian Games, an event that originated in 1850 and which, forty years later, was attended by the founder of the IOC, Pierre de Coubertin. There are numerous strands to Britain's Olympic history, but none link more directly to the modern Olympic movement than those that lead back to this small town in Shropshire.

Ever since that heart-stopping moment in Singapore on July 6 2005 when the president of the International Olympic Committee, Jacques Rogge, announced that the Games of the 30th Olympiad were to be staged in London, the whole issue of the Olympic and Paralympic Games has come to the fore in British public life.

Here, with no hyperbole intended, was history in the making. By winning the vote London was to become the first city since the modern Olympics were revived in 1896 to host a third Games, following on from the Games of the 4th Olympiad in 1908 and of the 14th in 1948.

For the nation's Olympians and would-be Olympians the decision offered the enticing prospect of competing for gold medals in front of their home crowd for the first, and almost certainly the only occasion in their lifetime.

For Londoners there arose the excitement, the anticipation and the potentially alarming costs and upheaval of hosting arguably the world's largest international event, sporting or otherwise.

And for the organisations and agencies tasked with the immense responsibility of preparing for and organising the 2012 Games, there was the challenge of delivering a daunting schedule of works after eight years of planning.

So many lives affected, so much to be done.

Inevitably, once work commenced on the main Olympic site in the Lower Lea Valley in 2006 it became evident that there were to be winners and losers. Local residents protested that an area some parties were dismissing as a post-industrial wilderness – littered with poor quality buildings and interlaced by stagnant backwaters – was in parts a haven of community life, with pockets of long established commerce, recreational use, allotments and wildlife. Meanwhile, as the effects of an unexpected credit crunch started to bite, questions were raised, and have continued to be raised as to the wisdom of investing £9 billion, nearly double the original estimate, ostensibly on a mere sporting event.

Could all this disruption and expenditure really be merited for just over four weeks of sport?

It is not for this book to tackle these issues, other than to comment that since at least the end of the First World War community activists and local politicians in east London have cursed a succession of governments for ignoring the needs of the area.

Nor can it be denied that those few weeks of sport in the summer of 2012 have kickstarted one of the most significant urban redevelopment programmes ever seen in Britain, bringing jobs, housing, transport improvements and the creation of the largest urban park this country has seen in the last hundred years.

In effect, redrawing the map of London.

From a national perspective it is also worth noting how, over the last two decades, sport has been repeatedly used as a catalyst to regenerate blighted areas. In common with art galleries and museums, the economic benefits of stadiums and aquatic centres, velodromes and arenas have been put to the test all over Britain, on Teesside and Wearside, in the Don Valley and the Taff Valley, in the Eastlands area of Manchester, where the Commonwealth Games took place in 2002, and in the East End of Glasgow, the focus of the forthcoming Commonwealth Games, due to be staged in 2014.

But it is from a historical, rather than a planning or economic perspective that this book seeks to contextualise the 2012 Olympic and Paralympic Games.

For not only do the Games amount to a great deal more than just 31 days of sport and ceremonies, they also represent the latest manifestation of a deeply rooted engagement between the British people and the philosophies and practices, real and imagined, of the ancient Olympic Games.

It is an engagement that predates the bid for 2012, and even the staging of the 1948 and 1908 Games. It predates also the contribution of British individuals to the formation of the IOC in 1894, and before that the staging of various Olympic-styled events around Britain, such as in Much Wenlock (see left), from the mid 19th century.

It is in fact an engagement that can be traced back at least four centuries, to when a fun-loving Catholic Royalist became involved in the running of his local Whitsuntide festival near the Gloucestershire town of Chipping Campden. The year, conveniently for those of us in search of neat straplines, was 1612. But much more important than that, Robert Dover's Cotswold Olimpicks, as they eventually became known, were the first recorded public games to have adopted the Olympic title since the ancient Games after which they were named came to an end, some 1,200 years earlier.

Quite possibly, as we discuss in Chapter Three, there were other 'Olimpick' Games in Britain during the same period, especially given that references to the ancient Olympics appear in the slightly earlier works of Shakespeare (as detailed in Chapter Two). But as far as historians have been able to ascertain, the Cotswold Olimpicks are the earliest to have been named as such, not only in Britain but anywhere in the post-classical world.

Once again therefore, it is no hyperbole to state that, with the obvious exception of Greece, no nation can claim to have nurtured such longstanding cultural and sporting links with the Olympics, ancient or modern, as can Britain.

This book is a study of those links. It is not, we emphasise, an attempt to somehow assert Britain's superiority within the Olympic movement. Other nations, such as France, Italy, Germany and the United States, plus of course Greece, have made equally significant contributions since the end of the 19th century.

Yet nor should we be afraid to celebrate the fact that Britain's Olympic heritage is unique, in a global context, or that, whether we view the coming 2012 Games with joy or trepidation, with indifference or even with hostility, there are elements within them that have, most assuredly, been 'Made in Britain'.

In 1996, when English football stadiums hosted the European Championships, a stirring terrace anthem called *Three Lions* was penned to emphasise the game's historic roots. Sung with gusto, at its core was the memorable chorus 'football's coming home'.

It would be overstretching the point to suggest that the return of the Olympic Games to London in 2012 be greeted by a similar expression of homecoming.

But Britain is, without doubt, familiar ground.

Olympianism and athleticism

The starting point is, of course, Olympia, the site of the ancient Games, held every four years in honour of the god Zeus, from at least 776 BC until around AD 393.

From the Renaissance onwards European scholars were captivated by details of the religious rituals and sporting practices reported to have taken place at Olympia, even if, for three centuries or more, their prime sources of information were an assortment of classical texts handed down through the generations, followed in later years by the accounts of travellers and antiquarians who had journeyed to the ruins. On which note, it is no coincidence that, as we relate in Chapter Two, the first travellers known to have identified and recorded the parlous state of the site at Olympia, albeit almost in passing, were three Englishmen, during the 1760s.

Patently for Christian scholars, the pagan rites and rituals of Olympianism were of academic interest only. But even if they could take nothing of spiritual value from the worship of Zeus, what was there in the Olympian cult of athleticism that might yield to modern nations something of the perceived strength and purpose of ancient Greece? Could Renaissance man be Olympian in body whilst remaining Christian in his soul?

Certainly Robert Dover, the central figure in Chapter Three, made no conscious attempt himself to recreate the ancient Olympics, either in form or spirit. Rather, it was left to others, through the medium of poetry, to make the connection between his annual Games and those of Olympia. In fact if Dover had any underlying philosophy, other than a clear love of merry-making and spectacle, it was as an opponent of Puritanism rather than as a proponent of athleticism.

Britain's earliest Olympic Games, therefore, were neither re-enactments of the ancient Games nor sports meetings in the modern sense. For the most part, throughout the 17th and 18th centuries they were simply rural festivals that assumed the name 'Olimpick' or 'Olympick' in the same way that today one sees events such as pea throwing in Lewes or black pudding throwing in Ramsbottom being mischievously described as 'world championships'. 'Olympick' was a badge of excellence, not of provenance.

Not that frivolity should ever be dismissed when considering these early Olympics. Their blend of sport, festivities and drinking was then, and remains in British sporting circles, an entirely serious business. Moreover, there were some tempting prizes to be won at these »

Seen here on tour at the Kobe City Museum in Japan in March 2011, this model of Olympia is one of Britain's most successful contributions to the dissemination of Olympic history. Built by model maker Kim Allen for the British Museum in 1980 and based on research by curator Judith Swaddling and illustrator Sue Bird, the model depicts Olympia in around 100 BC. Apart from several airings at the British Museum itself, with another to follow in 2012, the model has been exhibited all over Britain, Europe, the Far East, Latin America and the USA, and after over 30 years on the road continues to be in demand.

» Games, in the form of such coveted commodities as pigs, tea, gloves and belts, each more valued than any Olympian-style laurel wreath would have been.

That the term 'Olympic' was only loosely applied was further demonstrated in the early 19th century when it was increasingly adopted by the promoters of equestrian displays. One such individual was Britain's first black circus master, Pablo Fanque, best remembered for taking his Circus Royal to Rochdale in 1843, where it performed 'For the Benefit of Mr Kite' – as immortalised on the Beatles' album *Sgt Pepper's Lonely Hearts Club Band*.

Fanque's interpretation of the 'Olympian Games', and that of his counterparts in the world of showmanship, can readily be imagined; a burlesque blend perhaps of tricks on horseback and mock-chariot races.

Only from the 1850s onwards do we start to see in Britain a sustained effort to invest in the word 'Olympic' those philosophies and practices that would, in the 1890s, inform the nascent 'Olympism' of the early IOC.

As we will detail further in Chapters Four and Five, this development was a consequence, and also an expression of the steady 19th century shift in sporting culture from those essentially rough-and-tumble games and bloodsports of the pre-industrial era – cudgel fighting, cock fighting and the like – to the so-called 'rational' sports of the later Victorian period.

In the wider context this trend led to the emergence of such sports as Association football, rugby football and lawn tennis, with their written codes, specialised equipment, governing bodies and tailor-made arenas. But running parallel with their evolution there appeared at the Wenlock Olympian Games, first in 1850, a genuine attempt to translate the values of the ancient Olympic Games to the lives of ordinary Victorian citizens. Or at least, the perceived values.

William Penny Brookes, the Much Wenlock doctor whose ideas were to have such a seminal influence on the founder of the IOC, Pierre de Coubertin, was far more concerned with the moral and educational benefits to be accrued from sport than he was with sport *per se*. Indeed it was 'physical education' for which he campaigned most vigorously. Not the winning or losing, but the taking part, for all participants, rich and poor, youths and adults.

As we will often be reminded, Brookes' interpretation of the Olympian ideal, and that of many of his fellow British Olympians during the 19th century, bore little resemblance to what we now know was the reality of the ancient Games, where athletes were in effect hardened professionals who were handsomely rewarded for their efforts. But then we have the benefit of data arising from over a century of archaeological excavations at Olympia,

backed up by a wealth of historical research, whereas Brookes and his contemporaries had to rely almost entirely on the reading of available classical texts.

But in any case, as had been the case with Robert Dover, Brookes was primarily interested not in a strict interpretation of ancient Olympian ideals so much as adapting them to the times in which he lived.

This theme of continual adaptation and re-interpretation of Olympianism forms a thread throughout this book. Just as the ancient Games of the later Roman period differed from their earlier incarnation during the Classical and Hellenistic periods, each modern generation has sought to borrow from Olympia the qualities and characteristics that seem best to meet contemporary social and cultural demands.

A prime example of this is the importance attached to the Olympic torch relay, which sees runners bearing a 'sacred flame' from Olympia to the host stadium. On the surface it appears to be a truly authentic tradition, and yet it dates only from the 1936 Olympic Games in Berlin, where it was dreamt up by Nazi propagandists.

In the 19th century British Olympians proved equally adept at introducing rituals and practices that would later become enshrined in the modern Games.

In Chapter Five, for example, we will see how during the 1860s, the now accepted practice of awarding medals, rather than laurel wreaths, was introduced at Liverpool's Olympic Festivals, under the direction of the charismatic eccentric, John Hulley. One gold medal was awarded to the Festival's best overall performer, with silver medals being presented to the winners of individual events. (In fact the current hierarchy of gold, silver and bronze also emanates from Britain, having been introduced by the organisers of the London Games in 1908.)

Also from Liverpool in the 1860s came the strict requirement that only amateur athletes could take part in Olympic Festivals, and that, in contrast to the Wenlock Olympian Games, no monetary prizes would be offered. Both these principles would of course become central tenets of the IOC once it formed in 1894.

Another element of the modern Olympic movement to have first seen the light in Britain was the concept of a national body for Olympians. Formed in 1865, the National Olympian Association brought together the leading figures from Much Wenlock, Liverpool, Manchester and London. In Chapter Six we analyse why the NOA was ultimately unsuccessful and shortlived, despite making a promising start with its first annual Games at Crystal Palace in 1866.

By this time there were stirrings in Greece, where in 1859 a businessman and philanthropist, Evangelis

Zappas, had organised his own revivalist Games in Athens. Yet in the years to come it would be to England that the young Pierre de Coubertin would turn, time after time, in his own quest for knowledge.

Inspired by the novel *Tom Brown's School Days*, Coubertin made his first visit to England in 1883. In Chapter Eight we relate how in a subsequent visit he experienced, in his own words, something of an epiphany in the chapel at Rugby School, sitting by the tomb of his hero, Thomas Arnold. Coubertin would glean yet further inspiration from visiting Henley, where he saw in the strict practices of the Regatta Committee the essence of the amateur ideal. Here were Christian gentlemen whose faith in the cult of athleticism appeared to open a door to a new, affirmative form of masculine development. (Coubertin was no believer in female participation in sport.)

And then, through the pages of *The Times*, Coubertin gained another British mentor. For nearly forty years William Penny Brookes had espoused muscular Christian values, summed up by a line borrowed from the works of Juvenal, *Mens Sana In Corpore Sano*, 'a healthy mind in a healthy body'. For supporters of Brookes' campaign for physical education, the cult of athleticism was in itself not enough. Sporting excellence had to be accompanied by intellectual development and high moral values.

Prior to meeting Brookes in 1890, Coubertin's principal purpose had been to gather ideas from England and other nations that might usefully be applied in the French educational system. Thereafter, having seen the Wenlock Olympian Games in the flesh, he launched a somewhat different campaign, to garner support for a full scale international revival of the Olympics.

There can be little doubt, in an age of improving communications and international travel that, if not Coubertin, then someone else would have eventually embarked upon a similar mission. But whoever it might have been, in 1890s Europe there really was only one tried and tested model on which to base such a proposal, and that was the one found within sporting circles in Britain. Indeed the annual championships of the Amateur Athletic Association (AAA) were unrivalled anywhere in the world in terms of their organisation and performance levels.

Thus we can say that not only did British Olympians play a part in laying the philosophical foundations of a revival, but also that it was on the playing fields of England, and on the nation's running tracks and rivers, that the template for Coubertin's revivalist Games was to be found. How to lay a track, how to organise a multi-sport event, what rules to apply – all these practical issues had already been tried and tested in Britain.

In that sense, the modern Olympics have as much, if not more in common with a typical athletics meeting in Victorian Britain than they do with the format of the ancient Games as they were staged at Olympia.

That is not to say that the British welcomed Coubertin's proposals. Far from it. True, certain individuals did play key roles during the early years of the IOC after its formation in 1894. Charles Herbert, the Honorary Secretary of the AAA, was for example described by Coubertin as one of three most important figures in the organisation, along with himself and William Milligan Sloane, a professor of history at the University of Princeton. Also active in the early IOC was the Reverend Robert de Courcy Laffan, a one-time headmaster at Cheltenham College.

But overall, the majority of Britain's sporting administrators showed little or no interest. With a packed, and well established domestic sporting calendar already in place, what need did they have for an upstart tournament for rookie nations?

In Chapter Nine we will see how the staging of the Games of the 4th Olympiad in London in 1908 reflected this ambivalence, and in Chapter Ten, how in 1948 Britain seemed finally to embrace modern Olympism in its purest philosophical sense; that of a movement designed to bring nations together through the medium of sport.

One key component of Olympism – a term coined to differentiate the IOC's philosophy from that of the ancient cult of Olympianism – was, in Coubertin's words, 'physical superiority'.

In its post-Coubertin evolution Olympism was to gain a further strand by encompassing the participation of individuals who were not superior, but who had physical disabilities. In Chapter Eleven we relate how this seismic shift first saw light, again in England, in the spinal injuries unit of Stoke Mandeville Hospital.

And so two parallel narratives were to emerge during the 20th century. On one hand there grew in strength, purpose and inclusivity the Olympic Games of the IOC, with all its power, prestige and media exposure.

On the other there remained a very British brand of Olympianism, with its emphasis on community, localism and tradition. Robert Dover's Cotswold Olimpicks, having fallen into abeyance after 1852, made a spirited comeback during the 1960s. Much Wenlock's Olympian Games, a casualty of indifference during the 1930s, followed suit in the 1970s. Both Games continue to be staged annually, and are fully described in Chapters Three and Four.

In doing this, we shall also describe how a number of British historians from the 1980s onwards worked hard to persuade the IOC that the Cotswold and Wenlock »

British Olympian Denise Lewis tries out a prototype of the 2012 Olympic torch. As with so many Olympic symbols its design is loaded with meaning. Its three sides echo the three Olympic values of respect, excellence and friendship, the three words of the Olympic motto – *Citius, Altius, Fortius* (faster, higher, stronger) – and the three occasions on which London has hosted the Games. It also has 8,000 perforations, one for each of the runners expected to bear the flame from Olympia to London.

As we know, the torch relay has no historical links with Olympia at all. But then 'invented tradition', as defined by the historian Eric Hobsbawm, has always been something of a tradition in the Olympic narrative.

One of London's famed Blue Badge Tourist Guides shows visitors the scale of the 2012 Olympic site. Before the bid was won, at most only one or two tours passed this way per year. By mid 2011 that figure had rocketed to some 12–15 walking tours and 10–20 coach tours... per day. Between September 2007 and May 2011 the coach tours alone transported 185,000 tourists and official visitors, the Queen included.

This image was taken from the View Tube, a community venue offering information and facilities for tourists and schoolgroups. In February 2011 it celebrated its 100,000th visitor.

Never before has this part of London attracted so much interest.

≫ Games deserve to be acknowledged as integral parts of the official Olympic back story. That they succeeded, most of all on behalf of Much Wenlock, was borne out by the visit to the Shropshire town of the IOC President, Juan Antonio Samaranch, in 1994, as part of the organisation's centenary celebrations, and more recently by the choice of the name 'Wenlock' for one of the 2012 mascots ('Mandeville' being the other).

Much less acknowledged, at least so far, has been the contribution of the Liverpool Olympic Festivals of the 1860s. Hopefully Chapter Five of this book will serve to bring Liverpool's case to the fore of historical debate.

But as far as one other series of Olympic Games in Britain is concerned, there is surely no chance of any belated recognition by the IOC.

Chapter Seven tells the story of the Morpeth Olympic Games in Northumberland. Held between 1870 and 1958, the fact that the organisers adopted the tag 'Olympic' in around 1882, before the IOC was formed, is unlikely to swing mainstream opinion. For these were Games in which professional athletes were allowed to enter, where gambling was commonplace, and where monetary prizes were unashamedly on offer.

We include the Morpeth Games nevertheless in order to demonstrate that there can never be one single reading of Olympic history; that whether one follows the trail of the IOC Games, or the story of Britain's homegrown Olympianism, there are always alternative realities.

The road to 2012

At the outset we stated that Britain's engagement with the Olympics goes back to at least 1612. In the same vein it is important to recall that the road to 2012 did not begin in Singapore in 2005. In fact, by then Britain had been on the hunt for its third Olympic Games for some 30 years.

This quest began when, in 1975, the Greater London Council considered bidding for the 1984 Olympics as a means of regenerating the delapidated Isle of Dogs.

Then in February 1976 a Greater London Councillor called Roland Freeman proposed that instead London should bid for the 1988 Games, basing them in the derelict docklands area. To fund this, Freeman suggested, a national lottery should be set up.

The Conservative government of the day was not impressed. Nor was one civil servant. A 'load of codswallop' was his barbed reaction. But in any case, four years later the GLC finally voted against the plan, and it would be left to the financial sector to transform that part of the docklands which lies to the south of the 2012 site.

From London attention next switched to Birmingham. With full backing from the British Olympic Association (BOA) and, this time, from the government, in 1986 Birmingham put in a bid for the 1992 Games, choosing a site at Bickenhall, near the National Exhibition Centre.

Barcelona won on that occasion, although Birmingham's bid did at least get beyond the first round of voting, along with rivals Paris, Brisbane and Belgrade. The experience also persuaded Birmingham City Council to put forward Bickenhill as the site for a new national stadium in 1996, an attempt that also failed when Wembley was finally chosen as the preferred location.

But if there proved to be no lasting legacy of Birmingham's Olympic dreams, the same cannot be said for those of Manchester.

Manchester started planning its own Olympic bid in 1985, this time for the 1996 Games. Centred upon a site in the Trafford area, this bid also lost out in the second round of votes, Atlanta being the final winner. Undeterred, Manchester followed this up with a second bid, this time for the 2000 Games, based on a blighted area of east Manchester.

Again, the bid failed, this time having got through to the third round of voting, where it lost out to Beijing and to the eventual winner, Sydney.

Rather than give up, however, Manchester then adapted its plans and put in a bid for the Commonwealth Games of 2002. This was successful, and resulted in the construction of the £110 million City of Manchester Stadium, designed by Arup Associates to be converted into a football-only venue after the Games.

In a very real sense, therefore, Manchester's Olympic hopes did yield a concrete legacy, bequeathing not only the 48,000 capacity stadium where Manchester City now play, but also a 21,000 seat indoor arena, the National Cycling Centre, and two 50m swimming pools at the Manchester Aquatics Centre.

Birmingham and Manchester's experiences had the further effect of finally persuading the BOA and the government that if Britain was ever to host a third Olympics, the bid would have to come from London.

Thus the road to 2012 took three decades to negotiate, and is yet another reminder that Britain's engagement with the Olympics is by no means a recent phenomenon.

In search of Britain's Olympic heritage

Surveying the scene in the Lower Lea Valley today – with its 80,000 capacity Olympic Stadium, the magnificent velodrome, the sweeping lines of Zaha Hadid's Aquatics Centre and the mass of apartment blocks forming the athletes' village – it is hard to imagine that all trace of the 2012 Games might one day be swept away and forgotten.

But then it is the folly of every generation to believe that its achievements and monuments will last forever.

Apart from a memorial on the site of the Great Stadium at White City, and a single marathon distance marker, in Eton, there are no tangible commemorations of the 1908 Games; not even on those buildings that hosted some of the Olympic events and remain standing.

It is a similar tale for the surviving locations used in 1948. The new Wembley Stadium, it is true, has on display the bowl and pedestal that housed the Olympic flame (as featured on the cover), and also the two plaques recording the athletes who won gold medals in the stadium.

But elsewhere, nothing, or at least nothing formal, not even at the Wembley Arena or at the Herne Hill cycle track, the two most prominent surviving venues from those 'austerity' Olympics, nor at any of the other venues where lesser ranking or preliminary matches took place; the likes of Brentford's Griffin Park, Fulham's Craven Cottage and the Polytechnic Grounds at Chiswick.

In each of those cases and several more featured in Chapter Ten, the only record of anything Olympic-related ever having taken place there is in the record books.

As we see in Chapter Twelve, Britain's Olympians have been rather better served. Admittedly some of these commemorations are hardly more than tokenistic; the naming of streets after individuals, for example. But some, such as the statue of Sir Steve Redgrave at Marlow, and the commemoration of Mary Rand's record breaking long jump in 1964, at Wells, will surely continue to inspire the public for many years to come.

Then there are the artefacts left over from previous Olympics. In order to compile this book we have had to cast our net widely amongst a number of museums, archives and collections. The full extent of these holdings may be seen in the Credits section, and range from national institutions such as the V&A, the British Library and the National Archives, and from specialist collections at the River and Rowing Museum in Henley, the University of Westminster and Stoke Mandeville Hospital, to a host of local studies archives and the private holdings of members of the Society of Olympic Collectors.

In this respect, the coming of the 2012 Games has proved a great boon, galvanising the nation's curators and collectors to seek out anything and everything that has even the slightest Olympic connection.

Even so, there remains a considerable amount of material outside the public realm. At the time of writing, at various auction houses or on internet auction sites one could bid for any number of Olympic related pieces of ephemera; badges, postcards, ticket stubs, posters, handbooks and even medals.

How different will be the ephemera associated with the Games in 2012? Most likely, none will have come from any unofficial sources, given how closely the IOC, in protecting its brand and the interests of its commercial partners, now controls the use of any words or symbols associated with the Olympics. Certainly there could be no 'Olympic Games' in today's Morpeth.

Yet surprisingly, this was not Pierre de Coubertin's precise intention. In the August 1910 edition of *Revue Olympique* he wrote '…it is impossible to overemphasise the fact that the word "Olympic" cannot and should not be used except for gatherings of a variety of sports.' But he then added, 'The term is in the public domain. If you are not afraid of looking ridiculous, and if your efforts are considerable enough to be compared to what goes into organising a standard Olympiad, go ahead and use it. No one has the right to prevent you from doing so.'

Not so today. On the other hand, Coubertin also disapproved of women taking part in the Olympics, and could never have imagined such events as the Paralympics or the Special Olympics taking place. Nor, that within half a century of his death, barriers to the participation of professional athletes would also come tumbling down.

And so the world, and the Olympics, have moved on. Today the IOC summarises Olympism as being 'a philosophy of life, exalting and combining in a balanced whole the qualities of body, will and mind'.

How this, and other such lofty ideals have left their mark over the last four centuries in Britain, it is now our intention to investigate.

British historians have long played an active role in researching Olympic history, one reason why the International Society of Olympic Historians came to be founded at the Duke of Clarence pub in Holland Park, London, in 1991. The pub is no more, but the ISOH thrives. Among its founders were Ian Buchanan, Stan Greenberg and Peter Matthews. Other British contributors have included Peter Lovesey, Philip Barker and both Don Anthony – who threw the discus at the 1956 Olympics and who did much to advance the claims of Much Wenlock to its rightful place in Olympic history – and Francis Burns, who performed a similar role on behalf of the Cotswold Games.

But it was to be another Englishman who laid the trail, over two hundred years earlier…

Chapter Two

Olympia and Britannia

'Olympia has since been forgotten in its vicinity, but the name will be ever respected, as venerable for its precious era, by the chronologer and historian.'

So wrote the classical scholar Richard Chandler in *Travels in Asia Minor and Greece*, his account of how he, the architect Nicholas Revett (*above*) and artist William Pars identified the site of Olympia during an expedition from 1764–66.

No portraits of either Chandler or Pars have survived, but like Revett their work remains a vital source for scholars.

In 1764, at a time when all things pertaining to the classical world were held in thrall by English scholars and aesthetes, a party of three gentlemen set off on an expedition, their aim being to visit and record the sites and antiquities of Asia Minor and Greece, and to bring home any fragments they could find for further study.

Making up the party was an architect, Nicholas Revett (*left*), a young artist, William Pars, and the group's leader, a 27 year old classical scholar, Richard Chandler.

Backing the expedition was the London based Society of Dilettanti, formed in the 1730s by sundry aristocrats and scholars who had all been on the Grand Tour. Horace Walpole noted (in a letter to Sir Horace Mann, in April 1743) that although the 'nominal qualification' for membership of the Society was that candidates should have travelled to Italy, the real one was 'being drunk'.

But Chandler, Revett and Pars were no dilettantes. Instead, it was this trio who, during the course of an arduous two and a half year trek, and with a copy of Pausanius's 2nd century *Description of Greece* to hand, found their way to the lost site of Olympia.

No doubt other travellers had come across the site before. Had the English party not gone there, no doubt, in time, other scholars would have identified it. But it was no accident that it was Englishmen who searched for and first recorded Olympia in the modern world. For in Britain, perhaps more than in any other part of Europe, tales of ancient Olympia, and of the Olympic Games in particular, were already well entrenched in the popular imagination.

In the following chapter we will see how, since at least 1612, this fascination had already given rise to a series of 'Olympic' Games in the Cotswolds and other parts of England. But just as importantly, underpinning these games lay an engagement with the very notion of Olympianism itself.

Indeed the first ever recorded use of the word Olympian in the English language – according to the Oxford English Dictionary – is to be found in William Shakespeare's *Henry VI, Part 3*, penned in about 1591.

In the play, set during the Wars of the Roses, with the murderous Battle of Towton (which took place in 1461) in full flow, George Plantagenet addresses his fellow Yorkist, the Earl of Warwick, thus:

Yet let us all together to our troops,
And give them leave to fly that will not stay;
And call them pillars that will stand to us;
And, if we thrive, promise them such rewards
As victors wear at the Olympian games:
This may plant courage in their quailing breasts;
For yet is hope of life and victory. (Act 2, scene 3)

Just over a decade later, Shakespeare made a further allusion to the Games in *Troilus and Cressida*. In this instance, the Greek prince Nestor says to the 'gallant Trojan' Hector:

And I have seen thee pause, and take thy breath,
When that a ring of Greeks have hemm'd thee in,
Like an Olympian wrestling. (Act 4, scene 5)

As the more educated members of the audience would have known, the plot of *Troilus and Cressida* leaned heavily on the plot of *The Iliad*, Homer's epic poem of around the 8th century BC, which includes one of the earliest known references to the Olympic Games in literature. *The Iliad* had first appeared in English translation in 1598, and was one of a number of classical texts, including the works of Plutarch, Pindar and Herodotus, now available to English readers in printed form.

But before we look further at how these works brought alive the history of the Olympics to the scholars of 16th and 17th century Britain, and how they informed attitudes towards sport and sporting festivals in general, let us first remind ourselves of the ancient Games and their place in the classical world.

The Ancient Olympic Games

Held at a site called Olympia, near the town of Elis, in the western Peloponnese, the Olympian or Olympic Games formed one element of a religious festival dedicated to Zeus, that most omnipotent amongst the pantheon of all Greek gods. (To the Romans he was known as Jupiter.)

The earliest record of the Games dates from 776 BC, but it is certain they originated long before then. Some historians suggest that they may date from as early as 1300 BC. Taking place in the midst of summer, the Olympics were the largest of four festivals staged by the

Greeks in a four year cycle known as an Olympiad. In the first year of this cycle the Pythian Games, dedicated to Apollo, were staged at Delphi. The following year, the Nemean Games were staged in honour of Zeus, at Nemea. In the third year, the Isthmian Games took place at Corinth and were dedicated to Poseidon. The cycle then reached its climax with the Olympic Games.

From the 5th century BC onwards, essentially five types of sporting activity were contested at Olympia over a period of five days: running, jumping, throwing, combat and equestrian sports.

Before the Romans conquered Greece in the 2nd century BC, participation was limited to freeborn Greeks, and victors received only token honours, in the form of an olive wreath. Some were also allowed to have a statue of themselves dedicated in the Altis, the sacred part of the site forming the Sanctuary of Zeus.

In later centuries entrants came from across the Roman Empire – though none from Britannia were ever recorded – and while it is anachronistic to use such modern terms as amateurs and professionals, it is clear that many competitors were patronised (or sponsored as we would now say) to train and compete, and that for some athletes victory at Olympia brought immense wealth and status.

Three categories of individuals were banned from taking part and even from watching the Games: women, slaves and 'impious' persons.

One of the most important facets of the Games was the Olympic truce. This required that for the duration of the Games, all wars and disputes within the Hellenic world be suspended, and all competitors granted safe passage to Olympia.

By the end of the 3rd century AD the Olympics appear to have gone into decline. The last known official roster of victors appeared in AD 267, after which references to the Games become more sporadic, culminating in the last known Olympic victor, an Armenian prince, in AD 369.

Although we have no exact date for the final staging of the Games, they were formally proscribed as an anti-pagan measure in AD 393 by Theodosius, a veteran of military campaigns in Britannia and the last Emperor to preside over a single Roman Empire before it divided into eastern and western sections.

So, from at least 776 BC until AD 393, a period spanning nearly 1200 years, the Olympic Games formed an important part in the religious, political and cultural life of both the Greek and Roman spheres of influence. By comparison, the modern Olympics will celebrate only their 116th year in existence in 2012.

As for other sports festivals, after Theodosius's death they continued elsewhere for several centuries, for

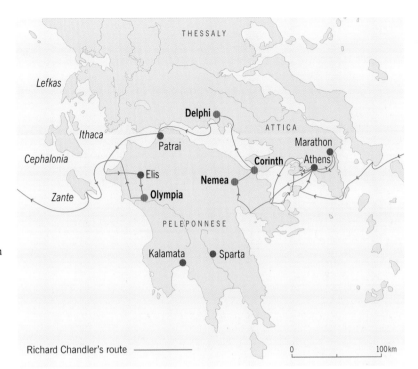

Richard Chandler's route ———————

0   100km

example in Antioch until AD 510, when they were finally banned by the Emperor Justinian.

Olympia itself, meanwhile, suffered from a series of devastating blows, man-made and natural.

In AD 426 the Temple of Zeus was burnt down by decree of the eastern Emperor in Constantinople, Theodosius the Younger. Christians then moved in and built a church, while looters helped themselves to stone from the crumbling buildings before the site was almost completely destroyed by a series of earthquakes between AD 522 and 551. The ruins were then gradually subsumed by erosion from the nearby Mount Kronos and by flooding from the rivers Alpheios and Kladeos, both of which flank the site. Within barely two centuries of the final Games, the site was lost under five metres of debris.

So overgrown and ruinous did Olympia become that for around 1,000 years its identity and location were all but forgotten. Until, that is, Richard Chandler and his party arrived in the mid 1760s.

The Olympics in classical literature
Although the physical evidence lay undiscovered for centuries, the Games themselves lived on in numerous records from the classical world, written by historians, »

The four year cycle of an ancient Olympiad began with the Pythian Games at Delphi, then moved on to Nemea and Corinth, before concluding at Olympia. After fourteen months travelling in Asia Minor the English scholar Richard Chandler and his party visited all four Games sites during 1765–66.

This is Discobolus, the discus thrower, a figure who appears in various portrayals throughout this book (*see for example page 129*). The original Greek bronze, attributed to Myron, was created in the 5th century BC. However this marble copy, discovered in Tivoli in 1790, dates from the first century AD. It was subsequently purchased by the British Museum in 1805, and although later found to have been wrongly restored, with its head pointing away, rather than towards the discus, it remains an enduring representation of the Greek cult of athleticism.

▲ Published in an American magazine, *The Century,* in April 1896, to coincide with the staging of the first modern Olympics in Athens, this illustration by the French artist **André Castaigne** portrays a victor at the ancient Olympic Games bowing before the towering **statue of Zeus**. The Games' revival inspired a legion of writers and artists to imagine how Olympia might have looked and how the Games were conducted.

One such individual was the English writer and cartoonist **Osbert Lancaster**, who just before the 1948 London Olympics penned his own witty, yet still pertinent description of the people most likely to have attended the ancient Olympics, and how for many of them sport was a mere sideshow to the Games' real purpose.

'The crowd which assembled in this spot every fourth year on the first full moon after the summer solstice would, one fancies, after one had got over the initial strangeness of costume and appearance and abandoned the preconceptions engendered in the classical Sixth, have gradually revealed itself as strangely familiar in all its diversity.

'The athletes themselves, as quarrelsome and self-conscious as prima-donnas, fresh from a training as specialized and prolonged, if in theory more intellectual, as that to which professional baseballers are subjected; the old afficionados, forever recalling bygone triumphs whose whole life consisted in a constant pilgrimage from Delphi to Nemea, from the Isthmus to Olympia; the horsy contingent who came solely for the chariot racing and the maiden gentlemen whose interest in the competitors was not entirely inspired by a passion for sport; for all these it would not be hard to find parallels at Newmarket or Lord's.

'But in addition there would be a number of the other types whose modern counterparts could only be found at St. Moritz and Le Touquet – the international good-timers, the "café society" of the Mediterranean world. Half-Asiatic princelings from Lydia and Cappadocia, the Maharajahs of antiquity, rich beyond dreams of avarice, with their hosts of hangers-on and strings of the most expensive bloodstock; Syracusan magnates with recently acquired fortunes and strong colonial accents; international bankers and financiers from Alexandria and Antioch and aggressive Roman tourists playing the role of the Transatlantic millionaires whom facially, to judge by the evidence of their portrait busts, they so strangely resembled: it was to the long-continued patronage of such visitors that the organizers of the festival were accustomed to look for their principal support.

'How munificent that support could on occasion prove is shown by the remains of the elaborate fountain, supplied with running water brought from a considerable distance and at immense expense, presented by that ostentatiously generous old culture-snob, Herodes Atticus.

'However, for all their seeming familiarity, this public was largely Greek, and in one respect, therefore, the atmosphere would have differed considerably from that prevailing at any Anglo-Saxon gathering; however various the reasons which had drawn all these patrons to the extreme west of the Peloponnese from all over the Mediterranean world, reasons of sport, of pleasure, of patriotism or purely snobbish, all would pursue in common an intense and insatiable passion for politics.

'The truce enforced by religious sanction that prevailed, no matter what contests were raging elsewhere, not only at Olympia itself but also for the period of the games along all the roads leading to it, provided the ideal opportunity for the representatives or agents of a dozen semi-independent cities and states to take soundings, cement alliances, dissolve coalitions, detach by persuasion or bribery a rival's supporters, and for a month the shady groves of the altis must regularly have witnessed as much undercover activity as the corridors of the Hofburg during the Congress of Vienna or the pump-room at Homburg in the days of Edward the Peacemaker.'

from *Classical Landscape with Figures*
Osbert Lancaster (1947)
© by permission of Clare Hastings

poets, philosophers and geographers who had either attended the Games in person or whose knowledge of the Greek world was sufficient to describe the events.

Homer, as noted earlier, mentioned the Games in *The Iliad*, when Nestor recalled his father sending a team of horses to compete in a chariot race at Elis. As the poem was composed in the 8th or 7th century BC, this remains one of the earliest known references to the Olympic Games in literature.

The Greek poet Pindar (c 522–433 BC) wrote victory odes to celebrate his patrons' achievements at Olympia.

Herodotus (c 484–425 BC) alluded to the Games on several occasions. For example, in Book II of *The Histories*, he described a delegation from Elis going to Egypt 'to boast that the fairest and finest institution in the world was their own Olympic Games, and to claim that not even the Egyptians, for all their superlative wisdom, could come up with anything comparable'. In Book V he related how Alexander the Great took part in running races at the Games, and in Book VIII he reported how, much to the amusement of a Persian observer, victors were rewarded only with garlands of olive branches. 'They make excellence rather than money the reason for a contest!'

Further descriptions of the Games appear in *Geographica*, written by the Greek traveller Strabo (c 63 BC – AD 24), and in the biography of Alexander the Great, written by Plutarch (c AD 46–120).

The Greek philosopher Epictetus (c AD 55–135) used metaphors from the Olympic Games to illustrate points about life and duty, while one of the fullest accounts was that of the great traveller and geographer Pausanias (c AD 143–76), whose *Description of Greece* Chandler took with him on his travels in the 18th century. Crucially, Pausanias provided detailed descriptions of Olympia's buildings and religious ceremonies, as well as writing about the myths and legends surrounding the Games' origins, and also about many of the sports that were common during his lifetime.

Even in the 2nd century AD, Pausanias was in no doubt as to the exalted status of what he saw. 'Many are the sights to be seen in Greece, and many are the wonders to be heard; but on nothing does Heaven bestow more care than on the Eleusinian rites and the Olympic games.'

So it was that throughout the centuries during which the actual site remained lost to the world, Olympia and the Games lived on in literary form – albeit not all of it accurate and much of it highly mythologised.

Not that these literary records were widely available. Far from it. The works of Pausanias, for example, appear to have received only scant attention after his death, and by the 15th century only three copies of his *Description of Greece* were known to have survived, all apparently copied inaccurately from one original manuscript.

More importantly, Christian attitudes decreed that these classical works were to be considered not as important historical documents but as pagan literature to be suppressed, with their stories of Zeus and Apollo and of sporting prowess and athletic contests.

The classical world rediscovered

If Olympianism lay forgotten during the medieval period, in common with so many other cultural aspects of the classical world it emerged blinking from the vaults as a result of the Renaissance, and more specifically the invention of the printing press, which allowed ancient texts to be more freely distributed and read across Europe.

Henry VIII endowed England's first professors of Greek at Cambridge University in 1540 and at Oxford the following year. Plutarch's *Lives of the Noble Greeks and Romans* appeared in translation in English for the first time in 1579, courtesy of Thomas North, in an edition dedicated to Elizabeth I. Shakespeare was said to have borrowed extensively from later editions of this work.

An English translation of Herodotus then appeared in 1584, attributed to one BR (possibly Barnaby Rich), who played fast and loose with the original, anglicising much of the content, but whose efforts nevertheless did much to popularise Olympian ideals.

Further evidence that classical references to sport were finding a wider audience came in 1595, with the posthumous publication of poet and courtier Philip Sidney's *Defence of Poesie*. Sidney criticised the Greek poet Pindar for his unbridled enthusiasm for the Olympics, but blamed this not on Pindar, but on the importance that his patrons placed on the Games:

'And where a man may say that Pindar many times praiseth highly victories of small moment, matters rather of sport than virtue; as it may be answered, it was the fault of the poet, and not of the poetry, so indeed the chief fault was in the time and custom of the Greeks, who set those toys at so high a price that Philip of Macedon reckoned a horserace won at Olympus among his three fearful felicities.'

Clearly this admonition did not deter later poets who wrote in praise of the Cotswold Olimpicks. As we shall learn, our prime source of information on the early years of these Games is a collection of poems published in 1636, entitled *Annalia Dubrensia* in honour of the Games' founder, Robert Dover. Throughout these works are found references to the Pythian, Nemean and Isthmian Games. But more common are the words 'Olimpick', »

The poet and courtier Sir Philip Sidney (1554–86) believed that poetry should teach its readers virtue, and felt that odes dedicated to sport had no lessons in them. But while he may have disapproved of the Greeks for investing too much emotion in the Olympic Games, he was hardly a killjoy.

In fact he rather excelled in that favourite sport of the Tudor monarchs, a form of jousting known as tilting, which would later be revived as 'tilting at the ring' at the Much Wenlock Olympian Games.

Sidney lived a colourful if short life, much of it overseas, before dying from a wound at the battle of Zutphon in the Netherlands, aged just 31.

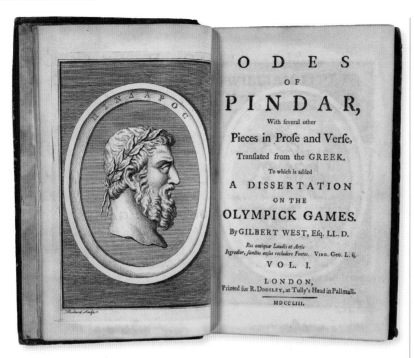

▲ Between 498–444 BC, the Greek poet **Pindar** composed a series of *Victory Odes*, celebrating the triumphs of athletes at the Olympian, Pythian, Isthmian and Nemean Games. First translated into English in the 16th century, the Odes were praised by Philip Sidney for their form and structure, if not for their celebration of sporting achievement.

Shown here, from the library of Columbia University, New York, is an edition translated by the author Gilbert West, published in London in 1753, together with West's *Dissertation on the Olympick Games*.

A typical extract is from Pindar's *Ode for Epharmostus of Opus*, winner of the wrestling 466 BC.

That which is inborn is always the best; but many men strive to win glory with excellence that comes from training.

Anything in which a god has no part is none the worse for being quelled in silence.

For some roads lead farther than others, and a single occupation will not nourish us all.

The paths to skill are steep; but, while offering this prize of song, boldly shout aloud

That this man, by the blessing of the gods, was born with deftness of hand and litheness of limb, and with valor in his eyes. (Ode IX)

》 'Olympick', 'Olympicke' and 'Olympicks', making it patently clear which of the Greek Games was ranked most highly in England at the time.

Rediscovering Olympia

The next discernible wave of interest in the ancient Olympic Games occurred in the 18th century, when, as noted earlier, Olympia was at last rediscovered by Richard Chandler's party in the 1760s.

Born in Elson, Hampshire, in 1737, Chandler was educated at Winchester College and both Queen's and Magdalen Colleges in Oxford. While at Magdalen in 1759 he published his first book, *Elegiaca Graeca*, on classical poetry, followed in 1763 by *Marmora Oxoniensa*, a catalogue of the inscriptions found on the Arundel marbles. These works led a year later to Chandler being commissioned by the Society of Dilettanti to lead the expedition to Asia Minor and Greece, 'in order to collect informations, and to make observations, relative to the ancient state of those countries, and to such monuments of antiquity as are still remaining'.

Finding Olympia, it should be stressed, did not form part of the Society's brief. Instead, Chandler and his two companions – the 43 year old architect Nicholas Revett, himself a veteran of previous trips to Italy and Athens, and the 22 year old artist William Pars – were simply told to make their headquarters for the first twelve months in Smyrna (now known as Izmir) in western Anatolia, and from there 'make excursions to the several remains of antiquity in that neighbourhood... as you shall, from the information collected on the spot, judge most safe and convenient'.

The party left Gravesend in June 1764, and after a productive but often perilous fourteen months, trekking through Asia Minor, sketching ruins, recording inscriptions, collecting samples and dodging plague and civil wars, travelled on to Athens for the Greek part of their expedition in August 1765.

For the next few months, Athens occupied their attention, before they set off on various excursions, for example to the site of the Nemean Games, to Marathon, Corinth, Delphi and eventually, in around June 1765, two years into their expedition, to Elis. This was the town whose inhabitants had been the guardians of Olympia and in whose *gymnasia* many of the athletes had trained.

What follows is taken from Chandler's own account of the expedition, entitled *Travels in Asia Minor and Greece*, and published in two volumes, in 1775 and 1776 respectively.

From Elis, Chandler wrote in Volume Two, 'Olympia was distant about three hundred stadia, or thirty seven miles and a half'. (The ancient Greek measurement of a *stade* was the equivalent of 600 feet, or just over 192 metres, and is the root of the word *stadion*, or stadium in Latin, one *stade* having been the distance run in the early foot races.) In other words, the approximate location of Olympia was known. But what lay there, no-one other than local inhabitants appears to have known.

Had circumstances been different, Chandler might not have been the first European scholar since antiquity to record the site. That honour may well have fallen to the German art historian, Johann Winckelmann, considered by many to be the father of modern archaeology as a result of his excavations at Pompeii and Herculaneum. But although Winckelmann wrote of his desire to find Olympia, he never visited Greece, and by the time Chandler's expedition account was published, he was dead; murdered during a robbery in Trieste in 1768.

Equally, Chandler's account might have been very different had his party arrived earlier on in their travels, when he and his colleagues were fresher. As it is, his entry on Olympia in *Travels in Asia Minor and Greece* is all too brief, and quite untainted by any sense of triumph or self-congratulation at having identified the site.

First, Chandler set the scene by summarising what Pausanias had written 1,500 years earlier about the Sanctuary at Olympia and the numerous religious practices routinely performed by the people of Elis. Sixty altars had been erected to various deities, according to Pausanias. Animal sacrifices had been especially common, not least because the smoke helped disperse the swarms of gnats which plagued the river valley and which, centuries later, gave Chandler's party a sleepless night on their arrival in the region.

Surveying an area stripped by looters and overtaken by natural disasters, Chandler wrote that, ever since the towering statue of Zeus – sculpted by Phidias and decked in gold, ebony and ivory – had been removed by the Romans to Constantinople, 'Olympia has since been forgotten in its vicinity'.

Here, in full, is Chandler's account of what he saw:

Early in the morning we crossed a shallow brook, and commenced our survey of the spot before us with a degree of expectation, from which our disappointment on finding it almost naked received a considerable addition.

The ruin, which we had seen in the evening, we found to be the walls of the cell of a very large temple, standing many feet high and well-built, the stones all injured, and manifesting the labour of persons who have endeavoured by boring to get at the metal, with which they were cemented.

From a massive capital remaining it was collected that the edifice had been of the Doric order.

At a distance before it was a deep hollow, with stagnant water and brick-work, where it is imagined was the stadium. Round about are scattered remnants of brick buildings, and vestiges of stone walls.

The site is by the road-side, in a green valley, between two ranges of even summits pleasantly wooded. The mountain once called Cronium is on the north, and on the south side the river Alpheus.

And there, without further ado, the description ends.

In the following section the party moves on to the nearby village of Miràca, where 'our approach occasioned some alarm' amongst a group of shy men, women and children 'employed in harvest-work'.

Had Johann Winckelmann been present we might have learnt more. Perhaps excavations would have been planned.

In his following chapter Chandler describes a French architect, Joachim Bocher, who had been visiting ruins to the south of Olympia, of what would later be identified as the Temple of Apollo Epicurius, at Bassae. But of Olympia itself no more was said. Instead, Chandler's party carried on up the valley for two hours, dined on some fowls, and then headed wearily back to Pyrgo and the coast, from where, in July 1766, they sailed to the island of Zante for some much needed rest.

Nearing the end of their expedition, Chandler wrote, 'We had experienced since our leaving Athens frequent and alarming indisposition. We had suffered from fruits, not easily eaten with moderation; from fatigue; from the violent heat of the sun by day, and from the damps and the torments inflicted by a variety of vermin at night.'

By now his companions were complaining, their servants were ill, while the captain of the vessel who had brought them to the Peloponnese 'had grown mutinous'. Lingering in or around Olympia was therefore no longer possible, or seemingly desirable, and after several further scrapes and setbacks, and one or two narrow escapes, on November 2 1766 the party finally arrived back at Bristol.

Their return, it has to be said, was not accompanied by any public proclamations of 'Olympia Found!'

Rather, reports of their findings took years to be published and circulated beyond the Society of Dilettanti.

The first report, *Ionian Antiquities, or, Ruins of Magnificent and Famous Buildings in Ionia*, appeared in 1769. In 1774 the Clarendon Press in Oxford then published Chandler's records of the many inscriptions he had noted down on his travels.

Finally, as noted earlier, in 1775 a full account of the first year of the expedition was published under the title *Travels in Asia Minor*, followed in 1776 by the second »

Peasants tend their goats amid the ruins of the Temple of Apollo at Didyma, as depicted by William Pars, the promising young London artist who accompanied Chandler and Revett to Asia Minor and Greece.

Held by the British Museum, this is one of 28 Pars watercolours reproduced in the highly influential *Ionian Antiquities*, published by the Society of Dilettanti in 1769 and reissued in numerous editions thereafter.

Alas, none shows Olympia, no doubt because the party seemed only too keen to leave the area to escape the gnats.

volume, *Travels in Greece*, in which the description of Olympia appeared.

At the start of the two volume work, in his Dedication to the Society of Dilletanti, Chandler wrote, 'The spirit of discovery, which prevails in this nation, will ever be reckoned among its most honourable characteristics'.

As such, he continued to travel and to write on classical and early Christian history and literature. He also served as a proctor at Oxford in the 1770s, and then became a vicar in Hampshire in 1779. Combined editions of both volumes were republished as *Travels in Asia Minor and Greece* after Chandler's death in 1810, and can be accessed today via the internet.

Nicholas Revett, meanwhile, lived to the age of 83, but died a poor man after modest success as an architect, artist and man of letters. For his part, William Pars became known as a pioneer of neo-classical art whose work would be widely exhibited in London. However, he died in Italy in 1782, aged just 40.

Between them, Chandler, Pars and Revett occupy hardly more than a footnote in the history of the Olympic Games. But as Britain entered a new era of discovery, industry and expanding horizons in the late 18th century, there could be no doubt that, thanks to their discoveries, Olympia would be not forgotten again.

Olympian references abound

In August 1773, the novelist and diarist Fanny Burney attended the Tingmouth (or Teignmouth) Races in Devon. As was typical of such rural gatherings, many other sporting events other than horse racing were to be enjoyed, including foot races, an ass race, a cricket

During the 19th century the terms Olympic or Olympian Games often referred to equestrian displays, as in this advertisement in the *Derby Mercury* of August 30 1854. Pablo Fanque, Britain's first black circus master, is best remembered for taking his Circus Royal to Rochdale in 1843, where it performed 'For the Benefit of Mr Kite' – as immortalised on the Beatles' album *Sgt Pepper's Lonely Hearts Club Band*.

BY PERMISSION OF THE WORSHIPFUL THE MAYOR, THOS. MADELEY, ESQ.,
And under the Patronage of the
EARL of CHESTERFIELD and LORD STANHOPE.

PABLO FANQUE, with his unrivalled EQUES-TRIAN TROUPE, will perform in the WHITE SWAN YARD, DERBY, for FOUR NIGHTS longer, with the LARGEST COMPANY of FEMALE EQUESTRIANS in the Kingdom; the First Equestrian and Gymnastic Artists of the day, and the MATCHLESS STUD of TRAINED HORSES and PONIES, who are not to be equalled in their Performances by any Establishment travelling.

The whole will go through their Wonderful and Extraordinary Feats, introducing New and Novel Features in the Olympian Games and Scenes of the Circle.

Commencing at half-past Seven.

Grand Fashionable MID-DAY PERFORMANCES On FRIDAY, and SATURDAY, Sept. 1st and 2nd.

Boxes, 2s.; Pit, 1s.; Gallery, 6d.

August 29th, 1854.

match and a competition common at that time in which members of the public were invited to catch hold of the greased tail of a pig. Although Burney disliked the cruelty involved with this last contest, and found a wrestling match to be 'a most barbarous diversion', her diary records how she was most impressed by a rowing race contested by five boats crewed by women.

One of Burney's party, a Mr Crispen, commented after the rowing, 'Games such as these... ought to make future events be dated universally from Tingmothiads, as former ones were from Olympiads'.

Fifteen years later in Hendon, Middlesex, according to an unsourced newpaper cutting from June 9 1786, on Whit Tuesday there took place 'a burlesque imitation of the Olympic games'. In this, 'the first prize was a laced shift, which was run for by four lasses in the neighbourhood, one of whom was distanced, and the prize adjudged to a damsel called Nan Peacock. The second prize was a gold laced hat to be grinned for by six candidates, who were placed on a platform with horses' collars to exhibit through; over their heads were painted in capitals *DETUR TETRIORI*; or, The ugliest grinner shall be the winner.'

As we will learn in the following chapter, grinning, or 'gurning' contests, also formed part of Robert Dover's Cotswold Olimpicks (and remain so today).

According to the London weekly, *Bell's Life*, a rather more serious attempt at an Olympic revival was proposed in November 1832. Its promoter was a character who might himself have stepped out of a Fanny Burney novel. Operating under the splendid moniker of Baron de Berenger, Charles Random was an entrepreneur, marksman and inventor of a waterproof gun, who earlier in life had served a prison sentence for stock exchange fraud.

In 1831 he took over the grounds of Cremorne House in Chelsea, turning part of them into 'The Stadium', or, as the prospectus also called it, the 'British National Arena for Manly and Defensive Exercises, Equestrian, Chivalric, and Aquatic Games, and Skilful and Amusing Pastimes'. This, the Baron intended, was to become home to The National Club, offering tuition for a variety of sports, including shooting, fencing and boxing, plus swimming and rowing in the adjacent River Thames.

If Berenger's proposed six day Olympic Games ever did take place in 1832, alas no reports have survived. Nor do we know anything of Berenger's later proposal to stage an Olympic Games in 1838, to celebrate the coronation of Queen Victoria. London society, it would appear, was not yet ready for his ideas, and so in the 1840s the site evolved into a rather more typical pleasure garden of the period, offering amusements, fêtes and spectaculars, rather than organised sporting contests. Known subsequently as Cremorne Gardens, the grounds were eventually sold for development in the 1870s, and were later largely covered by the Lots Road Power Station. But Berenger's legacy is at least remembered by the presence of Stadium Street (*see right*), while a small section of the former Cremorne Gardens was reopened to the public in 1982.

Played in Britain will return to the site in a forthcoming study *Played in London*. However one aspect of Berenger's enterprise does merit further mention in the present context, and that is his emphasis on the capacity for sport and exercise to build character amongst the upper echelons of society.

It was for their 'national games', the Baron declared in his prospectus for The Stadium, that the ancient Greeks and Romans had developed their 'superiority in muscular exertion and skill, and that mental loftiness, that noble daring'. From the Roman poet Juvenal he also threw in the phrase – *Mens Sana In Corpore Sano* (a healthy mind in a healthy body) – that over the ensuing decades would become something of a motto for those who espoused the cult of muscular Christianity (including the promoter of Liverpool's Olympic Festivals during the 1860s, as featured in Chapter Five).

In other words, Berenger imagined a form of Olympics that transcended the rustic frivolities of greased pigs and grinning contests.

Meanwhile, just as commonly during the late Georgian and early Victorian period the words 'Olympian' and 'Olympic Games' were attached to commercial entertainments and to exhibitions of sporting prowess, rather than to genuine athletic contests. On September 6 1790, for example, *The Times* reported that 'The Olympic Games, which have been neglected for such a length of time, seem to be again revived.'

But what was meant by the term 'Olympic Games'?

'Among those which stand foremost in the present age,' *The Times* article went on, was Mr Foster Powell's 'Pedestrian feats, as exhibited at Astley's' (that is, Astley's Amphitheatre in London, a venue famed otherwise for its equestrian displays).

Similarly, on February 13 1794 *The Times* announced that an eight-mile, four-in-hand charioteering race was to be staged at Newmarket, between Nanny Hodges and Lady Lads, for the colossal sum of 500 guineas. Regardless of whether or not cash prizes evoked the true spirit of Olympianism – of sport for sport's sake – the newspaper declared that the race signified 'something like a revival of the Olympic Games to supply the turf gentry and the rapid

MEMBERS of the NATIONAL CLUB, cultivating various skilful and manly exercises at the STADIUM at CHELSEA, being a WESTERN ARENA for such PURSUITS.

decay of horse-racing, which at present is in a galloping consumption'.

The word Olympic also came into vogue for places of entertainment. Hence in Liverpool there opened the New Olympic Circus, while in London, off the Strand, in 1806 Philip Astley, proprietor of the aforementioned Amphitheatre, opened the Olympic Theatre, offering riding lessons during the day and circuses in the evening.

In 1815, in an advertisement in *The Times* of August 19, Mr Gyngell's travelling variety show was announced to be visiting Peckham, Stroud, Bartholomew, Edmonton and Croydon Fairs, promising 'Hydraulicks, Hydrostatics, Deceptions, Musical Glasses, Sagacious Birds, Astonishing Dogs, Olympic Exercises, Equilibrium Wire', and Mr Paap, 'the celebrated Dutch Dwarf'.

From another notice in *The Times* of July 5 1839 we learn that visitors to the Vauxhall Gardens in London could watch a 'novel entertainment called the Curriculum or Olympic Games' involving 50 horses and 12 ponies.

Clearly the promoters of these spectaculars had only a vague notion of what the Olympics had been, and in one instance, of where they had originated.

Thus on October 28 1857 Madam Macarte's Magic Ring and Grand Equestrian Establishment in Edinburgh advertised in the *Caledonian Mercury* a show in which 'the extraordinary Evolutions of the Gymnastic Professors will forcibly recall to the Classic mind the old Olympian Games – the days of Rome and her "Colosseum", wherein the "Athletes" strive with each other before countless multitudes.' »

A lithograph from 1831 shows 'members of the National Club cultivating various skilful and manly exercises' at Baron de Berenger's shortlived Stadium at Chelsea, the site of which has since been marked by Stadium Street.

The Royal Borough of Kensington and Chelsea
STADIUM STREET, S.W.10

» The words 'Olympic' and 'Olympian' had, then, become a useful, catch-all term for a variety of entertainments and sports. But even if such events hardly amounted to a revival of the Olympics, as some newspapers suggested, the very fact that the idea of a revival was being voiced was at least significant, and in the mid 19th century would lead to some genuine attempts to recapture what was deemed to be the true spirit of the ancient Games.

Following in the wake of Robert Dover's 17th century Cotswold Olimpicks (see Chapter Three) there would appear Olympic or Olympian Games at Much Wenlock in Shropshire from the 1850s (Chapter Four), in Liverpool during the 1860s and 1890s (Chapter Five), and at Morpeth in Northumberland from the 1870s (Chapter Seven). National Olympian Games were also staged in various towns and cities during the 1860s and 1870s (Chapter Six).

Running concurrently with these sporting festivals were more discoveries at Olympia itself.

Olympia excavated

After years of turmoil in Europe as a result of the Napoleonic Wars, it was the French who followed in the footsteps of Richard Chandler, but in their case with the intention of excavating the ruins for the first time.

Organised by the Expédition Scientifique de Morée in tandem with France's military intervention in the Peloponnese, these initial excavations, led by Abel Blouet in 1829, focused on buildings within the site, such as the Temple of Zeus, and resulted in various treasures and some fragments of metopes being sent back to Paris.

After this, the Greek government understandably became rather more protective, and it was not until 1875 that another excavation, this time led by the German archaeologist Ernst Curtius and funded in part by the

German government, began an authorised and more scientific dig at Olympia.

Over the next six years, the German team uncovered and recorded large parts of the site. They concentrated on the sanctuary and the religious buildings which lay at the heart of the ancient complex: the Temple of Zeus and the Temple of Hera. Over 14,000 artefacts came to light.

No trace was found of the Statue of Zeus. This wonder of the ancient world had been dismantled and taken to Constantinople by Theodosius' court antiquarian, a eunuch named Lausus, back in the 5th century AD, and had subsequently been destroyed in a fire. However, Curtius' excavation did yield two spectacular finds: a statue of Nike, the Greek goddess of victory, by a sculptor called Paionios, and a statue of Hermes, the messenger of the gods, by the acclaimed Praxiteles.

Both German finds were put on display in a new museum opened by the Greek government, close to the site. From Lausus to Blouet, Olympia had suffered quite enough from looters.

Later archaeological digs then shifted the focus from Olympia's religious sites to its sports facilities.

In the 1930s another German team worked on the stadium, the gymnasium and the bathhouses, while later projects concentrated on the workshops and other buildings, and on revealing more of the site's earlier history. A century of excavations would thus transform the shallow grove of stagnant water and broken stones that Chandler had found so disappointing into a thoroughly documented site that UNESCO recognised as a World Heritage Site in 1989.

All this lay in the future at the time of Curtius' excavations. But the German archaeologist started a crucial process of discovery. Moreover, the publication between 1881 and 1897 of a six volume report on Curtius' findings did much to gain the excavations worldwide publicity. In newspapers and magazines and courtesy of lectures (such as one delivered by the American archaeologist, Dr Charles Waldstein, to the Royal Institution in May 1890), the story of Olympia was now, at long last, being backed up by tangible evidence.

Inevitably these findings had an influence on those in the world of sport. In Britain, at just the time when newspapers were reporting on the latest German excavations, Radcliffe Olympic Football Club formed in Nottinghamshire in 1876, followed a year later in Lancashire by Blackburn Olympic FC (see left). In 1882 the Corinthians FC, famous for their adherence to amateurism and fair play, were founded by former public schoolboys in London. By contrast, during the early 1890s the Olympic Bowling Club was formed by tradesmen

In 1883, just as more news was emerging of the excavations at Olympia, Blackburn Olympic became the first working class club to win the FA Cup – to the horror of certain FA members who questioned the players' amateur status and their unusual levels of fitness.

in Liverpool, and Rushall Olympic FC by miners near Walsall. During the Edwardian era there would then follow a spate of southern-based amateur football competitions with names such as the Isthmian, Athenian and Spartan Leagues.

By then this worldwide interest in all things Greek and classical had resulted in the rebirth of the ancient Olympics under the aegis of the French aristocrat, Baron Pierre de Coubertin. But it was a rebirth in which British individuals and organisations had played key roles.

Olympia in 20th century Britannia

Although it took some years to seep into the public consciousness, the formation of the International Olympic Committee (IOC) in 1894 and the staging of the first modern Olympic Games in Athens two years later resulted in a much clearer and more defined sense of what was meant by the terms Olympic and Olympian.

Indeed from 1908 onwards it was the IOC's version of the Olympics that came to dominate, underpinned by the emerging philosophy known as Olympism.

Other usages of related words came and went, particularly in the wake of the 1908 and 1948 Games in London. For example the White Star Line launched the RMS *Olympic* from Belfast in 1910 (a sister ship to the *Titanic*). In London, the Olympic Sound Studios were set up in the 1950s. In addition, there have been countless businesses and Greek restaurants similarly named. But in the sporting context the phrase 'Olympic Games' soon came to mean only one of two things: the ancient Games, or the IOC's quadrennial summer and winter series that continues to the present day.

Today, any use of the word 'Olympic' is closely monitored by the IOC in an effort to protect the integrity of the Games and its governing body, and to avoid any exploitation of the Olympic brand by anyone other than the IOC's commercial and media partners, who pay handsomely for their involvement.

Yet the lesson of history is that over the centuries the words Olympic and Olympian have meant many different things to different people in different circumstances. Hence, there are still Olimpick Games in the Cotswolds as there were when Shakespeare was alive, and there are still Olympian Games in Much Wenlock, as there were in Dickens' day. These local survivals defy modern branding, as the IOC itself has in recent years come to acknowledge, not least by recognising officially their part in the back story of Coubertin's modern Olympics.

Inevitably there will always be attempts, many of them innocent, to apply the 'Olympic' tag to events that have nothing to do with the official Games.

So, during the run-up to the 2012 Olympic Games, when London becomes the first city to host a modern Olympics for a third time, marking a period when public fascination with all things 'Olympic' appears at an all time high, a plethora of unofficial and informal uses of the Olympic label has appeared. Primary schools rebadge their annual sports days as Olympic Games. Town councils organise Pancake Olympics on Shrove Tuesday. Online knitting communities run the Ravelympics to encourage people to knit clothes during the Games, while anti-sport campaigners have advocated a Lazy Olympics.

Patently, these initiatives have no connection with the IOC. Nor, on the whole, are their promoters seeking to undermine the official Olympic brand. Rather, they are the inheritors of a long tradition, in which ordinary people have borrowed freely from classical Greece in order to lend their events a touch of glamour and an image of excellence. Each has sought to interpret Olympianism in ways that make sense to them, according to their time and place.

Britain's Olympic heritage, as a result, is as much concerned with traditional themes of carnival, localism, education and amateurism, as with the more modern themes of internationalism, sporting prowess, professionalism and boosterism.

Here, then, are the British Olympics, starting not in 1908 at White City, nor at Athens in 1896, but in the Cotswold town of Chipping Campden in 1612.

Cashing in on the wave of publicity surrounding the German excavations, in 1886 the proprietors of the recently opened National Agricultural Hall in Kensington, London, decided to stage circuses and adopt the name Olympia. It has stuck ever since, as seen here on the Grade II listed Empire Hall on Hammersmith Road, designed by Joseph Emberton and opened in 1929.

Chapter Three

Cotswold Olimpick Games

Medals await their winners at the Cotswold Olimpicks, held annually just outside Chipping Campden. Taking place originally over two days, on the Thursday and Friday of Whit Week, in their modern incarnation they are held on the Friday after the late May Bank Holiday. Organised by the Robert Dover's Games Society, they are usually referred to today as the 'Olimpicks'. But where the name 'Olympick' has been used in old texts we have retained this spelling.

Our quest to chart the heritage of Britain's very own Olympic Games will lead us to many a scenic spot. But none is more beautiful than that of a steep turf ridge lying between the Gloucestershire town of Chipping Campden and the nearby village of Weston-sub-Edge.

Forming a natural amphitheatre and offering stunning views across the Vale of Evesham, Dover's Hill is the setting for an annual gathering known as the Cotswold Olimpicks. These date back to at least the 1620s, but by a happy coincidence, may well have gained their 'Olimpick' tag as early as 1612, exactly four hundred years before the 2012 London Olympics.

Some sceptics might argue that for all their provenance and quasi-sporting content, the Cotswold Olimpicks were, and remain, little more than an endearing English rural gathering, with no meaningful links to the wider narrative of the ancient or modern Olympics.

Certainly, several of the sports practised on Dover's Hill, in 1612 as in 2012 – the likes of shin kicking, single stick fighting and tug-of-war – owe little to Olympia. Nor is there a stadium on the site, a gymnasium, any temples, nor any permanent buildings at all. On most days of the year visitors can walk through the area and sample the views without knowing that here is a site that has been staging sporting contests for longer than almost any other historic sportscape in Britain.

Yet despite these caveats, there can be no doubt that the very existence of the Cotswold Games, and the philosophy that underpinned them, helped to sow the seeds of a wider English movement that, in the 19th century, would ultimately lead to Athens in 1896.

What is also significant is that in the spirit of the ancient Olympians, the original promoter of the Cotswold Games, Robert Dover, intended the gathering to act as a unifying force, using the joy of sport and of friendly competition to bring peace and harmony to a community in danger of being torn apart by conflicting ideologies.

The first British Olympics, in fact, grew out of a very British struggle between religion and popular culture.

English rural sports and festive gatherings

We know from many sources that sports and games played a key role in the festivities of English people in medieval England, whether it was cockfighting,

bull baiting or football on Shrove Tuesday or, for the privileged classes, jousting tournaments held to celebrate royal birthdays and weddings. We also know that the authorities regularly tried to suppress everyday games amongst common people, such as skittles and bowls, partly to preserve the Sabbath, but also because such pursuits distracted men and youths from archery practice and were frequently accompanied by gambling, drinking and general unruliness.

However, by the late 16th and early 17th centuries attitudes towards games and physical recreation came to reflect a wider schism, a schism that at its most basic level arose between those who sought to maintain England's Catholic identity, and those of a puritanical leaning who wished to impose upon the nation a stricter, more pious form of Protestant faith.

Beyond the purely liturgical arguments, a number of cherished practices came under attack; for example the decoration of churches, the celebration of Saints' Days, the organisation of Church or Whitsun Ales (by which church wardens raised money by selling ale at festive gatherings), and even the seemingly innocent practice of dancing around a maypole, deemed to have been rooted in pagan beliefs.

Almost inevitably, sports and games were targeted too, as Catholic and Protestant, Royalist and Parliamentarian interests fought for the body and soul of England, the pendulum swinging one way and the other until the Restoration in 1660 and the Glorious Revolution of 1688 settled the matter in favour of a constitutional monarchy and the Church of England.

Although it would be a gross simplification to categorise the struggle purely as Puritans versus Pleasure Seekers, two tracts from the period are worth noting for their diverging attitudes towards traditional customs.

Phillip Stubbes' *Anatomie of Abuses* (published in 1583) railed against the corruption and dissolution of the period, against Popish practices, the despoiling of the Sabbath and the evils of theatrical performances.

On the subject of games held in May, or on Whitsunday or 'some other time of the yeare', Stubbes complained how 'every Parish, Towne, and village, assemble themselves together, both men, women and children, olde and young, even all indifferently: and either going all together, or dividing themselves into companies, they goe some to the woods, and groves, some to the hills and mountaines, some to one place, some to another, where they spende all the night in pleasant pastimes, and in the morning they returne bringing with the Birch boughs, and branches of trees, to deck their assemblies withal.

'And no marvell, for there is a great Lord present amongst them, as Superintendent and Lord over their pastimes and sportes: namely, Sathan, Prince of Hell'.

Countering this prejudice were various landowners and even churchmen who saw no harm in organised jollity, as long as it did not interfere with Sunday worship.

In 1617 King James I offered his verdict.

Published initially to settle a dispute in Lancashire, but extended to cover all England in 1618, the *Book of Sports* listed those activities which James considered permissible, such as archery, dancing, leaping, vaulting 'or any other such harmless recreation', and also, in direct contradiction of Stubbes, the holding of 'May-games, Whitsun-ales and Morris-dances, and the setting up of May-poles'.

Not all recreations were sanctioned. James prohibited the baiting of bulls and bears, and also bowling, a game usually carried out in alleys attached to inns.

To spread the message, ministers of the church were ordered to read passages from the *Book of Sports* to their congregations, an order repeated by James's successor, Charles I, in 1633. Any minister refusing to carry out this duty risked losing his position.

By responding to the more permissive tenets of the *Book of Sports*, rather than bowing to the gloomy dictates of the Puritans, Robert Dover's Cotswold Olimpicks were, therefore, no mere innocent diversion. They were instead a statement of loyalty to the king, and to the cherished notion of what later nostalgics would call 'Merrie England'. Or to put it a different way, as the modern Olympics are to British society in 2012 – as contentious as they are popular, as divisive as they are inclusive – so too were the Cotswold Games in 1612.

Robert Dover

Born into a middle-ranking Catholic family in Great Ellingham, Norfolk, in either 1581 or 1582, Robert Dover's career would appear to provide an object lesson in how an individual could, with good sense and the right connections, negotiate the fraught moral byways linking and dividing England during the early Stuart period.

Educated at Queens' College, Cambridge, in 1599 Dover was sent to earn his keep by working for a priest at Wisbech Castle. This was where many Catholics who had escaped execution were sent. Although Catholic himself,

Dover came from a family of 'church papists'. That is, they attended their local parish church and were therefore officially tolerated. (To encourage this stance non-attendance at church was penalised by the considerable fine of twelve pence per absence.)

To continue his studies Dover then moved to Gray's Inn in London, where, as Celia Haddon has suggested (*see Links*), he would have found himself in an environment in which entertainments, revels, sports and pageants were common, at a time when Shakespeare's latest plays were being staged to admiring audiences.

Dover might also have been exposed at Gray's Inn to various works of Greek literature, Pindar's Olympian Odes included. Indeed, Dover dabbled in poetry himself, prompting one London priest to describe him as superior to the respected Edmund Spenser.

After being called to the bar, Dover left London for the Cotswolds where two, and possibly three of his siblings already lived, and where he started practising as a lawyer. In June 1611 he settled down with the widow of a Bristol merchant in a house in Saintbury. Apart from occasional trips back to London, Dover would stay in Gloucestershire for the rest of his life, living at various times in Saintbury, Chipping Campden, Childswickham and Barton on the Heath.

Dover's Olimpicks were not conjured out of the void. Quite possibly they were not called the Olimpicks for some years. Instead, as historians such as Francis Burns have been at pains to emphasise (*see Links*), Dover would have attended the region's annual Whitsuntide festival – a gathering no different from many found in all parts of rural England – and only then, in later years, developed it into a larger event. »

A measure of how deeply James I's *Book of Sports* divided opinion is that on May 10 1643, London's public executioner burnt a copy at Cheapside. Earlier that day Puritans pulled down Cheapside Cross, with its statues of the Pope and the Virgin Mary, in order to 'cleanse that great street of superstition'. This engraving, probably by Wenceslaus Hollar, is from a collection by John Vicars in the British Library, entitled, *A Sight of ye Trans-actions of these latter yeares* (1646), helpfully designed to be read by men 'without spectacles'.

From the National Portrait Gallery, this is Endymion Porter (1587-1649), as portrayed by the Dutch artist Daniel Mytens in 1627. Groom to the bedchamber of both James I and Charles I, a friend and patron of artists, an occasional diplomat and briefly a Member of Parliament, Porter lived a colourful life. His royal connections, his Catholic leanings and his family home in the Cotswolds made him a natural supporter of Dover's Olimpicks. Like many Royalists, though, he fell from grace during the Civil War, and spent his twilight years in exile and poverty, before returning to England shortly before his death.

›› In taking on this role Dover had two advantages. Firstly, by all accounts he was an outgoing, witty and popular man who loved putting on a show. Secondly, in addition to his status as a respected newcomer to the area, he had connections with the court of James I. Crucially, these links meant that Dover knew exactly how far he could go in developing the local Whitsuntide games, and that anyone attending them would understand that the activities bore a royal stamp of approval.

At a more fundamental level, thanks to a courtier called Endymion Porter (*left*), Dover was able to parade at the Games wearing a set of clothes that had once belonged to James. In an age when items such as hats, jackets, ruffs and shoes were regularly handed down the social scale, being able to sport the king's cast-offs, even outdated ones, was celebrity indeed.

Dover thus had a showman's sense of what the public wanted and the wherewithal to provide it.

Just as importantly from a historical perspective, he also had a number of friends and supporters who were prepared to state in poetic form just how much they admired him and his Games. Published in 1636 and reverentially entitled *Annalia Dubrensia* (the Annals of Dover), this collection of poems has provided later generations with the best surviving impression of what Britain's first Olympics were like.

Not least, the illustrated frontispiece from the 1636 edition (*see opposite*) provides the only known visual reference to the Games during those early years.

Sports and games on Dover's Hill

As the frontispiece of *Annalia Dubrensia* delightfully suggests, Dover's Games were, as described by Christopher Whitfield (*see Links*), a 'conscious protest against the puritanism of the age'.

Presiding over the proceedings in the lower foreground is Dover himself on horseback, resplendent in King James' cast-off finery. As this is the only known image we have of Dover, too detailed an analysis would be unwise. But here at least he appears to have a benign, rather than a domineering presence, an impression which the poems that follow reinforce repeatedly.

Then, as today, the landscape appears similarly benign, offering a contrast between the slopes of Dover's Hill and the flatter but still undulating pastures both at the top of the ridge and below. The sports that required more space, such as hare coursing (to the right of Dover's feathered hat and above the tents to the left) and horse racing (to the left of Dover's hat), took place lower down in the Vale of Evesham. As such they would not have been viewable from the ridge in their entirety.

As can be seen, on the level areas a number of tents were erected. As well as providing refreshments, these also housed games of chess and cards. In front of the tents we see a group of eleven men enjoying a picnic with two large tankards set before them.

Dotted around we see sports that would have appealed to a broad range of participants from all classes: trials of strength involving the throwing of hammer and poles, combat sports involving sticks and swords, and, below the swordsman (top right), an unarmed sport subsequently known as shin-kicking. Elsewhere there are women dancing and men jumping and performing gymnastic exercises. All in all, exactly the type of frivolous activities that Phillip Stubbes had counselled against.

But perhaps the most enchanting image is that of the small castle mounted on the hilltop, with cannons firing out of two side turrets and a pennant fluttering in the breeze. It is tempting to imagine that this miniature castle is merely an artistic device. In fact, such structures, formed from timber, were common to pageants and celebrations of the period.

From the woodcut we cannot be sure of the scale of the castle. But clearly it had to be large enough to house at least one adult, and be sufficiently robust to bear the weight and recoil of two or more small cannons. At the same time, such mock castles could not be too heavy as they were usually pulled along on wheels or floated on water. Dover's castle appears to have been mounted on a round base, suggesting that it was designed to swivel in the wind, in the same manner as a post mill form of windmill.

Dover's castle was purely for effect, to provide a focal point, to create a loud noise and to excite the crowds. Also, the fact that real gunpowder was used offered further proof of Dover's contacts in high places, and his trustworthiness. When not in use, presumably the castle was dismantled and placed in storage until the following year.

Overall, the impression from this frontispiece is one of pastoral fun and games, imbued with convivial spirit. But at what point did the 'Cotswold Games' become elevated by the tag 'Olimpick'? Could it be that the word was by then in common use for traditional sporting festivals?

In his diary of 1620 (*see Links*), Symonds D'Ewes, an undergraduate at St John's College, Cambridge, described how, just south-east of Cambridge, the splendidly named Gog Magog Hills, 'notorious as a place of resort', were to be the venue of a bull baiting. In itself this was not surprising, since baiting had ››

COTSWOLD GAMES.

Frequently reproduced in facsimile but rarely seen in its original form, this is the wonderfully designed frontispiece of the first edition of a collection of verses by various poets called *Annalia Dubrensia, Upon the yeerely celebration of Mr Robert Dovers Olimpick Games upon Cotswold-Hills*.

Published in London in 1636 by Matthew Walbancke, a bookseller of Gray's Inn Gate, this copy is held by the British Library. It contains 33 verses, but this woodcut is the book's only illustration. Indeed, it is the only visual record that we have of the early Olimpicks.

Annalia Dubrensia was subsequently reprinted in 1720, 1877, 1878, and at least four times during the 20th century. The most recent edition was issued by the Robert Dover's Games Society in 2004, with an introduction by Francis Burns, who served for over 30 years as secretary of the Society before his death in 2011, and whose research has informed much of the material in this chapter.

William Hole's portrait of the 50 year old Michael Drayton, completed in 1613 and published six years later, shows the poet in an apparently disgruntled mood, and deliberately so. Despite the enthusiasm he showed in his later life for Robert Dover (*right*), during the reign of James 1 Drayton was often critical of behaviour and attitudes within court circles. Thus he chose to be portrayed as a 'satiric laureate'. That is, he wore the laurel crown of a poet laureate, but with barely disguised disdain.

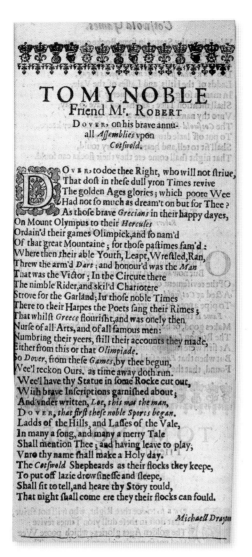

▲ Written by **Michael Drayton** (*above left*), shortly before his death in 1631, this is the opening poem in *Annalia Dubrensia*. Here we see Dover, 'that first these noble Sports began', as the direct descendent of Hercules, the mythical founder of the ancient Games. Drayton portrays the 'brave annual assemblies upon Cotswold' as a pastoral idyll, with shepherds and the 'Ladds of the Hills, and Lasses of the Vale' all joining in a merry celebration. By honouring Dover, and by entwining classical references with visions of bucolic harmony, Drayton set a tone that several later contributors emulated with evident enthusiasm.

been banned from the Market Square in Cambridge, presumably as a result of the *Book of Sports*. But then D'Ewes goes on to say of the Gog Magog Hills that as well as the baiting, 'all such exercises as bowling, running, jumping, shooting, and wrestling are to be practiced there for a month or six weeks, under the designation of the Olympic games'.

Alas there the entry ends, and in the absence of any other references, we can only guess as to whether the use of the word Olympic in this instance was a one-off in 1620, or even something D'Ewes had simply heard being mentioned casually by fellow students.

But then this is a subject that invites speculation from so many angles. Were the Gog Magog Games already established, as were the Cotswold Whitsuntide gatherings? If so, might Robert Dover have attended them during his period at Cambridge in the 1590s? Or, conversely, could the promoters of the Gog Magog Games have been inspired by the Cotswold Games?

Another speculation that has occupied historians for decades is the question of whether Shakespeare made references to the ancient Olympics, as noted in the previous chapter, because he knew Dover and had perhaps attended the Cotswold Games (see for example Jean Williams' article on what she calls 'The Curious Mystery of the Cotswold "Olimpick" Games', listed in our Links section).

Robert Dover and the Olympic connection

Whether or not the Cotswold Games had the tag Olimpick or Olympick from the early years of Dover's involvement, we cannot say. But they were certainly labelled 'Olimpick' by the time *Annalia Dubrensia* was published in 1636. As noted on the previous page, the book's subtitle reads 'Upon the yeerely celebration of Mr Robert Dovers Olimpick Games upon Cotswold-Hills'.

Francis Burns, who analysed *Annalia Dubrensia* in great detail (*see Links*), argued that the Olympic connection may simply have stemmed from the first of the poems, written by Michael Drayton in 1631 (*see left*), and that later contributors then picked up and developed this theme.

Whether true or not, the collection's contributors certainly demonstrated their knowledge of ancient texts. Several of the poets made references not only to the Olympics but also to the Nemean, Pythian and Isthmian Games, and to the nature of the sports and rituals performed at these Games.

To modern readers the tone of most of the poems appears slavishly sycophantic. In his foreword, the publisher Matthew Walbancke writes that for reviving the ancient Games that had been otherwise 'utterly abandoned and their memories almost extinguished', Dover was 'an Hero of this our Age'. Later on Dover is addressed as 'noble and fayre', 'jovial', 'heroic and generous minded', 'unparalleled and much honoured', as the 'great inventor and champion of the English Olympicks' and, lest we forget, 'the great architect and ingineere of the Famous, and admirable Portable Fabricke of Dover Castle…'

As Burns notes, four of the contributors were related to Dover and five lived locally. Four had been to Gray's Inn. Five had taken holy orders, one was a doctor, and several were connected with legal matters. Probably best known of the poets was Ben Jonson, who penned a short piece praising Dover for honouring the memory of the blessed James I, and for the fact that the Games advanced 'true love and neighbourhood' in the face of hypocrites, 'who are the worst of subjects'. Indeed, as might be expected in a work published during the decade that led up to the Civil War, hypocrites and Puritans were as much reviled as the purity and ideals of the Olympics were praised.

A typical passage was that of John Trussell. Bemoaning the loss of traditional rites and celebrations, he wrote:

All public merriments, I know not how,
Are questioned for their lawlessness, where by
Society grew sick; was like to die
And had not the jovial DOVER well invented
A means whereby to have the same prevented,
Love, Feasts, and friendly intercourse had perished,
Which now, are kept alive by him, and cherished.

In other words, Robert Dover's Olimpicks were more than a revival. They were a riposte to reformers, and a reminder to the English that if they wished to attain the greatness of the Greeks, they would be wise to retain sporting contests as part of their national ethos.

This certainly appeared to be Dover's own view. In a poem in which he congratulates his 'poetical and learned noble friends' for their efforts, he responded with disarming vagueness as to what had inspired him:

I cannot tell what planet ruled, when I
First undertook this mirth, this jollity,
Nor can I give account to you at all,
How this conceit into my brain did fall,
Or how I durst assemble, call together,
Such multitudes of people as come hither.

Of course it is possible he was being disingenuous, leaving it to others to make the Olympic connection, for otherwise his only comment on the matter was this:

Whilst Greece frequented active sports and plays
From other men they bore away the praise;
Their Commonweath did flourish, and their men
Unmatchèd were for worth and honour then…

But, Dover warns, the Greeks forsook such pastimes 'and unto drinking did themselves betake', with the result that they were no longer men 'but moving lumps of clay'. Yet Dover's final message suggested that his real motive was not to attack drinking but to promote honest, pure and simple fun.

Let those that be of melancholy form,
And pensive spirits, fret themselves, and storm;
Let snarling Envy bark, pine and grow mad;
Let carping Momus pouting be, and sad;
And let Content and Mirth all those attend,
That do all harmless honest sports defend.

Or as we might say today, 'Lighten up everyone, it's only a game'.

Chipping Campden and the Civil War
If the contributors to *Annalia Dubrensia* are to be believed, by the 1630s Robert Dover's Cotswold Olimpicks were attracting large numbers. None of the poets gave figures, but their descriptions of 'brave assemblies' and 'heroick meetings' certainly suggest large crowds.

The Games had also become sufficiently well known to London theatregoers for the dramatist Richard Brome to slip a reference to them into his comedy of 1641, *A Jovial Crew*. In the play, two sisters, Meriel and Rachel, and their suitors Hilliard and Vincent, consider fleeing their rural backwater for some sinful escapism:

Hilliard: *What think you of a journey to the Bath then?*
Rachel: *Worse then t'other way. I love not to carry my*
*   health where others drop their diseases. There's no sport*
*   i'that.*
Vincent: *Will you up to the hill top of sports, then, and*
*   merriments, Dovor's Olimpicks or the Cotswold Games?*
Meriel: *No, that will be too publique for our recreation.*
*   We would have it more within our selves.*

Not surprisingly, the Games' reputation for revelry would soon prove to be their downfall. After decades of simmering division, the Puritan axe was about to fall.

By the time Robert Dover arrived in the area in 1611, Chipping Campden had developed into what chronicler William Camden called 'a mercat towne well peopled and of good resort'. »

Glowing in the sunlight of a 1950s summer's day, these are Sir Baptist Hicks' almshouses on Church Street, Chipping Campden. In the distance stands the tower of St James' Church.

Built in 1612 for local pensioners at a cost of £1,000, and now listed Grade I, the almshouses stand out even in a town richly endowed with historic buildings (256 of which are listed).

Consisting of twelve dwellings they form a terrace which, in plan, takes the shape of the letter I, for *Iacobus*, the Latin version of King James' name. Four hundred years on, each house is still in use.

>> In previous centuries a key point along the trading route between Wales and London, Chipping Campden was dominated by the late 15th century church of St James', its scale a reminder of the wealth that wool had once brought to the area.

In 1605 James I had granted the town a charter, while further prosperity would emanate from a London merchant and moneylender to the king, Sir Baptist Hicks, who bought the manor some time after 1608 and built himself a lavish stately home, Campden Hall. He also commissioned a new market hall and a terrace of almshouses (*left*), both still wonderfully extant. As inscribed on his monument in St James' Church – he died in 1629 – Hicks was said to have donated £10,000 towards 'charitable uses'.

When the Civil War erupted in 1642, Chipping Campden found itself caught between the two rival factions. Indeed some of the war's key sites, at Warwick, Gloucester and Oxford, lay nearby, and in 1645 Campden Hall was burnt down by retreating Royalists in order to prevent it being used by the advancing Parliamentarians.

Clearly in such dire circumstances, to stage the Olimpicks, an event so closely linked to the Royalist cause, became impossible, and in 1644 the vicar of St James', William Bartholomew, cancelled that year's Games. In ancient Greece it was said that the Olympics went ahead whatever the military conflicts of the day. Not so in 17th century England, nor indeed in the 20th century, when war prevented the modern Olympics from being staged on three occasions, in 1916, 1940 and 1944.

Back in 1644, the cessation of the Cotswold Games must have struck a devastating blow to Robert Dover, a man who in legal matters was said to have placed great emphasis on conciliation and compromise. He died six years later, in 1650, and lies buried in a barely discernible grave at St Lawrence's Church, Barton-on-the-Heath.

Restoration and revelries
In common with so many facets of English popular culture, the Cotswold Olimpicks were revived following the Restoration of the monarchy in 1660. Exactly when this revival occurred is unclear, but from two literary works identified by Francis Burns we know for sure that the Games were once again firmly part of the local Whitsun calendar by the early 18th century.

The two sources are *Hobbinol – or The Rural Games*, a 1740 poem by William Somervile (itself a revised version of his earlier piece called *The Wicker Chair*, dating from 1708), and *The Spiritual Quixote*, a novel by Richard Graves, published in 1773. Both pieces are, to a degree, satirical, and, in common with *Annalia Dubrensia*, need to be judged as imaginative texts based on real events, rather than as factual accounts. However, both provide a sense of what the revived Games were like, and how the spirit that had prevailed before the Civil War had returned.

In *Hobbinol*, although Somervile does not mention Dover's Hill or Dover himself by name, the rural games referred to in the subtitle are 'the May-Games' which took place in or around the Vale of Evesham and Kiftsgate, clearly the same location as used for the Cotswold Games between 1612–43.

For his part, in *The Spiritual Quixote* Graves calls the Games 'Dover's Meeting' and the 'Dover's-hill revel'. As for the location, he describes 'a large plain on the Cotswold-hills' and, elsewhere, 'the plain called Dover's-hill', dotted with booths and tents offering refreshments.

Disappointingly, neither text mentions any attempt to revive the famed Dover's Castle, and both portray the gatherings as rough and even violent in nature, in terms of the Games themselves and the prevailing atmosphere.

For example, as well as the usual dancing, feasting and drinking, *Hobbinol* includes graphic descriptions of wrestling and of a cudgelling match in which a player called Tonsorio is smashed on the head and then has a wooden staff rammed into his 'gaping jaws'. Not surprisingly at this point, 'Sore maim'd; with pounded teeth and glotted gore, Half-choked, he fled.'

In *The Spiritual Quixote*, billed as 'a comic romance', Graves has his protagonists, a pompous Methodist preacher called Geoffrey Wildgoose and his servant Jerry Tugwell, describe the Games as a 'heathenish assembly' where 'great irregularities were practised'.

In a voice reminiscent of Philip Stubbes, Wildgoose asks, 'Dost thou call that sport, where so many poor souls are devoted to destruction, by drinking, swearing, and all kinds of debauchery? These wakes or revels are the devil's strong-holds, whence he issues forth, and takes captive the poor deluded people at his pleasure.'

Once again cudgelling is described, and once again heads are broken. When Wildgoose then harangues the crowd for their 'anti-christian... more than paganish recreations' they respond by pelting him and Tugwell with horse dung. It is a moment of pure slapstick.

Both accounts describe a foot race for young women, an event that was common to 18th and 19th century sports meetings, usually involving unmarried girls running in immodest clothing (as described at Hendon in 1786, *see page 18*). Also typical were the prizes; functional yet coveted items such as gloves, hats, and smocks. The gloves, wrote Somervile, were especially alluring; 'seam'd with silk and fringed with gold', while the young lady who won the smock race was apparently assured of marriage:

See here this prize, this rich laced smock behold,
White as your bosoms, as your kisses soft:
Blest nymph! Whom bounteous Heaven's peculiar grace
Allots this pompous vest, and worthy deems
To win a virgin and to wear a bride.

As was said of Dover's earlier Olimpicks, the 18th century Games attracted a range of spectators. From *Hobbinol*, this was the scene before the women's race:

See, on yon verdant lawn, the gathering crowd
Thickens amain; the buxom nymphs advance,
Usher'd by jolly clowns: distinctions cease,
Lost in the common joy, and the bold slave
Leans on his wealthy master, unreproved.

This intermingling of the social classes, in which 'distinctions cease', forms a familiar theme in accounts of rural gatherings of the period. At cricket matches and in the cockpit, the farmhand and the aristocrat, the slave and his master, came together to enjoy sports and games, and especially gambling. (As GM Trevelyan memorably wrote in 1942, in *English Social History*, 'If the French noblesse had been capable of playing cricket with their tenants their chateaux would never have burnt'.)

From local newspaper reports it appears that the Cotswold Games continued in this vein well into the 19th century, maintaining a flavour of 'Merrie England' as the real England became steadily transformed by industrialisation and urbanisation.

Surviving posters from the early 19th century show that the Games, and the hill on which they took place, continued to bear Robert Dover's name. 'Dover's Meeting' is the most common appellation. But the 'Olimpick' tag, albeit spelt variously as 'Olympick', 'Olimpic' or 'Olympic' also persisted, the term by now, as discussed in the previous chapter, enjoying a much wider currency than had been the case in the early 17th century.

The Games themselves were evolving too. Wrestling, backswords, horse and pony races, sack races, dancing, and jingling (a kind of blind man's bluff) were all regularly listed on the early 19th century posters.

Significantly, and contrary to the perceived spirit of the ancient Games (if not the reality), cash prizes were now being awarded by local patrons and publicans, supplementing the usual array of clothing and belts on offer. Notably, in 1818, twelve guineas were offered for the backswords competition, and in the following year for the horse race, five guineas in the sweepstake, with 30 guineas added. These were decent sums, suggesting that the organisers were keen to attract the best contestants.

A. Walker del. et Sculp.

Also, thanks to the coming of the railways in the 1840s, the attendances started to grow. One opponent of the Games, the Rector of Weston-sub-Edge, estimated that as many as 30,000 spectators had attended one year, bringing chaos and misery to this rural backwater. And where before any violence had largely been channelled into the sports themselves, there now appeared reports of unruliness amongst the crowds.

Writing in 1877, ER Vyvyan, the editor of a new edition of *Annalia Dubrensia*, was unflinching in his damnation, claiming that the Games had become 'the trysting-place of all the lowest scum… of Birmingham and Oxford'. Many of the newcomers he dismissed as 'roughs and undesirables from as far away as the Black Country'.

Yet while other contemporary accounts – for example the duty diary of the local police superintendent – suggest that there was nothing extraordinary about the crowds or their behaviour on Dover's Hill, the Games became an easy target for the new Puritans; if not for the protection of morals then at least for the protection of property. 》

It is from this poster of the 1851 Cotswold Games that the date of 1612 has been established as the event's inaugural year.

The key phrase is under the heading, where it reads in small print, 'It is now two hundred and thirty nine years since that noble generous and heroic gentleman, Mr Robert Dover, instituted the highly celebrated and renowned Olimpic Games, for which this true and distinguished Festival claims precedence of all others, and which are now patronized by Church and State, and esteemed by all brave, true and free spirited Britons, who admire those ancient and manly exercises for which this kingdom is so justly famed.'

That the organisers made this claim there and then was no doubt owing to the establishment the year before of the Much Wenlock Olympian games, sixty miles to the north west, in Shropshire.

Robert Dover, it will be recalled, had moved to the Cotswolds in June 1611, so the 1612 claim is by no means unreasonable.

DOVER'S

MEETING, 1851.

It is now Two Hundred and Thirty-nine years since that noble, generous, and heroic gentleman, MR. ROBERT DOVER, instituted the highly celebrated and renowned Olimpic Games, for which this true and distinguished Festival claims precedence of all others, and which are now patronized by Church and State, and esteemed by all brave, true and free, spirited Britons, who admire those ancient and manly exercises for which this kingdom is so justly famed.

On Thursday in the Whitsun Week,

The good old times will be revived with a spirit of hilarity, and a generous subscription for the amusement of Her Majesty's subjects, commencing at TWO o'clock, with

TWO DOZEN OF BELTS
TO BE
WRESTLED FOR,

To contend for which, Dons of high Blood and Metal are required to be on the Turf, The Sports of the day will conclude with DANCING FOR RIBBONS, JUMPING IN SACKS, JINGLING MATCH, and various other Amusements, too numerous to praticularize.

ON FRIDAY AT TWO o'CLOCK,
The Sports will commence with
WRESTLING for BELTS,
AFTER WHICH, A
HURDLE RACE

For a Handsome Silver Cup, of the value of £5., or in Specie.

Heats twice round Dover's Hill, over five flights of fair hunting hurdles to carry eleven stone each. Enterance One Pound each. A winner of any Race in 1851, to carry 7lbs. extra; Horses under fifteen hands high to be allowed 7lbs. for every inch, the horses to be entered at Mr. Wm. Drury's, Swan Inn, Campden, before twelve o'clock on the day of the Race. Open to horses of all denominations. Three to start or no Race. The winner to pay 5s. for scales and weights.

A GRAND DISPLAY OF BACKSWORDS.

The Silent Evening will be ushered in by a MERRY DANCE, to commence at Nine o'clock.
GOD SAVE THE QUEEN !!!

EXCELLENT BANDS OF MUSIC WILL ATTEND EACH DAY. No Person will be permitted to erect a Booth upon the Hill, for the Sale of any sort of Liquors or Ale, without paying £4. before Monday the 9th of June, or £1. extra will be charged (which will free him from any other demand ;) to be paid to MR. DRURY, Swan Inn, Campden. All Stalls for Cakes, Oranges, &c. to be paid for according to size. A Person will be appointed to conduct the Sports, and his decision shall be final, or whom he may appoint.
[Pearce. Pr. Evesham.]

>> Sport in 19th century Britain, in line with so many other areas of life, was becoming more sanitised and less violent. Thus, the formation of the Society for the Prevention of Cruelty to Animals in 1824 led to eventual bans on cock fighting and animal baiting. The 1835 Highway Act led to the banning of traditional Shrove Tuesday football matches on public roads.

This trend, combined with a growing fear amongst the authorities of large crowds assembling, would eventually kill off the Cotswold Games for the second time in their history. In 1850, with the backing of the local church, a group of landowners successfully applied to have Dover's Hill enclosed, thereby threatening to split up the playing areas into fields too small for the Games.

And so it was that the 1852 Dover's meeting proved to be the last for nearly a century.

By 1872, when John Marius Wilson wrote about Chipping Campden in his *Imperial Gazetteer of England and Wales*, Dover's Olimpicks had passed into history. The entry read simply, 'The Cotswold games, instituted in the time of James I., and sung by Ben Jonson, Drayton, and other poets, were held on Dovers-hill'.

The 20th century revival

As will become evident in following chapters, the various Olympic games that emerged during the second half of the 19th century were quite different in character. In an age of increasingly rational recreation, there was seemingly little appetite for the more traditional games of the Cotswolds.

Nevertheless, while Britain's Olympic torch was passed on to guardians elsewhere, the site of the Cotswold Games retained the name of Dover's Hill, and remained sufficiently important to local people that they fought for its protection when developers threatened in the 1920s.

Leading the campaign was the illustrator FL Griggs. A prominent member of the Arts and Crafts Movement and of CR Ashbee's Guild of Handicrafts, also based in Chipping Campden, Griggs had moved to the town in 1903 and often walked on Dover's Hill. It was where he proposed to his wife. He even renamed the Georgian building in which he lived Dover's House. With help from his neighbours and from the social historian GM Trevelyan, Griggs won the battle, and in 1929 Dover's Hill became the property of the National Trust.

From that moment on, it seemed only a matter of time before those individuals leading the revival of interest in English folklore between the wars would turn their attention to resurrecting the Games. Yet, as it transpired, it was a group of ordinary local people who took the initiative, inspired by the mood of celebration stoked up

by the Festival of Britain in 1951. Using the best possible template for their efforts, *Annalia Dubrensia*, in May that year an impressive pageant was staged, led by a local man, J Haydon, dressed up as Robert Dover, with a small wooden castle forming part of the parade.

Inevitably these first Games of the modern era included new events, such as boxing for men and pillow fights for women. There were family races, obstacle races, donkey races, a tug-of-war, and a competition for throwing horseshoes. More traditional was the contest to climb a greasy pole in order to win a leg of mutton, while a pig was donated as the prize in the bowling competition. Another notable revival was the shin-kicking contest.

As well as the Games, the week long celebrations included a firework display, a carnival, Morris dancing and a play.

Interestingly, the one aspect of the old Games that the organisers chose not to revive in 1951 was the use of the word 'Olimpick'. Given that London had staged the modern version only three years previously this was perhaps surprising. Instead, the new celebrations were described, as they had been in the 19th century, as 'Dover's Meeting' or as the 'Dover's Hill Games'.

It was intended to repeat the Games the following year, in 1952, but an outbreak of foot and mouth disease put paid to that. Thereafter the impetus must have been lost because it was not until May 1963 that Dover's Hill once again witnessed a Whitsuntide celebration, in the form of a bonfire attended by two local men dressed as Robert Dover and Endymion Porter. This was repeated in 1964 and 1965, after which, on July 22 1965, four local residents met to form the Robert Dover's Games Society.

It is this organisation that has run the Games in its current incarnation, from June 1966 to the present day, under the name of 'Robert Dover's Cotswold Olimpicks'.

Chipping Campden's town crier whips up the Festival of Britain spirit as Robert Dover's Games were finally revived in 1951 after 99 years in abeyance. It was not until the 1970s that the word 'Olimpicks' was reintroduced, and the 1980s before recognition was granted by the British Olympic Association that the Cotswold Games were indeed part of Britain's Olympic heritage.

The organisers of the 2012 Games followed this up by sending an official flag to the town in August 2008, where (*below left*) it was received by the Honourable Philip Smith, president of the Robert Dover's Games Society, and Mayor Chris Jones.

Key to map:

1. Dover's Hill
2. Kiftsgate Stone
3. Campden House
4. Dover's House
5. site of Old Campden House

▪▪▪ route of five mile run
▪▪▪ route of torchlit procession

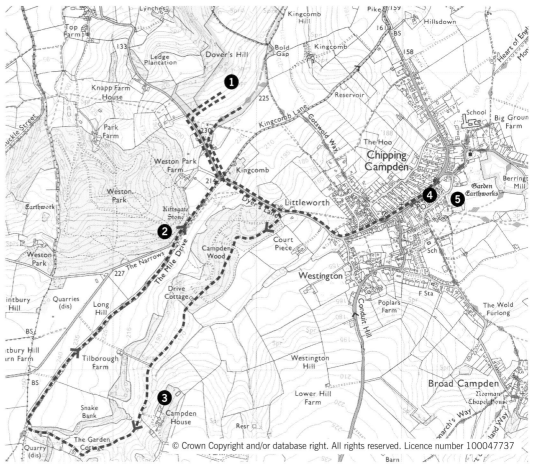

© Crown Copyright and/or database right. All rights reserved. Licence number 100047737

▲ It is fitting that the Cotswolds, known poetically if not geographically as the heart of England, should have been the birthplace of the first of our British Olympics.

For most visitors to the modern day Games, the picture postcard town of **Chipping Campden**, a firm favourite with tourists, forms the main gathering point, offering a rich assortment of historic, honey-coloured buildings, ranging from Jacobean to Arts and Crafts in style. Its stunning High Street, hardly altered in layout since the medieval period, was once described by GM Trevelyan as 'the most beautiful village street now left on the island'.

From the centre of Chipping Campden, **Dover's Hill** lies about a mile to the north-west, and is divided into two areas, known as the upper arena – a long flattish field accessed from the lane – and the lower arena, in a dip bordered by woodland.

Most spectators sit on the steep turf ridge that provides the transition between the two arenas (see opposite).

Before its enclosure was finally effected in 1853, the area used for the Games was essentially open land, running west of Kingcomb Lane. As can be seen, just west of the lane is a feature known as the **Kiftsgate Stone**. This was where, in the medieval period, meetings of the Court of the Hundred of Kiftsgate were held, with the accompaniment of sports and revelry. It was these gatherings that may well have laid the foundation for the Whitsuntide celebrations which Dover took over in 1612.

The route marked in blue is the one followed by the torchlit procession which traditionally ends the day of the Games, leading from the bonfire on Dover's Hill to the town centre, where the celebrations continue until the small hours.

It is 7.30pm on a Friday evening in May 2009, as a loud blast from a cannon signals to the crowd assembled on **Dover's Hill** that **Robert Dover** and his esteemed friend **Endymion Porter**, played by two local men, Father John Brennan and Paul Dare, are about to enter the lower arena on horseback (*right*).

Accompanying their grand entry are twelve kilted members of the St Andrew's Pipe Band, watched by the Scuttlebrook Wake Queen and her attendants (the Scuttlebrook Wake being a Whitsun tradition started in Chipping Campden in 1938).

From the topography it is easy to see why this elevated spot is so suited to sporting events, and although Dover's Castle may nowadays only be a stage-set backdrop to the proceedings, the sweeping views of the Vale of Evesham have barely changed since Dover's lifetime.

Today's Cotswold Olimpicks are watched by crowds of up to 3,000 and are squeezed into a two hour period.

Many of the local children will have already competed earlier in the day, not on Dover's Hill but in the Scuttlebrook Races, held on Chipping Campden's High Street. Kicking off the evening programme on the lower arena is an obstacle race for teams, one of several events to determine the Championship of the Hill.

Shortly after this, a five mile cross-country race starts, taking the runners through the grounds of Campden House at Coombe, south west of Dover's Hill (not to be confused with Sir Baptist Hicks' Old Campden House, of which only two freestanding banqueting halls remain in the centre of Chipping Campden).

For the rest of the evening the events are divided between the upper and lower arenas.

▲ After the opening ceremony, the 2009 Cotswold Olimpicks get under way with the **Championship of the Hill**, a series of relay races contested by teams of four, many of them representing local pubs and churches.

Very much in the spirit of the classic television series *It's A Knockout* the wheelbarrow race requires each team to carry bales of straw over an obstacle course. After each leg an extra bale is added, with the final leg seeing the smallest member of the team perching on the top.

Another race requires the four team members to ski in unison across the turf (*above right*).

Rather more serious is the tug-of-war (*above*), contested by men and women, typically from pubs, rugby clubs and young farmers' clubs. Apart from the running race, this is the only event that has ever been mirrored by the main Olympics, a tug-of-war tournament having formed part of the London Olympics in 1908 (*see page 110*).

One other link is that, however informal or light-hearted the games might appear – the Hill being no place for purist or puritan – every winner is rewarded with a medal, cup or trophy, formally presented by the President of the Robert Dover's Games Society.

▲ A contest that more than any other keeps alive the 17th century spirit of rough play, **shin-kicking** has become the iconic event of the Cotswold Olimpicks. As the T-shirts say, come to Dover's Hill and 'Get the shin kicked out of you!'

Gone are the iron-tipped boots once worn by 19th century kickers, some of whom, it was said, would harden their shins with coal hammers. But if the footwear has become less lethal since the Games' revival in 1951, shin-kicking remains a tough contact sport, and one for which the attendance of paramedics is occasionally necessary.

The rules are simple. Two contestants – usually, but not always male – face up, each gripping the other by the shoulders. They are dressed in white coats, to represent the smocks worn by shepherds, and have straw taped to their shins or stuffed down their trouser legs.

The 'stickler', or referee, then gives the signal. Kicks must be aimed between the ankle and knee, but players may also hook their feet behind their opponent's legs to force a fall. The first shin-kicker to floor his rival wins. Bouts can last from ten seconds up to five minutes.

Shin-kicking is a knockout event, so with up to twenty contestants usually entering it can take the best part of two hours before the gruelling best-of-three final takes place around 9.00pm, forming the climax to the programme on the lower arena.

In the single stick contest (*left*), entrants aim to strike their opponents with a slender ash rod. They can target any part of the upper body. Like shin-kicking, this is a sanitised version of a much older, bloodier sport, and is a reminder that for all its jollity, Merrie England had its violent side. Also taking place on the upper arena are displays of cudgel fighting, as illustrated on page one.

▶ Donning a leather horse collar and pulling an ugly face may not be an activity to which many young hopefuls aspire when they dream of winning medals. But the point of **gurning** (thought to derive from the word 'grinning') is that anyone can have a go and, on Dover's Hill at least, become an Olympian in the process.

There is, at the same time, a genuine historic resonance in this apparent frivolity. For contests such as gurning, shin-kicking and single stick fighting are not just quaint re-enactments of old traditions. They form a reminder of how activities that seem innocuous to us today were once emblematic of the struggle for religious and social freedom in the 17th century.

Robert Dover was no radical, and his Olimpicks were never entirely given over to the Lord of Misrule. Yet there remains something still proudly anachronistic about the Games that seems to have endured over four centuries. It is as if, in the balmy Cotswold air up on Dover's Hill, the modern world has been left behind, for a few hours of innocent fun. No flashing scoreboards. No booming music. No numbered tickets or seats. Indeed, no seats at all. Only a grassy bank with occasional thistles for unsuspecting behinds.

Nor do any of the sports require expensive equipment. There was a dalliance with motorcycle scrambling in 1968, piano smashing in 1970 and professional wrestling in 1971. But traditional sports have lasted the best.

Of course the modern world cannot be entirely excluded. There is a tent selling merchandise from the **Robert Dover's Games Society**, and one might easily spot a foreign television crew hoping to capture one of those classic 'Merrie England' moments. There is also a ban on alcohol, although for medicinal purposes some shin-kickers apparently manage to circumvent this.

Glowing in the firelight stands Robert Dover, played fittingly in 2009 by Father John Brennan, the Roman Catholic priest of St Catharine's in Chipping Campden. It was of course Dover's Catholic heritage that informed his attitude to religious control and puritanical teachings.

Another concession to modernity came in 2010, when for the first time since the Games' revival, the towering **bonfire** – traditionally lit at the end of the evening by the Scuttlebrook Wake Queen – was moved from the upper to the lower arena, where it could be kept under tighter control, away from the crowds. The dramatic crowd scene shown above left, from May 2009, is therefore unlikely to be repeated.

Bonfire apart, the long arm of health and safety officialdom seems refreshingly absent from Dover's Hill. Instead, the Cotswold Olimpicks combine all the finer elements of a community sports day with the fun of a funfair and the laid-back vibe of a music festival.

Above all, the Games give us a precious sense of the spirit in which Britain's Olympic heritage was born; in a field, in the countryside, on a Whitsuntide holiday, with a long night of carousing in prospect.

▲ After the medal ceremonies have ended, as the bonfire's embers die down and the bells of St James' can be heard striking eleven in the distance, it is the turn of the crowd to become the spectacle. With torches (and inevitably mobile phones) held aloft, families and friends, spectators and participants, old and young, leave Dover's Hill for the mile long walk back into Chipping Campden, the night sky bathed in a gorgeous glow.

At the edge of the town, the torches are extinguished in a skip – there are thatched cottages still to pass – and as the front of the procession nears the centre, a band starts up in the town square. Meanwhile, on the far side of the square a garish, raucous funfair spews out light and noise across this usually reserved Cotswold townscape.

On the Saturday comes the Scuttlebrook Wake; the May Queen is crowned, children dance around the maypole, morris dancers celebrate the coming of summer and a fancy dress parade winds its way through the streets.

As in 1612 so in 2012, Britain's oldest Olimpicks remains the most local of affairs, but with a place firmly at the heart of our national story. The old Puritans would be appalled, but Robert Dover would surely have approved.

Chapter Four

Wenlock Olympian Games

Cast in zinc alloy and coloured bronze, this is one of the medals awarded at the annual games of the Wenlock Olympian Society. The medal incorporates the Society's traditional logo, consisting of the letters WEN and a padlock – a visual witticism of the kind much beloved by the Victorians.

If Robert Dover's Cotswold Olimpicks were redolent of Merrie England, the next British Olympics to become established, in the Shropshire town of Much Wenlock, from 1850 onwards, were a Victorian attempt to rationalise the Olympian ethos and make it a force for the physical, educational and moral improvement of the working classes.

The instigator of these Wenlock Olympian Games was William Penny Brookes, a local doctor and magistrate.

To begin with, Brookes' Games were little more than a well organised sports day for local inhabitants. However, their reach soon extended to other parts of Shropshire, before gradually gaining a national influence during the 1860s (as following chapters will relate).

Most crucially of all, the Wenlock Olympian Games were to have a direct and lasting impact on the values and goals of Pierre de Coubertin. As we stated in the Introduction, throughout the 1880s Coubertin's main concern had been the study and teaching of physical education in other countries, with a view to improving matters in his native France. Only after his visit to Much Wenlock in 1890 did he turn to campaigning for a modern revival of the Olympic Games.

Initially Coubertin acknowledged the influence that the Wenlock Games had had upon his thinking (*see opposite*), only for him to later omit all references from the official IOC narrative. Fortunately, however, after lobbying by British historians this omission was finally rectified when, in 1994, one of Coubertin's successors as President of the IOC, Juan Antonio Samaranch, visited Brookes' grave and paid tribute to the doctor for his role as 'the founder of the Modern Olympic Games'.

So when the Shropshire Tourist Board claims that Much Wenlock is 'the home of the modern Olympics', it is no idle boast.

Nor are the Wenlock Olympian Games of historic interest only. Following periods during the 20th century when they went into abeyance, they have enjoyed an unbroken sequence since 1977, and today could be said to be as strong as ever. Partly this is owing to the strenuous efforts of local volunteers, to whom we are grateful for much of the material in this chapter.

But also it is owing to increased interest arising from London's successful bid to stage the 2012 Games, and from the decision, in May 2010, to name one of the two 2012 mascots 'Wenlock' – the other being 'Mandeville', named after Stoke Mandeville (*see Chapter Eleven*).

Much Wenlock

With a current population of around 2,600, Much Wenlock – or Wenlock for short – lies 35 miles north west of Birmingham and five miles south of Ironbridge, the heartland of Britain's industrial revolution.

Ironbridge may be a bigger magnet for tourists, but in other respects Much Wenlock meets all the criteria one would wish for in a small market town. Local butchers, bookshops, tearooms and delicatessens line the High Street, and there is plenty of historical interest, including the ruins of Wenlock Priory, which date back to the seventh century and are now managed by English Heritage, a Tudor Guildhall and a town museum (*below*).

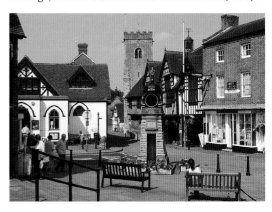

'In truth, Wenlock is a happy place. I do not know whether there is any other town that is so well provisioned with everything that a progressive and generous municipality can make available to its citizens. The moment one sets foot there, one senses the privileged nature of the place.'

Pierre de Coubertin
La Revue Athlétique December 25 1890

By the mid 19th century Much Wenlock was an established trading and administrative centre serving the needs of the surrounding agricultural community.

British sport was in the midst of great change at this time. While the majority of working people were becoming urbanised and their spare time increasingly constricted by the unrelenting demands of the industrial timetable, for the sons of the social elite, public schools such as Eton, Harrow, Rugby, Winchester and Shrewsbury (twelve miles north west of Wenlock), were starting to codify sports such as football, rugby and athletics.

As a result of this growing regulation, sport – which in the 18th century had become so tainted by its association with gambling, hunting, animal baiting and passive spectatorship – regained at least some of the nobler characteristics that had been handed down from the Greeks, and subsequently celebrated by the scholars and poets of the 16th and 17th centuries.

'Rational' recreation, as this emerging form of sporting culture became known, had no truck with the kind of alcohol-fuelled, rough play that characterised the Cotswold Olimpicks. Rather, the new puritans of the Victorian era invested in sport a whole range of improving qualities. From sport a boy, or man, though not yet many a girl or woman, could learn discipline, loyalty, team spirit and fair play, all qualities that would stand them in good stead in their adult lives, not least should they be called to arms in the service of the Empire.

For these individuals, many of whom equally embraced the precepts of 'muscular Christianity', the added virtue of amateurism, of sport for sport's sake, was also of paramount importance.

So it was that although certain forms of traditional sport and play would survive this period and endure well into the 20th century, it was largely the morally driven, public school ethos that set the agenda and established a benchmark in British sport during the second half of the 19th century. Here was a cult that cut across social classes – there would be many 'amateurs' amongst working men too – and one that was soon to be exported around the Empire and beyond.

William Penny Brookes

Born in Much Wenlock in 1809, William Penny Brookes is remembered as the town's most eminent Victorian.

After going to London as a young man to undergo his medical training, Brookes spent further spells in Paris and Padua. But once he returned to his home town in 1831 he would live there for the rest of his life.

In addition to his work as a doctor and as a Justice of the Peace, Brookes threw himself into a succession of

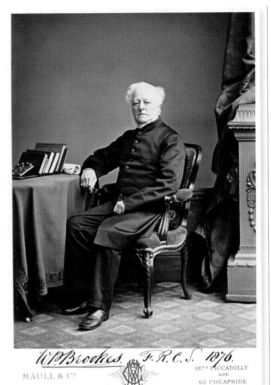

W.P. Brookes. F.R.C.S. 1876.

MAULL & Cº

187ª PICCADILLY
AND
62 CHEAPSIDE

improvement schemes: the surfacing of local roads, the construction of a new Corn Exchange, the provision of a gas supply and, crucially, the construction of a railway line linking Much Wenlock to the neighbouring towns of Wellington and Coalbrookdale, thereby opening up routes to major centres such as Birmingham and Oxford.

As an archetypal Victorian gentleman with interests in history, geology, botany, and education, Brookes was also firmly committed to the improvement of people. At first, this philanthropic work focused on education. Thus in 1841 he established in Much Wenlock the Agricultural Reading Society, in effect a lending library, out of which grew classes in music, fine art, and natural history. For the town's children, Brookes helped to set up a National School in 1847.

But improving minds was only one part of his agenda, for as a doctor he grew equally aware of how physical recreation could offer benefits too. In this, Brookes was arguably ahead of many of his contemporaries, seeing in the public school attitude towards sport a philosophy that could equally help other sectors of society. »

In his later writings on the origins of the modern Olympics, Pierre de Coubertin failed to mention William Penny Brookes by name. Yet in December 1890, in *La Revue Athlétique,* he wrote, 'The fact that the Olympic Games, which modern Greece has been unable to restore, are being revived today is due not to a Hellene, but to Dr WP Brookes.'

This portrait was taken when Brookes was aged 67 and still lobbying on behalf of the National Olympian Association. Brookes' biographer, Catherine Beale (see *Links*), has noted how his commitment to public works started when, aged 15, he accompanied his father, also a doctor, on his rounds, and saw the conditions in which rural workers lived.

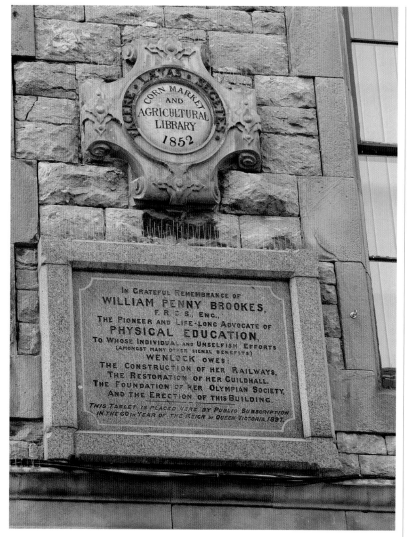

▲ These plaques are to be seen on the Grade II listed **Corn Market and Agricultural Library**, opened on Wenlock's High Street in 1852. While the business of agriculture was carried out on the ground floor, on the upper floor a meeting room, a library and 'a house for the librarian' were established for the Agricultural Reading Society. The lower plaque, erected at the time of Victoria's Diamond Jubilee in 1897, pays tribute to the recently deceased Brookes, that 'pioneer and lifelong advocate of physical education' and bringer of 'many other signal benefits' to the town. The **Wenlock Olympian Society** is still based in the building.

≫ It was with this improving mission in mind that in February 1850 Brookes set up a sub group within the Agricultural Reading Society. Clearly a man with a classical education, he named this group the Wenlock Olympian Class.

As declared in the minutes of the first meeting – still kept by the modern day Wenlock Olympian Society in a handsome leather binding – the class' brief was 'the promotion of the moral, physical and intellectual improvement of the inhabitants of the town & neighbourhood of Wenlock and especially of the Working Classes by the encouragement of out-door recreations and by the award of prizes annually at public meetings for skill in Athletic exercises and proficiency in intellectual and industrial attainments'.

In keeping with the ethos of rational recreation, this was to be a tightly governed body, with a Committee of Management, umpires, financial accounts and an annual subscription of 'not less than one shilling'.

Significantly, unlike Pierre de Coubertin's later vision of an Olympic revival, there was no attempt at Wenlock to impose amateur values. Instead, funded by subscriptions and donations, cash prizes were offered from the start. However, the inclusion of prizes for intellectual as well as for athletic attainments did echo ancient Greek precedents.

The first Wenlock Olympian Games

Eight months after its formation, the Wenlock Olympian Class staged its first Games on October 22 1850. The venue was the town's main recreational space, the racecourse, which had been laid out in 1807.

There was a cricket match, with a prize of 22 shillings for the winning side and an additional five shillings for the highest scoring batsman. In the football competition £1 was offered to the first team to score three goals.

The athletic programme, meanwhile, consisted of foot races for juveniles and adults, and competitions for 'leaping in height' and 'leaping in distance'.

Prizes ranged from 2s 6d for the winner of the under-nine's race up to ten shillings for the adults and for the quoits tournament. These were handsome prizes; ten shillings was then slightly more than the typical weekly wage of an agricultural labourer.

Of course such financial incentives were not in keeping with how later amateurs would characterise the Olympian ideal. Nor, apart from the foot races and arguably the quoits (a popular throwing game that was often mistakenly linked with discus throwing) were the sports on offer derived from the ancient Games. Rather, Brookes adopted the title 'Olympian' to add gravitas, to

inspire his fellow townsmen, and to emphasise to the Games' participants that they were engaged not merely in sports but in self-improvement and the greater good of the community.

As with Robert Dover's Cotswold Olimpicks, the Wenlock Olympian Games were therefore based on what would be described by historians today as an 'invented tradition'. This was imagined classicism rather than a faithful re-enactment.

Unlike the Cotswold Games, however, the spirit underlying Brookes' efforts was decidedly modern.

Each event was strictly regulated. The foot races were organised in age groups. Leaping events were decided by finite measurements. The team games were to be played according to the ethos of the public schools.

A great success the first event was too, at least according to a local newspaper, *Eddowe's Journal*. A total of £10 15s had been raised in donations and subscriptions, it was reported, and this had been sufficient to cover the day's entire costs and to ensure that the Olympian Games would, as Brookes hoped, become an annual event.

Two important changes marked the first decade. »

▲ Taken at the **Wenlock Olympian Games** on Windmill Field in June 1867, this is believed by the **Wenlock Olympian Society** to be the world's oldest photograph of a sporting event at which spectators are present. (Earlier, posed images taken at Scottish bowls clubs exist, but none show matches or events taking place.)

Capturing the pageantry that was central to the Games, the photograph shows the end of the procession, as the officials dismount from their carriage, watched by lines of smartly dressed guests and competitors, including men mounted and ready for the tilting. Note how the man closest to us watches the camera rather than the parade.

On the brow of the hill can be seen the remains of a mid 17th century windmill. Its sails had been destroyed by lightning in 1850, so in 1859, James Milnes Gaskell, the local landowner and MP, paid for it to be 'fitted up'. Although unlikely to have been used for spectators, it was said at the time that from its summit 'an excellent view' could be 'obtained of the Games and the surrounding country'. That view from the windmill remains excellent, but still not for the public. Nor, owing to tree growth, can the Games be viewed from the slopes any longer.

For the most prestigious events at the Wenlock Olympian Games, medals eventually replaced cash prizes, as amply demonstrated by HW Brooke, a member of London's German Gymnasium, who won the 1869 Pentathlon.

Below is the WOS's First Class Medal, presented to Dr Brookes in 1867.

The motto *Arte et Viribus* is bordered by a lyre, a sculpted bust, an artist's palette, a bat, ball and tilting lance, a sword and a rifle. Several other Wenlock medals were cast from the same mould.

➤➤ In 1858 the organisers moved the Games from the racecourse to an area north of the town, known both as Windmill Field or as Linden Field. This area remains the venue to the present day, and is formed partly by a public recreation ground and partly by the playing fields of Wenlock's comprehensive school (named, almost inevitably, after William Penny Brookes).

A second development followed in 1860 when the Olympian Class split from the Agricultural Reading Society to form a separate Wenlock Olympian Society.

From the WOS's lovingly preserved minutes and its excellent collection of artefacts, and from extensive press reports, a detailed history of the Wenlock Games throughout the rest of the 19th century emerges.

We learn for example that for the second Olympian Games, held in September 1851, archery and hurdling were added, and various regulations tightened up. Each football team, for example, was limited to 15 players, while in the hurdles the rules required 'over seven hurdles to be clearly leaped without knocking'.

Rather less serious was a foot race for 'old women', the prize being a pound of tea. As reported by the *Shrewsbury Chronicle*, the contestants 'acquitted themselves remarkably well, considering the disadvantage under which they laboured in not being provided with the "Bloomer costume" attired in which they would have run capitally'. Mrs Mary Speake claimed the prize – described as 'woman's much-loved herb' – while runner-up Anne Meredith 'was rewarded for her exertions by a smaller prize out of the same canister'.

The account book for the 1851 Games duly includes the entry, 'Tea for old women – 5s'.

Many other novelty events would follow. In 1854 there was a blindfold wheelbarrow race, in 1856 a sack race, and in various years donkey races, pole climbing, jingling matches (a form of blind man's bluff with bells) and a once popular game of team tag called 'prison base'.

Some events were added for soldiers. In 1893, for example, there was a Balaclava Melee, named after the Crimean War battle of 1854, in which teams of mounted troopers armed with sticks had to knock the plumes off each others' helmets. Two years later, cavalrymen competed in a Gimcrack Race, in which the riders had to stop their horses at set intervals to put on a pair of boots, take a drink and smoke a cigar.

The range of serious events was also extended. In addition to the staples of athletics, archery, football and occasionally cricket, rifle shooting was introduced from 1860 onwards and cycle racing from the 1870s.

Two other new events had more historic roots. The first, introduced during the late 1850s, was the faux medieval equestrian event of 'tilting at the ring' (*see opposite*), a non-contact form of tilting, which was itself a form of jousting that had evolved amongst courtiers during the Tudor and Stuart periods.

The second, introduced at Wenlock in 1868, was the pentathlon, a competition based in structure if not in sporting content on the ancient Olympic Games. The five sports varied over time, but were essentially tests of either speed or strength. In 1868, for example, contestants raced over hurdles, climbed a 55 foot rope, threw a 35lb stone, and jumped for length and height.

Significantly, winners of both the pentathlon and the tilting at the ring, on a horse, were awarded medals only, whereas the winner of a competition for tilting from a pony ('not exceeding 13 hands') received a medal and £5 in cash. Thus there emerged a divide between those who competed for money, because they were either professional athletes or in need of extra income, and those, perhaps men of greater means, who competed solely for the glory. In other words, professionalism and amateurism existed side by side at the Games, seemingly without any embarrassment or sense of contradiction.

There also arose a division between those events in which only local entrants were allowed, and those for which outsiders were permitted.

As noted earlier, Brookes originally conceived the Games as being for working people in the 'town & neighbourhood'. However, in 1859, clearly with a view to attracting more spectators and adding excitement, the organisers announced that the one mile foot hurdle race, for which the prize was £5, was 'open to all England'.

The only condition was that the winner and runner-up of this event, who might well be professionals, could not enter any of the other races.

A separate half-mile hurdle race, worth £2 to the winner, was meanwhile open only 'to persons residing not more than 10 miles from the Guildhall, Wenlock'.

Similar conditions of residency were placed on competitors in the tilting at the ring, while certain races for juveniles were limited to Wenlock parishioners.

It is also noticeable from the WOS minutes how for younger contestants, cash prizes were, over time, replaced by the award of books.

Intellect and industry

William Penny Brookes made clear that 'intellectual improvement' was one of the prime aims of the Much Wenlock Olympian Class.

In 1852, therefore, a programme of 'intellectual and industrial' activities was introduced, aimed mainly at local children, and in some instances open only to pupils of ➤➤

Seen here at the 1887 Wenlock Olympian Games, tilting at the ring was a simplified version of a medieval test of strength and horsemanship. The aim was for the rider to capture on his lance a ring hung from a crossbar (which the WOS minutes from 1858 tell us had been supplied by Mr Edwards, a wheelwright, at a cost of 22s). In order to deter professional jockeys, only local gentlemen were allowed to enter, the prize being, from 1859 onwards, a silver trophy, called the Forester Cup, worth £10. In true Olympic style, from 1860 winners were also crowned with laurel wreaths, as shown below left. Dating from 1887, this photograph shows Charles Ainsworth being crowned by Miss Serjeantson, daughter of the rector of Acton Burnell, a nearby parish. This was Ainsworth's third triumph in the tilting. Dr Brookes can be seen to the right of Miss Serjeantson, wearing the medal shown opposite. This medal, and a tilting lance, can be seen today in the Wenlock Museum.

▲ The Wenlock Olympian Society's penchant for pomp and ceremony is exemplified by this collection of Games regalia, one of several displays devoted to the Olympian Games housed in the **Wenlock Museum**.

On the left, in front of a photograph of Thomas Yates, the Herald of the Games in 1887, is his burgundy coloured ceremonial collar and his hat, complete with its white plume. On the right are some artefacts associated with tilting at the ring, including a red and gold saddle cloth, decorated with tassels and the ubiquitous Wenlock logo. These costumes and accessories give a real flavour of the historical character that Brookes wished to bestow on the Games. Ceremonial costumes added dignity to the event, and helped to make it a memorable day in the town's calendar.

Almost inevitably, the museum itself has a link to Dr Brookes, for it was at his behest in 1878 that the local board of ratepayers sanctioned its construction, originally as a Market House. In 1919 the building became the Memorial Hall, and for some years it served as a cinema, before being converted into the present day museum and tourist office in 1974.

>> the Wenlock National School. For girls under 14 there was a competition for the 'neatest and quickest sewing', rewarded with a book for the winner and calico for the runner-up. Knitting contests were also instigated.

For their part, in 1853 boys under the age of 14 were offered books for competitions in arithmetic and writing. Later categories were to include recitation, Bible history, English history, drawing and 'glee singing'.

The subject of one of the essay competitions set in 1860 says much about the organisers' social standing. Its title: 'On the political importance of the Middle Classes'.

In the same year, the ancient Olympian tradition of poetry was revived with a prize being offered for the best ode dedicated 'To the Victor in the Tilting Match'.

The winner was Jonathan Douglas of Shrewsbury, who in the spirit of *Annalia Dubrensia* from 1636, linked the England of his day to the glories of ancient Greece:

O England! Wise as thou art free –
Glorious and great forever be!
While virtue crowns thine honour'd name
May prescient genius guard thy fame:
Forget not in the blaze of courts,
The people's joys, the people's sports;
Like Greece – which in her mighty prime
Pluck'd Immortality from Time –
Thou to thy manly pastimes cling!
Still may thy poets weave the rhyme,
Thy great and good
Of gentle-blood,
Still wreathe, as now,
The victor's brow,
And guerdon still award for Tilting at the Ring!

A 'guerdon' is a prize or reward, which in the case of the poetry competition was £4 in cash, rather than a laurel wreath, which given the tone of the winning ode might have been more historically apt. On the other hand, Jonathan Douglas was almost certainly the editor of the *Shrewsbury Chronicle* at the time and therefore a professional writer.

Nevertheless, medals and trophies, pomp and ceremony – such as inviting local dignitaries to crown the tilting champion (*as seen on page 43*) – did much to raise the Wenlock Olympian Society's profile and to ensure that the local community took pride in the Games.

The pre-Games procession was intended to have a similarly uplifting effect. In 1851 this set off from Wenlock town centre at 9.00am and was made up of 'competitors, bearers of implements of the Games, Committee & friends, with flags and a good brass band'.

Perhaps not everyone was keen to take part because in 1859 competitors had to be warned, 'No persons, whether adults or boys, will be allowed to contend in the Games, unless they join in the procession'.

The Society's accounts show some of the costs involved in this pageantry, with fees being paid to flag bearers, brass bands and bell ringers. Other suppliers included florists, bakers, carpenters, wheelwrights, farriers and stationers, while the Crown Inn was used as an assembly point for the parade, and the Raven Inn on Barrow Street often hosted post-Games dances and accommodated important visitors.

The Games' economic benefits to the town increased still further when, as noted earlier, the new railway line linking Wenlock to Birmingham opened in 1860 (having been partly financed by Brookes himself).

The *Wellington Journal and Shrewsbury News* reported that trains bringing visitors to the 1870 Games had been 'fifteen to a carriage designed for eight!' One estimate towards the end of the century put the number attending the Games at 5,000.

Yet Brookes' ambitions did not stop at Wenlock.

To Shropshire and beyond

In May 1860 Brookes wrote to the mayors of several Shropshire towns, including Shrewsbury, Ludlow, Bridgnorth, Wellington and Oswestry (where as we saw on page 4 there had been 'Ho-Limpyc Gaymes' in 1834). His proposal was that an annual Shropshire Olympian Games be held by participating towns 'in rotation'.

Perhaps in reaction to this letter, a month later 'Olympic Games' were staged as part of Shrewsbury's annual show at The Quarry, an area of parkland and walks to the west of the town centre, in a loop of the River Severn. But these Games were hardly reported on and took the lowest billing on the show's poster, subordinated to such entertainments as 'Cupid and the Stag', put on by the town's tailors, drapers and skinners and 'Queen Catherine', performed by local flax dressers.

Brookes' suggestion did find eventual favour, however, and on Whit Monday and Tuesday in May 1861 the newly convened Shropshire Olympian Society staged its first county-wide Games on a site near Wrekin Hill, just south of Wellington and ten miles from Wenlock.

Hugely popular they were too, attracting an estimated crowd of 14,000. Not only that, but to the satisfaction of those within the Olympian movement who advocated rational recreation, the overall tone of the event was deemed to have been solidly respectable.

At least this was compared with a previous gathering to have taken place in Wellington, five years earlier. >>

Tom Sabin from Coventry, winner of the three mile race at Wenlock in 1877 and 1878, poses with his Ordinary (only later was the name Penny Farthing adopted). Below is the cup he won in 1877, part of the WOS's collection at the Wenlock Museum.

According to *Bicycling Times*, Sabin was a 'fair specimen of what an athlete should be' because he worked on his family's farm and did not smoke.

In April 2010 a Tom Sabin Memorial Challenge Ride was held between Coventry and Wenlock.

In his later years, William Penny Brookes wrote of his hope that a Wenlock Olympian might one day compete in a modern Olympic Games. Harold Langley from Birmingham was the first to fulfil that dream.

Seen here with the pentathlon medal that he won on Linden Field in 1923, Langley, a member of the Sparkhill Harriers, represented Great Britain in the triple jump at the 1924 Paris Olympics.

Langley later went on to serve as an athletics judge at the 1948 Olympics in London.

» Held to celebrate victory in the Crimean War, these 'Grand Rejoicings' had, in addition to the usual wheelbarrow races and climbing the greasy pole, included one contest offering five shillings to anyone able to seize in their mouth a live eel from 18 inches of water. Such Games, complained one pamphleteer, amounted to 'a revival of barbarism' and were 'not only frivolous but calculated to lower the dignity of human beings to a level with the inferior creation'.

The 1861 Shropshire Olympian Games were, by contrast therefore, a definite mark of progress. In true Wenlock Olympian style the day started with a procession from Wellington's Market Square to the field at the Wrekin. The packed programme included foot races on the flat and over hurdles, quoits, putting the stone, tilting at the ring, jingling, single-stick combat and rifle shooting. Prizes ranged from ten shillings for the under-ten's 100 yard dash to £3 for the adult's half mile race. As at Wenlock there were also prizes for poetry, art, sewing, knitting, arithmetic and English history. The best needlewoman won a work box, for example, while the winner of the history competition won a writing desk.

The following year the Shropshire Olympian Games were held at Wenlock, effectively merging them with the town's own 1862 event. No other town came forward for 1863, but in September 1864 Shrewsbury acted as host.

The venue was again The Quarry, while the sporting programme was similar to that of Much Wenlock, but with added wrestling, a sword exercise carried out by the Shropshire Yeomanry, and a series of swimming, rowing, sculling, punting and coracle races on the River Severn. Unlike Wenlock, only medals were awarded, with entry forbidden to professionals.

To accompany the Games the Shropshire Olympian Society issued a pamphlet, loftily entitled *Opinions of Eminent Men on the Importance of Physical Education and Out-Door Gatherings for Healthful Recreation and Athletic Exercises.*

This document, held by the Shropshire Archives, offers a perfect summary of the Victorian philosophy of rational recreation. Consisting of extracts from newspapers, books and speeches on the value of physical exercise, penned by sundry politicians, lawyers, teachers, churchmen and historians, the pamphlet's tone is best summed up by a passionate speech made by Mr Justice Bayle in 1858:

'I do not believe that a more useful thing can be done in any large town... than to encourage and assist the youth of the country in out-door exercises and recreations, which improve the health, increase the stature, mature the courage, and fire the pluck of our youth, on which, God knows, the very existence of the country depends.'

John Hulley, the self-styled Gymnasiarch of Liverpool, who we will meet in the next chapter, was quoted arguing that state-funded gymnasiums would 'contribute more towards raising us up a healthy, brave, manly, and handsome race of men and women'.

In a similar vein was a statement by the Liberal politician and then Chancellor of the Exchequer, William Gladstone, who declared that 'physical training, by manly sports and otherwise, is a matter at all times deserving of careful attention, and that no education can be considered complete from which it is excluded.'

But could these fine words be matched by deeds?

Certainly at The Quarry – famous then as now for its annual flower shows – the scene was set for a memorable gathering. Bedecked in a colourful array of flags, shields and coats of arms, the park's centrepiece, in an area known as the Dingle, was a statue of Hercules. Originally displayed at Condover Hall, this was a copy of an Athenian statue known as the Farnese Hercules. Indeed it still stands in the Dingle and is listed Grade II, as is Quarry Park (on English Heritage's Register of Parks and Gardens of Special Historic Interest).

Over the statue, according to the *Shrewsbury Chronicle*, was erected a 24 feet high arch, bearing Latin mottos of the Shropshire Olympian Society, including *Palmam qui meruit ferat* (let him who earns it bear the reward) and *Civium virtus civitatis tutamen* (the virtue of the citizens is the strength of the city), and the motto of the host town itself, *Floreat Salopia*.

Unfortunately the Games themselves were not allowed to flourish. Heavy rain cascaded down The Quarry's slopes, creating a muddy track for the athletes, and the Games turned out to be the last held by the Shropshire Olympian Society at county level.

However this was not the end of Brookes' attempts to popularise the Olympian cause beyond Wenlock. While continuing to support the annual Wenlock Games, he embarked on two further campaigns.

The first concerned the setting up of the National Olympian Association in 1865, an organisation supported by several representatives from Shropshire (as detailed in the following chapter). In fact the NOA's Games in 1868, 1877 and 1878 were all staged in the county, in Wellington, Shrewsbury and Hadley respectively, when no other hosts came forward, and as late as 1890 there was a body calling itself the Shrewsbury Olympic Society, holding its meetings in the Corn Exchange.

Brooke's second effort was directed rather further afield, towards Greece itself. For as he discovered, interest in an Olympic revival was not confined to England, and had resulted in revivalist Games being staged in Athens in November 1859. Open only to Greeks, the Games had been organised by a wealthy businessman and philanthropist, Evangelis Zappas.

Learning of this, Brookes made contact with Zappas via the British Embassy in Athens and donated £10 towards a prize, which was duly named the Wenlock Prize. It was won by Petros Velissarios of Smyrna for being, according to the *London Review*, 'the best runner in the longest race'.

Two further Greek Games were held in Athens in 1870 and 1875, but unlike their English counterparts, the idea did not take root. In the meantime, Brookes' gift to Zappas was reciprocated in 1877 when King George of Greece sent a silver trophy in recognition of Queen Victoria's 40th year on the throne. Brookes donated this to the National Olympian Games, held in Shrewsbury that year, and went on to lobby various figures in the Greek political and educational establishments, both in Athens and in London, in order to drum up interest in the idea of an Olympic revival.

We will return to these efforts, to Brookes' contacts with Pierre de Coubertin, and to Coubertin's own visit to Much Wenlock in 1890 in later chapters.

But to continue the Wenlock story, while efforts elsewhere in Shropshire faltered, the Olympian Games on Linden Fields continued uninterrupted throughout the latter years of the 19th century, and proved robust enough to survive beyond the death of William Penny Brookes on December 10 1895. Alas, this occurred just four months before the doctor's cherished dream finally came true with the staging of the first modern Olympics in Athens in April 1896.

The Wenlock Olympian Games after Brookes

On May 26 1896, five weeks after the IOC's first Olympic Games at Athens ended, Linden Field staged the 45th Wenlock Olympian Games, the first to take place without the benign presence of Dr Brookes.

The programme contained the usual athletics and cycling, as well as a Gimcrack Race (*as explained on page 42*) and an equestrian hurdle event called the Victorian Cross race. In 1909 members of the Shropshire Yeomanry took part in two novelty events, a costume race and wrestling on horseback.

During this period cash prizes were phased out, but there were still other incentives, some of them supplied by Frank Peplow, a jeweller on the High Street. In 1911 the prizes included a case of fish knives, a cut glass decanter, a Gladstone bag and a pickle jar.

As in Brookes' day, the Games were preceded by a procession. In 1909 the Jackfield Brass Band led the way with *Round the Town* and Mendelssohn's *Old Romance*. »

▲ A float at the **Much Wenlock Carnival** in 1948 (*top*) provided a link between the town and goings on in the wider Olympic world. Perhaps to avoid any clash with events in London that summer, Wenlock's sporting programme that year was not described as Olympian in any publicity material. But a competition to thread a needle was at least reminiscent of Brookes' day.

Holding the Olympic torch is **Harold Lloyd**. In 1953 Lloyd became the first local athlete to take gold in the Wenlock pentathlon since 1870. Above he is seen winning the sprint element of the competition.

Modelled on the familiar figure of Discobolus (see page 14), the Norman Wood Memorial Trophy was donated to the WOS by the BOA in 2006, to commemorate the man who worked so hard to revive the Games in 1977. The trophy is awarded to the individual considered to have contributed most to the Wenlock Games in any one year. Winners so far have been recognised for organising the athletics programme, dealing with torrential rain on Games day, and helping to manage the laying of the new running track.

» After the Games, there was dancing on the bowling green or, if the weather was poor, in one of the local pubs.

The regional appeal of the Games is also evident during these pre-war years, as athletes from clubs in Birmingham, Coventry, Shrewsbury, Kidderminster and Wales regularly competed. They were joined in some years by entrants from Islington and Blackheath in London.

No Games were held during the First World War, but they were relaunched in 1921, starting poignantly with a rendition of *Lest We Forget*, followed by a full programme of cycling, quoits, tilting and a pentathlon featuring the high jump, the long jump, a 200 yard flat race, a half-mile hurdle race and the shot putt. When Harold Langley won the pentathlon in 1923, reports stated that 3,000 spectators were in attendance.

But there were also hints of a decline. In 1924, the year that Langley competed at the Paris Olympics, the tilting competition, so beloved by Dr Brookes, had to be cancelled 'owing to insufficient entries', while a reminder in the 1929 programme that betting was forbidden suggests that at a time of acute economic hardship the Wenlock Olympian Games were in danger of losing their integrity.

Nor did it bode well that instead of genuine sporting contests a series of what appear to have been circus acts were invited. Performing in 1929 were Madene and May, the 'Brilliant Equilibrists, Comedy Clowns on the Rolling Globe' and Silo, 'Greatest of all Trick Cyclists and One Wheel Wonder'. In 1931 it was the turn of Wun-Hi and Ching-Soo, the 'Funny Chinese Laundrymen'.

Rational recreation, it would seem, had given way to variety entertainment.

And so it was that with Brookes now a distant memory – four of his five children predeceased him, and his last surviving grandson died in 1925 – the Wenlock Olympian Society finally proved unable to keep the flag flying in the face of apathy, and by the time war broke out in 1939, the annual Games had all but petered out.

After the war, as seen on the previous page, there was at least a nod to the IOC's Olympics at Wenlock's 1948 Carnival, while the year 1950 signalled the centenary of the Wenlock Games. Accordingly a one day celebration, with procession and sporting events, took place on Linden Field and appeared to represent a new beginning.

There was still a distinctly carnival spirit, evident in an archery competition to burst balloons, William Tell style, and in prizes for the best decorated prams and tricycles. But the entry of runners from Wolverhampton and from the Birchfield Harriers in Birmingham suggests that the Games still had some appeal to genuine athletes.

Which they did, if only sporadically. There would be

further Games in 1951 linked to the Festival of Britain, and in 1953 to celebrate the Coronation.

But as the decade wore on, Linden Field on Games day appeared more like a local fête than a sports meeting. There was dancing around a maypole, beautiful baby competitions, Punch and Judy shows, 'modern dancing' in the Memorial Hall, Old Tyme dancing at the British Legion and a 'soup and hamburger novelty barbecue'. In 1953 a gymkhana was held. In 1962 the organisers experimented with clay pigeon shooting.

By the early 1970s, however, the momentum had once again run out and it was clear that for Brookes' Games to be restored as a serious sports meeting there would need to be a major effort.

The modern Wenlock Olympian Games

The Games in their current form, with the accent once again firmly on sport, stem from a revival which took place at the time of the Queen's Silver Jubilee in 1977.

It was driven largely by two local men, Norman Wood – appropriately enough a physical education teacher at the William Brookes School – and the mayor of Wenlock, John Simpson. Working with a group of like-minded volunteers, Wood and Simpson resurrected the Wenlock Olympian Society, and while that year's Games were not formally titled Olympian, they had a strong sporting content. This included, for the first time in Wenlock, swimming and diving in the school's new pool, which flanked the Linden Field.

From that year onwards, the event flourished, with the word 'Olympian' being reintroduced in 1978, and Brookes' idea of educational and cultural activities being revived in 1979 in the form of an arts festival for local schoolchildren.

But just as important as the revival of the Games themselves has been the long overdue recognition of Much Wenlock's place in international Olympic history, and of William Penny Brookes' central role.

For this, much of the credit must go to the efforts of Norman Wood, and alongside him two men; Don Anthony, an Olympic scholar and chairman of the BOA's education sub-committee, and Roy Rogers, an international athletics official, who had acted as a timekeeper when Roger Bannister broke the four minute mile in 1954. All three worked hard at both local and national level to gain Much Wenlock its rightful place in Olympic history.

They were helped by historian Sam Mullins. Inspired by Birmingham's bid to stage the 1992 Olympic Games, Mullins wrote an influential pamphlet, *British Olympians: William Penny Brookes and the Wenlock Games*, published in 1986 by the Birmingham bid team. That same year, the BOA and the IOC sent representatives to what the Wenlock Olympian Society promoted as their 100th Games. Also in attendance at those Games was Pierre de Coubertin's great nephew, Geoffroy de Navacelle.

As noted earlier, this was followed in 1994 by the visit of the IOC President, Juan Antonio Samaranch, as part of his organisation's centenary celebrations. Samaranch gave the town's Olympic credentials a formal stamp of approval by making a pilgrimage to Brookes' grave, where he publicly acknowledged the doctor's legacy.

Wenlock's cause received further backing two years later with the publication of *The Modern Olympics: a Struggle for Revival* (*see Links*). In this, the American historian David Young drew heavily on the Wenlock Olympian Society's minute books, thereby furthering Brookes' reputation as 'a major figure in the Olympic movement'.

Royal visitors to Wenlock, meanwhile, included Princess Anne in 1990 and the Queen and the Duke of Edinburgh in 2003, when pupils from the William Brookes School put on a sporting display.

A further sign of recognition occurred in 1995 when an Olympic torch relay passed through Wenlock on its way from Athens to Bath, in advance of that year's European Youth Olympics, with the flame resting overnight by the memorial to Brookes in Holy Trinity Church.

Similarly, the Flame of Hope for the Special Olympics has passed through Wenlock twice, in 2005 and 2009.

Finally we come to the build up to the 2012 Olympics Games in London, a story in which Much Wenlock has played an active role. Cited in the bid document itself, the town has become a popular focus for pre-Games publicity, while the Games themselves have been attended by a number of prominent individuals. Helping to give out medals in recent years have been the Paralympic basketball player and now administrator, Philip Craven, the triple jumper Jonathan Edwards, the sprinter Ann Packer and cyclist Tommy Godwin.

David Moorcroft, a leading British distance runner of the 1970s and 1980s, even competed in the seven mile race at the Wenlock Games in 2010.

And of course also in 2010, as noted earlier, came the moment that meant so much to the Wenlock Olympian Society's dedicated band of volunteers; the unveiling of 'Wenlock' as one of two mascots for London 2012.

No longer just a curious part of Britain's sporting history, known only to a select few, Much Wenlock and its favourite son, William Penny Brookes, could at last claim their rightful place in the Olympic narrative.

Or to adapt a phrase, one small town in Shropshire, but a giant leap for the international Olympic movement.

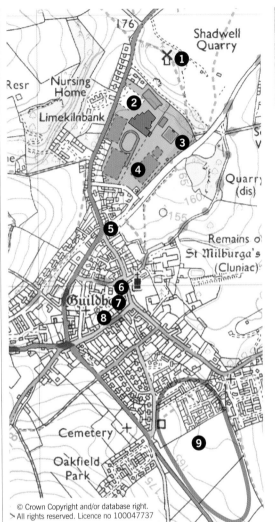

Wenlock's Olympian Trail starts at the museum and is denoted by a series of bronze markers. Covering just over one mile it takes in all the points of interest relating to the Olympian Games. The legacy of William Penny Brookes is everywhere; at the former schoolhouse and at the current school, at the old station, even an avenue of trees he planted at the entrance to Linden Field.

Key to map:

1. Windmill
2. William Brookes School
3. Bowling green and 'Coubertin oak'
4. Linden Field
5. National Olympian Association plaque (*see page* 77)
6. William Penny Brookes' house
7. Much Wenlock Museum
8. Corn Exchange and Agricultural Reading Society rooms
9. Site of Much Wenlock Racecourse (1807–1939)

Of all the memorials and plaques dedicated to William Penny Brookes, this marble tablet, in Much Wenlock's Grade I listed Holy Trinity Church, is surely the grandest.

There has been a church on the site since the 7th century, while the nave dates back to the 12th century. The tablet is positioned on the nave's southern wall, just inside the main door.

Beneath the relief bust – the only three-dimensional representation of Brookes that we have – is a summary of his achievements, while below is a biblical text, 'Be strong and of a good courage', taken from the book of Joshua. At the foot of the memorial is the familiar Wenlock device, with the letters WEN set inside a padlock.

The Brookes memorial was funded by public subscription 'as a mark of esteem and gratitude to a venerated friend and benefactor'.

As seen opposite, Brookes is buried in the Holy Trinity churchyard, in the family tomb.

▶ Opposite Holy Trinity Church, at **4 Wilmore Street**, stands the Georgian terraced house where, as yet another plaque records, William Penny Brookes Esq. JP, LSA, FRCS, was born in 1809 – his father was also a doctor – and where he lived for most of his life.

It was in this house that in October 1890 the 81 year old doctor entertained the 27 year old Pierre de Coubertin, and where in December 1895 he died, having been nursed by his daughter Adeline, the only one of his five children to outlive him. Moreover, all three of his grandchildren died childless, and so the Brookes family line died out in 1950. Coincidentally, a similar fate was to befall Coubertin's family, also during the 20th century.

It is impossible to visit Much Wenlock without coming across Brookes' extraordinary legacy.

Apart from the Wenlock Olympian Society and the Grade II listed Corn Exchange in which it is based on the High Street, there is the Market House (now the Museum), built at Brookes' behest, the Grade II* listed Gaskell Arms, where he used to deliver pre-Games speeches, the Grade II listed Raven Arms, where Brookes laid on a dinner for Coubertin during that 1890 visit, and the 16th century Grade II* Guildhall, where Brookes sat as a Justice of the Peace for over 40 years, surrounded by richly carved oak panelling and furniture that he had purchased on the town's behalf in 1848.

Elsewhere in Wenlock, on a street called the Bull Ring, stands the Priory Hall, which from 1848 to 1952 served as the town's National School. Brookes was instrumental in setting this up. On Sheinton Street stands Wenlock's last remaining gaslight. Brookes, almost inevitably, was a co-founder of the company that erected it. Around the corner stands the former railway station, another public utility Brookes helped to bring to Wenlock.

From there it is a short stroll to an avenue of trees, also paid for by Brookes, lining the entrance to Linden Field.

Finally, his grave (*below right*) lies in the Holy Trinity churchyard, overlooked by the Guildhall.

The plot, in which several other members of the family are buried, including Brookes' wife Jane, who died in 1885, is bordered by wrought iron railings made up of a succession of laurel wreaths, to symbolise Brookes' love of the Olympian ethos.

Understandably the grave forms one of the main stopping off points along the town's Olympian Trail, with many a wreath and bouquet placed accordingly. But most important of all, not least to the volunteers who keep alive the Wenlock Olympian Society, were the words of the IOC President Juan Antonio Samaranch, a visitor in 1994: 'I came to pay tribute and homage to Dr Brookes who was really the founder of the Modern Olympic Games.'

▲ Still standing sentinel over the Wenlock Olympian Games are the ruins of the Grade II listed windmill, now in a greatly improved state thanks to the efforts of the Much Wenlock Windmill Preservation Trust.

As noted earlier, trees now obscure much of the view of the games from **Windmill Hill.** One of the most imposing of these trees, next to the bowling green on Linden Field, is the **Quercus Concordia**, or Golden Oak (*above right*) planted by Pierre de Coubertin during his visit in October 1890 and bedded in with a libation of champagne. The original plaque (*above*) is now in the Wenlock Museum.

In July 1990, to commemorate the 100th anniversary of Coubertin's visit, a second oak was planted near the original tree by HRH the Princess Royal, herself a member of the International Olympic Committee.

Four years later a third tree was planted by the IOC President, Juan Antonio Samaranch, to honour William Penny Brookes.

During the preparations for the 2012 Olympics it was announced that an oak tree germinated from an acorn from the original 'Coubertin Oak' will be planted somewhere within the Olympic Park in London.

The modern day Wenlock Olympian Games take place each year over a weekend in July. Following the reconstruction of the William Brookes School and the laying of a modern athletics track in 2009–10, Linden Field has changed markedly. But, tilting apart, the range of activities remains much the same as in the 1850s, and the majority of participants still come from clubs around Shropshire, the Midlands and Wales, and at junior level, from local schools. The games are organised and staffed entirely by volunteers brought together by the Wenlock Olympian Society.

▲ The **Wenlock Olympian Games** are now a thoroughly modern affair, but there is one part of the programme that harks unashamedly back to their Victorian roots.

Attracting enthusiasts from across the region, this is a series of races and displays organised by the **Veteran Cycle Club**, featuring a cavalcade of beautifully maintained penny farthings, tourers, racers and even delivery bikes, many of them ridden by their owners in appropriate period dress. The climax of the event is a 'devil take the hindmost' race, seen here in 2009 (*above left*) and 2007 (*above right*), in which the last rider at the end of each lap drops out until only two remain for the final lap.

Another favourite at Wenlock since the Victorian era is the archery competition, organised by the **Bowbrook Archers** from Shrewsbury (*right*). It was an archer who became the first Wenlock Olympian to win a medal at the IOC's Olympic Games. Alison Williamson, then aged ten, came second at Wenlock in 1981, and went on to win the bronze medal in the women's individual event at the 2004 Olympics in Athens.

Using the newly opened facilities on offer in the **Much Wenlock Leisure Centre** – part of the William Brookes School, which flanks Linden Field – four events at the Olympian Games are staged indoors: volleyball, badminton and fencing (*above left*), plus swimming in the leisure centre pool. Other new events include golf, clay pigeon shooting and Kwik Cricket.

▲ In several respects the **Wenlock Olympian Games** resemble a typical school sports day, as after each event, competitors crowd round excitedly to check their times and positions. There is a diverse range of trophies and prizes to be won, such as the **Wenlock Plate**, awarded to the winner of the Male Veterans category in the road race, seen here held by Andy Wetherill, winner in 2007 (*right*).

In other ways, however, Much Wenlock echoes its grander Olympic counterpart. For example, every winner must mount the podium in order to receive a medal.

This distinct character gained a further layer in 2010 when LOCOG, the organisers of the 2012 Games, announced that one of the two official mascots would be named **Wenlock**. Seen above is the mascot's visit to Linden Field in July 2010, a visit much appreciated by the Wenlock Olympian Society's dedicated band of volunteers, who not only run the Games but also devote much of their spare time to maintaining the Society's archives, dealing with enquiries and showing growing hordes of visiting dignitaries and members of the world's press around the town. Few other market towns, and certainly no other community sports days, receive attention on that scale.

Seemingly ordinary, and yet unique, seemingly informal, and yet steeped in tradition, the **Wenlock Olympian Games** are indeed unlike any other sporting event in modern Britain.

Chapter Five

Liverpool Olympic Festivals

'There is no country in which manly exercises are so much in repute; and there is no town in the kingdom so well fitted to be the centre of the rapidly spreading movement as Liverpool,' commented the *Liverpool Mercury* on June 9 1864. Largely responsible for this was John Hulley (1832–75), a leading figure in the promotion of Liverpool's Olympic Festivals during the 1860s, and in efforts to establish a National Olympian Association.

For historians and scholars of Britain's Olympic history, the events described in our previous chapters on the Cotswolds and Much Wenlock will have been broadly familiar. Less so, almost certainly, the subject of this chapter; a series of 'Olympic Festivals' organised by a coterie of individuals and organisations based in Liverpool during the 1860s.

That these Festivals are so little known in Britain, even in the localities in which they took place, can largely be put down to the fact that, unlike the Games of Robert Dover and William Penny Brookes, they took place on only six occasions. Four were staged in Liverpool, in 1862, 1863, 1864 and 1867. Two were staged in Llandudno, north Wales, in 1865 and 1866.

Yet shortlived though they were, their significance in our wider narrative should not be overlooked. Not least is the fact that Liverpool's Festivals set a precedent that would be followed by the international Olympic movement of the 1890s, namely that entry be open only to amateur competitors.

As noted in the previous chapter, amateurism was not a major concern at Much Wenlock, where in some categories medals or trophies were awarded and in others the victors received prizes or sums of money.

Although clearly respectful towards Brookes, Pierre de Coubertin rejected this approach. His ideal was the athlete of ancient Greece, performing not for reward but for glory, not for money but for a simple laurel wreath.

Nowadays it is widely understood by historians that many victors at Olympia were rewarded in other ways, by patronage, favours and gifts. Nevertheless, for certain interest groups during the second half of the 19th century the mythologised ideal of the noble amateur of Olympia offered a convenient and overtly respectable model on which to base their own statements of intent.

Professionalism was of course their chief taboo. But in numerous instances this extended to a barely concealed dislike of competing against anyone who worked for a living. This was not only a British trait. The first Greek revivalist Games, held in Athens in 1859, were themselves open only to 'gentlemen'.

In subsequent years the Amateur Athletic Association, formed in Oxford in 1880, barred from its events anyone who had ever won a cash prize. The Amateur Rowing Association, founded in 1882, went further by banning not only professional watermen and rowers from its ranks, but also artisans, mechanics and indeed any individual who earned a living from manual labour. (Only in 1937 was this clause dropped.)

Association football effectively divided into amateur and professional camps from 1885 onwards, while in rugby, the issue of payments to players would lead in 1895 to a lasting split, between the Rugby Union and the Northern Union (known today as the Rugby League). In cricket it would result in amateur and professional players within the same team having separate changing rooms and even entering the pitch from different gates.

Never mind that amateurism was a luxury that only men of means could afford, or that many an 'amateur' – most notoriously the cricketer WG Grace – often received recompense under the counter or via third parties. Professionalism was *per se* anathema amongst the sporting gentlemen whose beliefs would help to lay the basis for Coubertin's own Olympian ideals.

Therein lies the historical significance of the Liverpool Olympic Festivals. They were the first modern Games to be named Olympic *and* to have amateurism at their core.

Moreover, the men behind them would play a key role in the formation of the world's first national Olympian association, at a gathering in Liverpool in 1865 (as detailed in the next chapter).

When the Liverpool Festivals were switched to the Welsh coastal resort of Llandudno for two years they were also the first Olympics to be specifically linked to tourism.

The legacy of these Festivals therefore belies the fact that only six were ever staged, and explains why historian Joachim Rühl, amongst others, has argued that they form 'one of the missing links' in the Olympic story.

Liverpool in the 1860s
At the time it launched its first Olympic Festival in 1862, Liverpool was a dynamic and thriving port city, enriched by its trade with the Americas and West Indies. Its population had grown from 82,000 in 1801 to 430,000 by 1861, the single largest group being Irish migrants fleeing the potato famine of the 1840s. Inevitably this influx, combined with the growth of trade and industry, had a major impact on the city's social and economic make-up,

and its infrastructure. Dense slums developed around the docks and in such areas as Dingle and Toxteth, while the city's professional and merchant classes moved outwards to the new suburbs of Sefton Park and Aigburth.

Two men share the credit for initiating the city's Olympic Festivals, Charles Pierre Melly and John Hulley.

The son of a successful cotton merchant, Melly was born in 1829 and educated at Rugby, a school where sport had famously assumed a central role under Thomas Arnold, headmaster from 1828–42.

On his return to Liverpool, living in what was then the village of Wavertree and working in the family business, Melly embarked upon a life of philanthropy and public service. He worked in several different areas (*see right*), but in the field of sport and recreation his first contribution was to finance a network of 'outdoor gymnasiums', starting on a patch of ground in the Smithfield Road area in 1858. Fitted with parallel bars, swings, seesaws and the like, this first gymnasium, or playground as we would call it, attracted nearly 7,000 users in its first month, according to the *Northern Daily Times*.

Three more followed in Wavertree, Toxteth and Kirkdale, all erected and supervised at Melly's expense.

In his capacity as chairman of the town council's Parks Committee, Melly also went on to play a lead role in the creation of Sefton Park in 1872 (as featured in *Played in Liverpool, see Links*).

John Hulley, meanwhile, was an important, if rather quixotic figure in local gymnastic circles.

Three years younger than Melly, Hulley had been trained by Louis Huguenin, a French gymnast who had started up classes on Cook Street, Liverpool, in 1844. By the 1850s Hulley was running his own gymnasium in a former billiard hall called the Rotunda, on Bold Street. It was at this gymnasium where that now familiar Latin motto, extracted from Juvenal's *Satires*, was adopted: *Mens Sana In Corpore Sano* (a healthy mind in a healthy body).

Whether or not this was adopted at Hulley's instigation we cannot be sure, but he certainly considered himself to be at one with the classical tradition. Most notably he took on the ancient Greek title of 'Gymnasiarch', and to widespread amusement sometimes appeared in colourful Turkish robes, Highland costumes or velveteen suits. A posthumous portrait of him in the *Liverpool Citizen* of February 25 1885 made great play of these 'harmless eccentricities' which did so much to make Hulley a well known and often entertaining figure in Liverpool life.

Melly's philanthropy, combined with Hulley's practical skills and persuasive powers, proved an ideal match. Both shared an enthusiasm for health, sport and exercise, and both were intent on promoting not only health and physical education amongst the working classes, but also setting an example of how they should 'play the game'. To Melly and Hulley that meant adopting a gentlemanly spirit, untainted either by prize money or by gambling. To spread this ethos, in January 1862 the two men founded the Liverpool Athletic Club (LAC), with Melly as president and Hulley as secretary.

Several of its earliest members came from branches of the Volunteer movement, a nationwide military organisation that had emerged a few years earlier in response to the perceived threat of invasion from France.

Liverpool's first Olympic Festival

Six months after the formation of the LAC, on June 13 1862, readers of the *Liverpool Daily Post* were greeted with a large advertisement (*reproduced overleaf*). Headed by the motto *Mens Sana In Corpore Sano*, the advertisement invited the public to attend a 'Grand Olympic Festival'.

Hulley expressed the hope that the Games would live up to the ancient traditions of Olympianism. 'No effort will be spared by the Committee not only to render the Festival worthy of its immortal title,' he declared, 'but also to make it the means of drawing more public attention to the important subject of physical education.'

As emphasised earlier, no professionals were to be allowed to compete, and no cash prizes were offered. Instead, this was to be an event primarily for 'Gentlemen Amateurs'. Similarly, with the cheapest tickets priced at one shilling for an unreserved place, and a seat in the stand costing two shillings in advance (or 2s 6d on the day), the organisers were clearly intent on attracting predominantly middle class and wealthy patrons.

Only one concession to non-gentlemen amateurs was made, and that was the provision of two silver and two bronze medals, plus 'other prizes which the Committee will decide upon on a future occasion', to be offered to 'the amateur frequenters of Mr Melly's Free Public Gymnasiums'.

As the list of local dignitaries and businesses supporting the event suggests, Hulley and Melly garnered considerable support. Retailers on Castle Street, Lord Street, Church Street, Bold Street and St James Street sold tickets. Liverpool's mayor, Robert Hutchinson, donated the Champion's Gold Medal, which in common with all the other gold, silver and bronze medals had been supplied by a local goldsmith, Joseph Mayer.

From the Volunteer movement, Colonel Sir John Jones and Major Faulkner were appointed as judges, while the bands of the 4th Lancashire Artillery Volunteers and the Childwall Rifles, the corps of which Melly was a captain, offered to provide music on the day. »

The cotton merchant **Charles Pierre Melly (1829–88) was one of Liverpool's most energetic philanthropists. In addition to his promotion of outdoor gymnasiums and the Liverpool Olympic Festivals he was active in the National Association for the Promotion of Social Science, the Working Men's Improvement Society, and in the setting up of Ragged Schools for working class children.**

Melly was also well known to Liverpudlians for endowing the provision of 43 drinking fountains across the city, at a time when suspect water supplies were a major health risk amongst the growing population.

Under its motto *Mens Sana In Corpore Sano* the Liverpool Athletic Club advertises in the *Liverpool Daily Post* of June 13 1862, the day before its first Grand Olympic Festival at the Mount Vernon Parade Ground.

Note the complicated hierarchy of prizes, with only five events deemed worthy of gold medals, one of which was for the essay competition. The others were for gymnastics, the steeplechase, the one and a half mile race and the 'four mile walking match'. There was also an overall Champions Gold Medal, donated by the Mayor, with all other events being rewarded with silver and bronze medals.

But who were the 'universally famed Lancashire Witches?' under whose 'distinguished patronage' the Festival was to take place? From a report of a regimental ball published in the *Lancashire Gazette* of January 7 1860 the title appears to have been a jocular one applied, no doubt by regimental officers, to the ladies of the county set.

"MENS SANA IN CORPORE SANO."

THE LIVERPOOL ATHLETIC CLUB
WILL CELEBRATE A

GRAND OLYMPIC FESTIVAL,
UNDER THE DISTINGUISHED PATRONAGE OF THE UNIVERSALLY FAMED

LANCASHIRE WITCHES,
AT THE

MOUNT VERNON PARADE GROUND,
ON SATURDAY NEXT, THE 14TH INSTANT,

When the following PRIZES will be offered for competition to Gentlemen Amateurs :—

THE CHAMPION'S GOLD MEDAL,
PRESENTED BY HIS WORSHIP THE

MAYOR, R. HUTCHISON, ESQ.

This Medal will be a beautiful specimen of workmanship, by our townsman, Mr. Mayer. It is in the form of a Maltese Cross. In the centre is a figure of Hercules, surrounded by a white enamelled ribbon, on which is inscribed the motto of the club, "Mens sana in corpore sano," in gold letters, and round that again is a wreath of laurels, in green enamel. This prize will be awarded to the most successful competitor of the day.

JUDGES :

COL. SIR J. JONES, K.C.B.,
AND

MAJOR FAULKNER,

Numerous other Prizes, also from the Establishment of Mr. Mayer, and specially designed for this occasion, will be contested for, and presented to the successful competitors by the President of the Club,

C. P. MELLY, ESQ.,

as follows :—

A Gold Medal or Ten Guineas for the best Essay on Physical Education.
One Gold, one Silver, and one Bronze Medal, for Gymnastics. Open to Members of the Liverpool Athletic Club only.
One Gold, one Silver, and one Bronze Medal, for a Steeple Chase of 1,200 yards.
One Gold, one Silver, and one Bronze Medal, for a One and a-half Mile Race.
One Gold, one Silver, and one Bronze Medal, for a Four Mile Walking Match.
One Silver, and one Bronze Medal, for Fencing.
One Silver, and one Bronze Medal, for Broadsword.
Two Silver, and two Bronze Medals, for Sabre v. Bayonet.
One Silver, and one Bronze Medal, for Jumping.
One Silver, and one Bronze Medal, for Leaping.
One Silver, and one Bronze Medal, for Vaulting.
One Silver, and one Bronze Medal, for Boxing.
One Silver, and one Bronze Medal, for Wrestling.
One Silver, and one Bronze Medal, for 120 Yards Race.
One Silver, and one Bronze Medal, for 300 Yards Race.
One Silver, and one Bronze Medal, for Half a Mile Race, for Youths.
One Silver, and one Bronze Medal, for Half a Mile Race, for the Club.
One Silver, and one Bronze Medal, for Throwing the Disc.
One Silver, and one Bronze Medal, for Throwing the Cricket Ball.
One Silver, and one Bronze Medal, for Indian Club Exercises.
One Silver, and one Bronze Medal, for Dumb-bell Exercises.
Also Two Silver, and two Bronze Medals, with other Prizes, which the Committee will decide upon on a future occasion, will be offered for competition to the amateur frequenters of Mr. Melly's Free Public Gymnasiums.
The Ground will be tastefully decorated for the occasion. A large and commodious

GRAND STAND

Will be erected, a portion of the basement of which will be fitted up for a Ladies' Refreshment-room ; the remaining portion will be used as a Refreshment-room for Grand Stand Ticket-holders only.
Tents will be provided for the competitors to dress in.
Numerous Flags, Military Trophies, &c., will be set up on different parts of the ground.
Several Military Bands will be in attendance, and no effort will be spared by the Committee not only to render the Festival worthy of its immortal title, but also to make it the means of drawing more public attention to the important subject of physical education.
JOHN HULLEY, Hon. Sec.
Proceedings to commence at Three o'clock.

Tickets may be obtained in Castle-street from Messrs. Mander and Allender, Webb and Hunt, Brett and James ; Lord-street, Messrs. Williams and Crook, Wynes, Oakes, Satchell, Mayer ; Church-street, Messrs. Tooke, Hime, Promoli, Lewis, Nodder, Horsfall, Jacobs, Thompson ; Bold-street, Ellerbeck, Nelson, Shand, Keet ; St. James's-street, Mr. Thompson ; Aigburth, Messrs. Pearson.
PRICES :
If taken before Saturday—Reserved Portion of Ground and Grand Stand, 2s ; Unreserved, 1s.
On Saturday—Reserved, 2s 6d ; Unreserved, 1s.

55476614

As for the sport, the *Liverpool Daily Post* expressed its pleasure that 'so many of the youths of the town and district' were taking an interest in physical education.

On the morning of the Festival, Saturday June 14 1862, clouds loomed. But fortunately the rain held off and the *Illustrated London News* was later able to report that some 9,000 people had paid for entry, forming a 'large and fashionable body of spectators', with the grandstand occupied principally 'by the gentler sex'.

The actual programme shared much in common with that of Much Wenlock. (This may simply be owing to prevailing sporting practices at the time, for although we know that Hulley and William Penny Brookes became firm allies by the mid 1860s, we cannot be certain Hulley attended any Wenlock Olympian Games before 1862.)

After the band of the 4th LAV had led a procession of competitors around the track at 3.00pm, Charles Melly, as president of the LAC, declared the Festival open and announced the first winner. This was a 21 year old Londoner, Edgar Athlestane Browne, who won a gold medal for contributing the best essay on physical education (a work that would later be read out at the Festival's medal ceremony, held in St George's Hall.)

Then began the Games, for as Melly declared, 'the principle of the Liverpool Athletic Club was action and not talking'.

Unfortunately for all concerned, however, the organisers tried to cram in rather too much action. As listed on the left, there were seven races, ranging from a 120 yard sprint – an event which gleaned the highest entry of 24 runners – to a four mile walking race.

Inside the track there were competitions for jumping, leaping and vaulting, for boxing and wrestling, for exercising with Indian clubs, and for throwing the disc and a cricket ball. For LAC members and affiliates there was also a gymnastic competition, plus, for the more military-minded, fencing, fighting with broadswords and one curious event, in which Hulley himself competed, called 'sabre v. bayonet'.

As it transpired, not all the proposed contests took place or were finished. On several occasions the crowd encroached on the competitors. Only one official time was recorded, that of J Tunstall's 35 minutes and 36 seconds in the four mile walk. One newspaper reporter complained of being unable to identify winners.

More embarrassingly, a boxing display staged between the LAC's boxing professor, Mr Wynes, and the day's winner, J Harrison, threatened to turn into a free for all.

But at least the organisers were able to announce an overall winner of the Mayor's Champion Gold Medal. Alexander Fairweather of the Athenaeum Gymnastic »

▲ From the *Illustrated London News* of July 12 1862 this wonderfully detailed and highly evocative etching shows the scene at the first **Liverpool Olympic Festival**, described here as 'the Volunteer Games', owing to the large numbers of participants from local Volunteer brigades, and to the fact that it took place on the **Mount Vernon Parade Ground**. This large expanse was located just east of Liverpool's town centre, between West Derby Road and Hall Lane, an area now dominated by the Royal Liverpool University Hospital.

On the far side of the 440 yard track, backing onto a church (no longer extant), is an uncovered grandstand, described as being close to Hall Lane, with the bell tents on the left serving as changing accommodation for athletes. In the foregound, the steeplechase, contested over a distance of 1,200 yards, is in full flight, with the twelve athletes – all dressed as jockeys it may be noted – running and leaping over fences in the wake of a horse and rider.

Around the infield, meanwhile, crowds gather in informal groups to watch various events taking place at the same time, including what appears to be boxing, broadsword fighting and gymnastic exercises on high bars.

There would be several instances during the afternoon when the sheer volume of spectators and a lack of crowd control led to chaos and confusion, while the LAC's over ambitious programme meant that some events had to cancelled before fading daylight finally brought the proceedings to an end at 9.30pm.

HAND SWING
Suspended from a Hook with a wire to allow of its being turned in any direction.

Gymnastics was one of the few branches of physical education in the 19th century in which leading proponents actively encouraged female participation. This etching was used to illustrate an essay entitled *Mens Sana In Corpore Sano*, written by EA Browne, which won him a gold medal at the Liverpool Olympics in 1862. John Hulley, a free spirit in several respects, wrote often of the need for women to share the benefits of sporting activity, and argued also that they be allowed to wear unconstricting costumes when swimming.

≫ Club in Manchester took the honour, having won both the Indian club exercises and the sabre v. bayonet contest, come second in both the vaulting and disc throwing, and third in the gymnastics.

Otherwise, failing light forced the rest of the programme to be halted at 9.30pm, Hulley and Melly having demonstrated that, an over-ambitious programme and inadequate crowd control notwithstanding, there was indeed an appetite for a modern version of the Olympics in a major city like Liverpool, just as there had been in a small rural town like Much Wenlock.

Liverpool's second Olympic Festival

A year later, on June 13 1863, the LAC returned to Mount Vernon for what they now billed as their 'Second International Olympic Festival', inviting not merely 'gentlemen amateurs' but 'gentlemen amateurs of all nations' to compete. This is the first explicit reference we have in our story of a British Olympic event attempting to reach beyond these shores.

Clearly there was great anticipation. Before the big day the *Liverpool Daily Post* carried notices from the police, advising spectators and horsedrawn vehicles on how to access the parade ground.

In a separate article entitled 'Our Olympic Games' the newspaper considered the Festival's links with the ancient world. Noting 'the eagerness with which we seek classical names and classical sanction for modern objects and pursuits', the writer concluded that in most instances the differences between the inspiration and the modern entity were too great to be meaningful. But not so attempts to revive the Olympics. 'If ever a name was fairly transferred from an ancient to a modern institution, it is in the case of those Olympic allusions by which the great athletic festivals of our day distinguish themselves from the mere sordid sporting contests that have rendered the very name of many exercises distasteful to the ear of a refined and highly civilised age.'

Or, put another way, rational recreation was closer in spirit to the sport of the ancient Greeks than any of the professional or gambling orientated sports meetings that had been the norm in the 18th and early 19th centuries.

The *Daily Post* then went on to state that the 'Olympic idea' held that 'the supremacy of physical excellence' set in essence 'a standard of manly perfectness'.

In fact as far as the *Daily Post* was concerned, thanks to Hulley and Melly, Liverpool's Olympic Festival was now 'the greatest' of all the modern festivals and, moreover, could be just the start of a much greater movement.

There could be little doubt, the newspaper went on, that the Festival's promoters 'would be quite willing to

see them assume the national importance of the great celebrations by which the physical condition of the Greeks was maintained at the high point at which it long remained.'

Lofty aims indeed. But what of the 1863 Festival itself?

Certainly the weather was better than in 1862, although heavy rain during the previous week rendered the running track heavy going. There were also more spectators, with one estimate suggesting a peak of 12,000 in attendance. To improve their view and to keep the crowds at bay a stage was erected in the infield for the boxing, wrestling and other combat sports. A Mr Graves had taken over Charles Melly's role as LAC president.

Otherwise, the programme was much as in 1862, starting with a procession at 3.00pm and the announcement of the winner of the essay competition. With an eye to a more concise timetable, events were scheduled to take place simultaneously (as has been standard practice at athletics meetings ever since).

There also appears to have been a concerted attempt to record times, even if those timings cannot be relied upon for accuracy. For example, we know that G Barker covered the four mile walk in 36.27 minutes, and that RH Merry won the two miles in 11.16 minutes. But the 120 yards was won by a Mr Wright with a scarcely credible time of 12 seconds (compared with the 1908 world record for the 110m, an equivalent distance, of 15 seconds). On the other hand, this may explain why Wright was immediately accused of being a professional. The accusation was overruled, but was an ominous sign of the splits that were to come in the wider world of athletics.

As for Hulley's hope that an international field might be attracted, reports suggest that this did not happen.

One final aspect of the 1863 Festival worth noting is that the Mayor's Champion received not only a gold medal but was also crowned with a laurel wreath, while all the victors were reported to have borne 'their honours modestly' just as those who had been 'worsted cheerfully submitted to their disappointment'.

The Olympic spirit, it would seem, was catching on.

Liverpool's third Olympic Festival

After the gains made in 1863, the LAC anticipated another bumper day for their third Festival on July 2 1864.

In the weeks beforehand, the *Liverpool Mercury* kept up the rhetoric of previous years. On June 9 it linked the Festival to the 'sound and philosophic notions of antiquity'. 'There is no country in which manly exercises are so much in repute; and there is no town in the kingdom so well fitted to be the centre of the rapidly spreading movement as Liverpool.'

On the morning of the Festival the *Mercury* wrote at some length on how Hulley and Melly's 'attempt to revive the games of the Olympiad' could improve the nation's health. As in the previous year there was to be a full programme of events. A 'large and commodious grandstand' had been erected and a decorative array of bunting and flags put out to enliven the scene.

But this sense of anticipation soon dissipated.

Firstly, owing to the sale of the Mount Vernon Parade Ground earlier that year, the LAC ended up having to hire another venue, the Zoological Gardens. Lying also on West Derby Road, just north east of Mount Vernon, the Gardens had been established during the 1830s in an old clay pit, by Thomas Atkins, the owner of a travelling menagerie. Atkins' claim to fame was that he had cross-bred lions with tigers to create a 'liger'. Following his death in 1848, however, the zoo had been relaunched as a pleasure garden and, as was commonly the fate of such enterprises in Victorian Britain, had acquired a somewhat dubious reputation, especially in the evenings.

This was not the venue's only drawback. The site itself was too small, allowing a running track of only one eighth of a mile, or 220 yards, to be laid out.

Then on the morning of July 2 the British summer did its worst. Torrential rain made the gymnastics and combat sports all but impossible, and turned the grass running track into a quagmire.

But in any case, either the weather or the unsuitability of the venue dissuaded most spectators from attending, leaving the LAC with no choice but to postpone the Festival until the following Saturday, July 9.

On this occasion all boded well. Colonel Sir John Jones was now in the president's seat. The Mayor, Charles Mozley, had once again donated the Champion's Gold Medal. As the *Liverpool Mercury* reported, there were also athletes from further afield, not just from Manchester but from Yorkshire, Warwickshire, Newcastle, London, and St John's College, Cambridge. All were attending, the *Mercury* reiterated, 'not in the sordid hope of winning so much money, but, as in the old Grecian times, simply for the honour which rewards success'.

But the day was beset with problems. Once again, as in 1862, the organisers proved unable to prevent the crowds from spilling onto the running track. Once again the programme overran, this time until 10.00pm. Even worse, a number of professional athletes turned up, and although barred from competing, happily took part in side events organised by wily local bookmakers. One such professional, Morton Brown from Liverpool, a man in his fifties, hopped a distance of 50 yards in just 18 hops.

Critics of the day would later blame the slip in standards on the salacious reputation of the venue. But in any case, by the time the medal ceremony was eventually held some days later it was apparent that Messrs Melly and Hulley were already preoccupied by another venture.

This was the laying of the foundation stone of a new building on Myrtle Street, the Liverpool Gymnasium, John Hulley's pride and joy. Opened the following year, this building will be featured more extensively in the next chapter, for it was there in November 1865 that a National Olympian Association was formed, in an attempt to repeat nationwide what Melly and Hulley had achieved with their Liverpool Festivals.

As for the 1865 Festival, this would be relocated to a new home, sixty miles to the west.

Liverpool's Olympic Festivals move to Llandudno

Although Cardiff is to host eight matches as part of the 2012 Olympic football tournament, it is not the first place in Wales to have staged an event styled as an Olympics.

Llandudno, on the north coast, can claim that honour.

Set between two rocky headlands – the Great Orme to the west and Little Orme to the east – Llandudno was in 1865 a small town that had come into being largely thanks to a new phenomenon, railway tourism. Its potential had first been spotted by Thomas Edward Lloyd-Mostyn, a baronet's son, who in 1849 bought up 832 acres of coastal land through an enclosure act, and in 1854 was elected MP for Flintshire.

Working with the Liverpool-based surveyor Owen Williams, within five years Lloyd-Mostyn had steered the Llandudno Improvement Act through Parliament, thereby beginning the transformation of what was mainly coastal marshland into a refined holiday resort. Streets were laid out on a grid pattern. Public buildings and a graceful promenade were erected, and in 1858 the all-important railway link was completed by the Chester and Holyhead Railway Company. A year later came the pier, enabling steam ships also to serve the new resort.

With fine sea bathing, clean air and a glorious backdrop of Snowdonia and the Clwydian Hills, and with such facilities as a croquet club, golf course and indoor swimming bath (in the basement of the Assembly Rooms), Llandudno soon became a prime destination, and not only for the new breed of middle class holidaymakers.

William Gladstone, Otto von Bismarck, the deposed French emperor Napoleon III, and Queen Elisabeth of Romania all visited, the latter describing Llandudno as 'a beautiful haven of peace'. Another visitor was John Hulley, who, on June 22 1864, wrote in the *Liverpool Mercury* on the benefits of sea bathing at Llandudno. »

Whereas several 19th century medals survive from Wenlock, the only representation of any medal from Liverpool's Olympic Festivals is this drawing from the *London Illustrated News* of December 12 1863. Depicting the Champion's Medal – awarded to the best performer at the Festival overall – in the centre of the Maltese Cross, mounted on a gold medallion, is the figure of the Farnese Hercules. Encircling this on a band of white enamel with gold lettering is the LAC motto, *Mens Sana In Corpore Sano*, a saying that was to become synonymous with the cult of 'muscular Christianity'.

》 Hulley was not the only Liverpudlian to appreciate its charms. When the poet Matthew Arnold visited in the mid-1860s he wrote of how 'The best lodging-houses at Llandudno look eastward, towards Liverpool; and from that Saxon hive swarms are incessantly issuing, crossing the bay, and taking possession of the beach and the lodging-houses.'

So it is not entirely surprising that after the relative disappointment of the 1864 Olympic Festival at the Zoological Gardens, Hulley should have decided to stage the 1865 Festival at this new resort, far away from the bookmakers of Merseyside and with the added bonus of being able to add swimming to the programme.

Besides which, as noted earlier, Hulley was already deeply immersed in the construction of the gymnasium in Liverpool, and, as we will learn in the next chapter, in the planning for a new national Olympian movement.

Llandudno's first Olympic Festival took place on Saturday, July 22 1865. The venue was the town's croquet lawn. Little was done to prepare the site apart from marking out a track and putting up all the usual flags and bunting. Instead of a grandstand, spectators gathered on the lower slopes of the Great Orme, which formed a natural amphitheatre, overlooking Llandudno Bay.

On the programme were all the usual events from Liverpool, but with one significant difference. The participants were boys, divided into two categories of under-12 and under-15. Press reports made great play of these lads' athletic prowess, their sporting behaviour and, almost inevitably, their potential in the future service of the Empire. And of course they were all amateurs too.

At 2.30pm the boys entered the arena, led by Wallace's brass band, and for the next three hours a good time was seemingly had by all, especially in the 100 yard hopping race. No unruly crowds. No bookmakers. As the *North Wales Chronicle* reported with pride, 'not a single contretemps occurred'.

Not all Hulley's preparations went to plan, however. After the afternoon programme the crowds were directed towards the seafront, where a men's 100 yard swimming race was scheduled to take place under lantern lights at 9.00pm, preceded by a Grand Procession of Illuminated Boats. But alas the boatmen Hulley had hired failed to materialise – they had been mysteriously double-booked – and so reluctantly the race had to be rescheduled.

Staging it on the following day, a Sunday, would have been quite out of the question, so instead it was held on the Monday, followed by a medal ceremony for Saturday's winners, conducted on a dais set up on the Parade.

Speeches extolling the virtues of athletic sports for promoting health, loyalty, discipline and 'gentlemanly demeanour' were made by a local dignitary, Colonel Hugh Molyneaux Walmsley, the son of a noted Liverpudlian, followed by Colonel McCorquodale of the Mersey Dock Board and Liverpool Gymnasium. Both men thanked Hulley for his efforts.

For one gushing correspondent to the *North Wales Chronicle*, Hulley's Olympics were the start of 'a new era'. Indeed what the town needed was more public entertainments. 'Llandudno was stepping on in the path of progress, towards that goal on the page of fame, which has so frequently been predicted concerning it.'

Two weeks after the Festival, reported the *North Wales Chronicle*, the Olympics remained 'a favourite topic of conversation'. But if 'the former gathering was a numerous one,' claimed the newspaper, 'a second would be far more so'.

Hulley agreed. The following March he returned to meet with Llandudno's Public Amusement Committee, consisting of hoteliers, publicans and retailers. His pitch for what he called somewhat inflatedly 'the fifth annual international Olympian festival of the Athletic Society of Great Britain', brimmed with confidence. (The ASGB, it would appear, was a title specifically adopted by the Festival organisers to lend the event greater prestige.)

The 1866 Festival, promised Hulley, would attract 10,000 visitors and some of the best adult athletes in the land. 'First-class men,' he insisted, 'the best men from the universities, officers in the army, and others of a similar class.' Such men were not, Hulley assured the Committee, 'men who competed for a living', and nor was he a mere 'showman'.

This postcard view of crowds gathering in Llandudno to hear a musical performance dates from the 1890s, but shows the terrain where the town's first Olympic Festival took place in 1865, on sloping turf at the foot of the Great Orme. The area remains as open parkland, with both the Grade II listed Queen Victoria Monument and the Toll House on Happy Valley Road, on the seafront (*centre right*), still standing.

Not that Llandudno's worthies needed persuading. William Hughes, the MP for Caernarvonshire, chipped in with ten guineas to start the fundraising. For his part the Mayor pledged to emulate his counterparts in Liverpool by donating a Champion's Gold Medal.

The 1866 Festival was held over three days, from Monday June 25 to Wednesday June 27.

This time, in anticipation of larger crowds, the venue was a field a mile to the east, closer to the Little Orme. This had room for a temporary grandstand, a 420 yard track and all the usual gymnastic equipment.

Starting off the Festival, as at Much Wenlock, was a procession of competitors led by a brass band, snaking its way from St George's Hall, on Mostyn Street in the centre of town, to what the local press called the 'Olympic arena'. At 3.00pm Colonel Walmsley delivered the opening oration, in which he followed remarks on the importance of physical recreation with a reminder that the field on which they stood was in fact 'historical ground... where Roman legions trod when they beat back the Britons...' and on whose soil 'the soldiers of the cruel Edward trod when they drove the Cymru to yonder mountain range'.

After the previous year's truncated programme for youths, the 1866 Festival schedule was as packed as during the earlier years in Liverpool. This time, however, more sensibly, two days were allowed for the athletics and gymnastics. On the third day – fortunately warm with few breezes – attention turned to the seafront, where the aquatic events were held by the Pier.

These consisted of swimming races held over 100 yards, a quarter of a mile, half a mile and a mile, as well as competitions for diving and for 'fancy swimming'.

Another Olympic innovation was an 'Ocean Yacht Race' which, despite its billing, was actually staged between Liverpool and Llandudno. Having started at 11.00am, it was won by a Mr Macfie, whose yacht sailed into Llandudno Bay at 6.30pm.

Later that evening there took place a Festival of Lights on the seafront, with the local boatmen this time turning up as promised, followed by a dance that proved so popular that it had to be switched from the Assembly Rooms to the beach.

But this was not quite the end, for a month later Hulley and his colleagues on the Llandudno Public Amusement Committee organised a junior Olympic Festival. Staged on the same field as the June event, and reportedly under the auspices of the 'Juvenile Athletes of Great Britain' – another title no doubt concocted by Hulley – it was contested mainly by the children of holidaymakers and drew a respectable crowd estimated at 4,000.

THE OLYMPIC FESTIVAL AT LLANDUDNO: THE FEAST OF LANTERNS.—SEE PAGE 16.

Judging by letters to the local press, both 1866 Olympic Festivals were well received. As seen above, they also gained Llandudno exposure in the *Illustrated London News*, ever supportive of Hulley's initiatives.

Yet there would be no further Olympics in the town.

Only one week after the junior Olympics, the first ever Games of the newly formed National Olympian Association took place in London (as detailed in the next chapter). Then in 1867, the Llandudno Public Amusement Committee found itself at Chester Assizes, accused of not paying the printing bills of a Mr RS Tomkinson. During the hearing it emerged that Committee members had had to stump up £50 each to cover the Olympics' losses.

'Some public-spirited individuals,' the prosecution barrister, Mr Giffard, commented scornfully, 'thinking it would be desirable to increase the prosperity of Llandudno, organised a committee to carry out certain amusements. There were to be concerts and all kinds of sports. There were to be grand entertainments and music, athletic games, Olympic games – whatever that might mean (*laughter*) – balls, concerts, and he knew not what.'

But not any more. Or at least, not in Llandudno.

The sixth and final Liverpool Festival

For two years Liverpool's Olympic Festivals had been effectively out of sight, if not entirely out of mind, in Llandudno. Meanwhile, the Liverpool Gymnasium had opened on Myrtle Street, and its two main supporters, Charles Melly and John Hulley, had become involved with the aforementioned National Olympian Association.

Hence, in 1867 there was an attempt to bring the Festival back to Liverpool. »

From the *Illustrated London News* of July 7 1866, this drawing depicts the Festival of Lights, in effect the closing ceremony of Llandudno's second Olympic Festival.

>> This time the events were staged at three venues, as had been the precedent set at the previous year's National Olympian Association Games in London. Naturally, the gymnastics, held on the evening of Friday June 28, were staged at the Liverpool Gymnasium. Yet proud though Hulley and his fellow LAC members must have been, it should be noted that on the same afternoon in Birmingham there also took place the second annual Games of the NOA. In other words Hulley's loyalties must have been split. Nor did this clash of schedules suggest much unity amongst leading Olympians.

It was also reported that yet again the Liverpool programme overran its schedule.

On the following day, June 29, the Festival's athletics events took place on 'a broad cindered course' at the Sheil Park Athletic Grounds, just east of the city centre. This time, as Hulley had long been promising, there was a genuine international flavour, with entrants coming from Paris and Marseilles as well as from Manchester, Northumberland, Sheffield, Shrewsbury and London (including representatives from the German Gymnasium and the War Office). There were also some new events, such as a hurdles race, and an extended one mile steeplechase, featuring 'a very stiff' ditch, ten feet wide.

During the two mile walk, one entrant called Farnworth suffered what we might call a wardrobe malfunction and had to be lent a spectator's coat in order to save the blushes of female spectators. It clearly did him no harm, though. He still won the race.

The athletics were followed on the evening of Monday July 1 with swimming races of 100 yards and of one mile, both staged in the River Mersey, off the Great Float at Birkenhead, on the opposite bank.

In terms of its scope and organisation, this was Liverpool's most ambitious Olympic Festival yet. Some 300 individuals in 28 disciplines had entered (the majority, 220, being for the athletics), further evidence that Liverpool was at the forefront of amateur sport.

But, emphasised Hulley in his speech that year, 'Olympic festivals are not the end of physical education. Physical education, or rather its dissemination, is the end. Olympic festivals are the means of securing that end.'

That said, the 1867 Festival would be the last of its scale held in Liverpool. The main reason for this appears to have been Hulley himself. Apart from his commitments to the Liverpool Gymnasium and to the NOA, Hulley caused a considerable stir in his home town by forming a relationship with the only daughter of a wealthy merchant, who was so opposed to the match that he locked her up on the day the couple were planning to get married.

This delayed the nuptials only by a day or two, but it did not help Hulley's social standing at a time when the Gymnasium's membership stood at its highest, yet its finances were starting to creak. Worse, Hulley developed a chest complaint, and was advised by his doctor to winter abroad. From what we know of his travels these were as adventurous as his life back in Liverpool, reportedly taking him across the Americas and on to North Africa.

But it was at the family home in Grove Street, Liverpool, where Hulley died, in January 1875, at the age of just 42.

As a Liverpool journal called *The Porcupine* reported on January 9, 'Mr Hulley had his whimsicalities, which sometimes offended and worried other people, but, looking at him now, as we have only the right to do, as a public man, it must be acknowledged that his enthusiasm and indomitable energy gave a stimulus to physical education in Liverpool which no other man was both willing and competent to impart.'

As for Hulley's great patron, Charles Melly, he died in November 1888, at the age of 59, it is said having committed suicide during a bout of depression.

The two men's beloved Gymnasium lived on, however, surviving various changes of ownership and a string of financial crises. It even witnessed two brief revivals of the Olympic spirit. Named the 'Grecian Games', these gatherings took place in February 1892 and November 1894 and were both attended by the French and Greek consuls in Liverpool.

By then the impetus for a revival of the Olympics at an international level already resided firmly with Pierre de Coubertin and others. But it is at least of interest to note that at both Grecian Games at the Liverpool Gymnasium every effort was made to reflect ancient traditions; for example, wreaths tinted in gold, silver and bronze were awarded, while the competitors turned out in togas provided by the local Greek community.

Also of note is that the 1892 Grecian Games were presided over by Herbert Gladstone, son of the former Prime Minister and president of the National Physical Recreation Society. Two years later Gladstone would be an adviser to Coubertin at the birth of the International Olympic Committee.

Otherwise, Liverpool's brief contribution to our Olympic story would lie largely forgotten for the next hundred years and more.

Liverpool's Olympic heritage

Few traces of any of the venues or events featured in this chapter can be seen today. As noted earlier, the Mount Vernon Parade Ground was sold in 1864 and the site is now dominated by the Royal Liverpool University

Hospital. Nor are there any traces of either the Zoological Gardens or of the Shiel Park Athletic Grounds. The Gymnasium on Myrtle Street, meanwhile, went into decline after its new owners, the YMCA, found it too large to maintain – its London counterpart, the German Gymnasium, proved equally ill-suited – and after two decades in use as offices for the National Health Service, the building was finally demolished during the 1970s. The Arts Centre of the Liverpool Community College now stands on the site.

There are also few traces of the two Olympic Festivals in Llandudno. The site of the 1865 Youth Games, the croquet green, became part of a leisure park called Happy Valley and in 1963 hosted the national Eisteddfod.

Today the site is marked by a Bardic Circle of stones from that event, still overlooked by the Great Orme and overlooking Llandudno Bay. The views over to Snowdonia are virtually unchanged from 1865.

The 1866 site, meanwhile, is an unmarked field, lying between the eastern edge of the town and the Little Orme.

Other points of interest include the pier, built in 1877. This replaced the original, which formed a marker in the swimming race in 1866. St George's Hall, at 74 Mostyn Street, where the athletes assembled before the 1866 Games, was a record store in 2010, although the façade of the Hall remains clearly discernible.

Concerning our two lead characters in this chapter, back in Liverpool there is a plaque to Charles Melly in the cloisters of the Unitarian Church in Ullet Road, and a memorial to him and other family members in the Columbarium of the Ancient Chapel of Toxteth, on Park Road. (One later member of the family was the jazz musician and writer George Melly.) A number of the Melly drinking fountains also remain in place, as seen right.

But the most significant efforts to rekindle interest in Liverpool's Olympic heritage have focused on the life and work of John Hulley. This has been researched by a number of historians, including Don Anthony, Joachim Ruhl, Ray Physick (author of *Played in Liverpool*, for *Played in Britain*), and by a family historian who shares Hulley's surname. Indeed it is largely thanks to Ray Hulley, a retired senior civil servant, formerly from Lancashire but now living in Hemel Hempstead, that we know more about the colourful Gymnasiarch than ever before, and that a website in his memory now exists (*see* Links).

Otherwise, Liverpool's chief contribution to the wider Olympic story must remain its stalwart adherence to the principles of amateurism. Three decades later this notion was to become central to Pierre de Coubertin's Olympic vision, and would remain a distinctive characterstic of the modern Olympics right up until the 1980s.

▲ It is owing to a campaign initiated by family historian **Ray Hulley** *(far right)* that **John Hulley's grave** in **Toxteth Park Cemetery** was restored and unveiled at a ceremony conducted on June 14 2009. In attendance, from left to right, were Olympic historian Don Anthony, the Reverend Graham Murphy and sports historian Ray Physick.

The grave's restoration was carried out by the John Hulley Memorial Fund in conjunction with F Welsby Ltd., monumental stonemasons, and received contributions from the British Olympic Association, the International Olympic Committee and numerous members of the public. Under Hulley's oft-quoted motto *Mens Sana In Corpore Sano* the gravestone reads, 'in loving and grateful remembrance of John Hulley, Liverpool Gymnasiarch, Co-Founder of the National Olympian Association 1865'.

Elsewhere in Liverpool are a number of the **drinking fountains** erected by Hulley's friend and patron, Charles Melly. Seen here on **Woolton Road** is one restored in 2007 following a campaign by The Friends of Liverpool Monuments (*see* Links).

Melly was thanked for his generosity in November 1861 with a candelabrum and silver plate, paid for by public subscription. According to the *Illustrated London News* this was 'as a token of the estimation in which he is held by his fellow-townsmen, rich and poor, on account of his public spirit and liberality...'

Chapter Six

National Olympian Games

One of Britain's foremost advocates of Olympianism was Ernst Ravenstein, seen here shortly before his death in 1913. Born in Frankfurt in 1834, at the age of 18 Ravenstein emigrated to London and became a respected cartographer and geographer. He was president of both the German Gymnastic Society (from 1861–71) and of the London Swimming Club, and with John Hulley co-wrote two manuals on the design of gymnasiums.

Until 1865, the various Olimpick, Olympian and Olympic Games and Festivals staged in Britain had essentially been local affairs. True, those in the Cotswolds, Much Wenlock and Liverpool attracted competitors from other regions, but in no sense could they be described as national events.

This changed when William Penny Brookes from Much Wenlock and John Hulley from Liverpool met up in Liverpool with other interested parties to form a new body, the National Olympian Association, in November 1865. The NOA's principal aim was to establish a National Olympian Games, to be held in a different city every year.

Given the founders' combined experience in organising local events, their commitment to the cause, and taking into account the growing popularity of athletics and gymnastics, this aim appeared to be an entirely logical and sensible progression to make.

However, for a variety of reasons that will become apparent, the National Olympian Games were not a long-term success. After the first two annual events, in London in 1866 and Birmingham the following year, in 1868 the NOA in effect retreated to Brookes' heartlands for a series of sporadic meetings at Much Wenlock and other Shropshire towns, culminating in the final NOA games in a village called Hadley, in 1883.

Failure though it was, the NOA nevertheless deserves to be fully considered for its role in Olympic history.

Firstly, it was the world's first national Olympian association, founded 29 years before the International Olympic Committee and 40 years before the British Olympic Association. Secondly, the NOA was the first organisation to attempt to bring together individuals and clubs from different disciplines, such as athletics, gymnastics, boxing, fencing and swimming, in order to create a national, multi-sport event.

Thirdly, the NOA was the first sporting body in Britain to lobby towns and cities in the hope of securing venues and financial backing for its annual games. As later administrators would discover when this process became common practice in the second half of the 20th century, this was no easy task.

Taking all these factors into account, the NOA was undoubtedly a construct ahead of its time. In other ways the NOA also helped strengthen Britain's Olympian ethos; for example it embraced amateurism, and actively promoted competitions for intellectual as well as sporting achievement. Also significantly, some of its leading exponents went on to create a later organisation, the National Physical Recreation Society, from which we can trace a direct line to the modern day IOC and BOA.

The NOA occupied, in other words, a vital, if ultimately shortlived place in the wider Olympic narrative.

Formation of the National Olympian Association

In July 1865, a week before the start of that year's Olympic Festival in Liverpool, John Hulley, Charles Melly and other members of the Liverpool Athletic Club visited London to meet their counterparts at the German Gymnastic Society in London. Both organisations were at the time putting the finishing touches to their grand new gymnasiums, so no doubt they had much to discuss about building works, construction costs and equipment. The Liverpool delegation was also keen to see the *Turners* (as German gymnasts were called) in action at the Society's annual display at Crystal Palace, in Sydenham.

Until that point, apart from Baron de Berenger's attempts in the 1830s (*see pages 18–19*), no-one from London had showed much interest in staging Olympic-styled events that were genuinely athletic (rather than equestrian). But the founder of the German Gymnastic Society, Ernst Ravenstein, was different. Because he saw in Hulley and Melly kindred spirits; perhaps because, being a German émigré, he had a less parochial outlook, and maybe because he also recognised that the gymnasium his organisation had just opened next to King's Cross station, in January 1865, would need all the support it could get, Ravenstein entered into a correspondence with the Liverpool duo.

The result was that when the Liverpool Gymnasium officially opened, on November 6 1865, Ravenstein attended, and with several other delegates stayed behind after the speeches for a meeting to discuss the formation of a National Olympian Association.

As the *Liverpool Mercury* reported the following day, the intention was to create 'a central association to systematise... and bring into focus' the many physical education, athletic and gymnastic clubs that were spreading all over the country.

»

◄ Costing £14,000 and probably the most expensive private establishment of its kind at the time, the **Liverpool Gymnasium** was one of several purpose-built gymnasiums constructed during this period. German and French teachers had popularised gymnastics among the upper classes in early 19th century London, but had always conducted their classes in adapted premises.

From the 1850s onwards, however, particularly as concerns grew about the fitness of British soldiers and sailors – compared, for example, to their Prussian counterparts – there arose a need for specialised buildings. Uppingham is thought to have been the first public school to have built a gymnasium, in 1859, closely followed by Radley College, Oxford, where gymnastics was taught by a Scotsman trained in France, Archibald MacLaren. MacLaren then advised the army on the construction of several gymnasiums at military training establishments, two of which survive, at Sandhurst (1862) and Brompton Barracks, Gillingham (1863). The oldest to survive from the private sector – Liverpool's having been demolished during the 1970s – are the former Royal Gymnasium in Brighton (1864) and, in London, the German Gymnasium (1865). More on this last building and its founder, Ernst Ravenstein, follows in this chapter, while further information on the Liverpool Gymnasium can be found in *Played in Liverpool* (see Links).

As for the nine delegates attending the **National Olympian Association's inaugural meeting**, from the minutes (*left*), apart from Hulley, Brookes and Ravenstein – Melly was one notable absentee – and subsequent newspaper reports, we know that Messrs Keeling and Lee represented the Athletic Society, which may well have been the same Athletic Society of Great Britain which Hulley had set up to organise the sporting elements of the Liverpool Festivals. Certainly both men had competed in the Liverpool Olympic Festival of 1864, Keeling in gymnastics and the all-rounder Lee in the 100 yards, the broadsword, and the sabre v. bayonet.

William Mitchell of Waterfoot in Lancashire (not Waterfost as printed in the minutes) won the hurdles at the 1863 festival, while Ambrose Lee was a promoter of amateur athletics from Manchester and had competed in the pole vault at the 1864 festival. Thomas Phillips represented Shrewsbury School, while John Murray was a member of the German Gymnastic Society in London.

The NOA's founding committee thus brought together the Liverpool and Shropshire Olympian movements with representatives from the two great athletic centres of London and Manchester. As importantly, they brought to the table organisational and practical experience, a mix that has characterised Olympian bodies ever since.

Of the few precious artefacts to survive from the National Olympian Association, the majority are in the collection of the Wenlock Olympian Society, having been found amongst the effects of William Penny Brookes.

This medal was struck for Brookes in 1866 to mark his election as first president of the NOA. On this side, Britannia crowns an athlete with a laurel wreath, circled by the motto, *Civium Vires Civitatis Vis* (the strength of the citizens is the power of the state), a variation of the motto later adopted by the NOA, *Civitum Virtus Civitatis Tutamen*.

On the reverse, surrounded by a laurel wreath, are the words 'National Olympian Association for Promoting Physical Education'.

Britain's early Olympians placed great emphasis on medals, as Brookes himself showed when attending the 1887 Wenlock Olympian Games (*see page 43*). The NOA medal is now one of several from his collection on display at the Wenlock Museum.

≫ From the minutes reproduced on the previous page, we can see two familiar characters, Hulley (in the chair), and Dr Brookes. It was at their insistence that the new organisation take the title Olympian, after a suggestion by JB Lee that it be called the Athletic Society instead. As the *Liverpool Mercury* reported, Lee was firmly advised that the term 'Olympian' had been preferred because it had a wider scope than athletics, and because of the organisation's intended emphasis on 'showing the advantages of combining mental with physical culture'.

Other resolutions adopted also followed now familiar themes in the Olympic narrative.

'Manly exercises' involving skill and strength would form the focus of the NOA's annual games, with medals, not money, as prizes.

The NOA would be a national organisation, with membership organised along county lines.

It would serve as 'a centre of union for different Olympian, athletic, gymnastic, boating, swimming, cricket, and other similar societies' and as a focus for a national annual competition open to 'all-comers', including international competitors.

Note, however, that the definition of 'all-comers' precluded professionals and women.

Intellectual achievements, meanwhile, would be recognised through an honorary membership scheme for 'persons who have distinguished themselves in literature, art, or science, or who have proved themselves benefactors to mankind'.

Here, then, were all the elements of a modern form of Olympism: amateurism, masculine sports, medals, a mix of physical and intellectual competition, and a Latin motto to sum up the organisation's ideals (*see left*).

Pierre de Coubertin, we should add, was at this time just two years old.

The first NOA Games, London 1866

Having set out such lofty intentions, the capital was the obvious choice for the NOA's inaugural Games. London's sporting culture, then, as now, was wider ranging than any other British city. Much of this, of course, was owing to its scale. According to the census, its population in 1861 was just over 2.8 million; that is, six times that of England's second largest city at the time, Liverpool.

Among its teeming masses, London was well endowed with ex-public schoolboys and university graduates who had gone on to form clubs and societies, such as the London Rowing Club, the London Swimming Club, and the London Athletic Club (originally the Mincing Lane Athletics Club), formed in 1856, 1859 and 1863 respectively.

The capital was also destined to become the focal point for a new form of sports organisation, the national governing body; the first of which, the Football Association, formed at the Freemasons Tavern in Great Queen Street also in 1863, two years before the NOA came into being.

London was similarly blessed with well appointed venues, such as Lord's (where several sports other than cricket were regularly staged), and numerous open spaces, such as Blackheath and Clapham Common, where sport, both amateur and professional, had flourished since the 18th century. London also played host to a number of well established events, such as the Oxford v Cambridge Boat Race, staged on the Thames since 1845.

This strength in depth, however, turned out to represent a major obstacle to the NOA, for there were plenty of powerful individuals already active on the London sporting scene – representing the universities, public schools, the Civil Service and other establishment institutions – who had no intention of falling in with a group of relatively unknown men from Liverpool, Manchester and Shropshire. It was not that they disagreed with the ideals of the NOA. Far from it. London's gentlemen were as anxious to promote amateurism and healthy activity as were Hulley and Brookes. But why run the risk of ceding London's place as the epicentre of amateur sport?

There may well have been other prejudices at play. After all, strictly speaking was not John Hulley himself a professional, in the sense that he was paid to manage and teach classes at the Liverpool Gymnasium? He was clearly an eccentric too, as his penchant for exotic costumes revealed. As for Ravenstein, a respected cartographer at the War Office he might have been, but he was nevertheless a German. And who was this Shropshire doctor, Brookes, with his preoccupation with Greek history, medals, laurel wreaths and tilting at the ring?

But whatever the nature or root of their objections, London's sporting elite certainly made clear their response to the NOA's proposals. Instead of joining up, they hurriedly formed a new organisation of their own, the Amateur Athletic Club.

As noted by Peter Lovesey in his official history of the AAC's successor body, the Amateur Athletic Association (see Links), 'It has to be said that the AAC prospectus, published in February 1866, bears signs of having been cobbled together over Christmas with no more purpose than to thwart the National Olympian Association.'

A few weeks later, in March 1866, just four months before the NOA's first games, the AAC then held their own 'first annual champion games' in the grounds of Beaufort House, in Brompton, west London. Its exclusivity can be gauged by the fact that entry to each event cost one guinea and that any athlete who competed in the NOA's games, or any 'open race or handicap' would be banned from any future AAC competitions.

This was hardly the spirit of co-operation that Hulley, Brookes and Ravenstein had sought. Yet they were not deterred, and at six o'clock on the evening of Tuesday, July 31 1866 – a month after that year's Olympic Festival at Llandudno (see page 63) – Britain's first National Olympian Games started with a splash, or at least with a swimming race, in the River Thames at Teddington, in south west London.

Once again demonstrating their ambition, the NOA's founders had decided to programme their inaugural games over three days, taking in three different locations. Interestingly, this was the model adopted by Pierre de Coubertin in his early thoughts during the 1890s.

Also noteworthy is the fact that the NOA chose to stage the swimming in the River Thames, rather than utilise one of the indoor swimming baths newly available in London. For example Lambeth Baths, opened in 1853 and home to the London Swimming Club (of which Ravenstein was president), had two pools of over 120 feet long and had often been used for competitions.

Swimming in the Thames, by contrast, was a more manly pursuit, even if the stretch past Teddington was not actually tidal, thanks to the construction of the Teddington Lock in 1811. (Teddington itself, a former village, had been absorbed into the outer belt of London suburbia by the arrival of the London and South Western Railway in July 1863.)

But however suitable the location, the weather proved far from ideal. Heavy rain fell and a strong north-westerly churned up the water and blew into the swimmers' faces, forcing some to drop out.

Despite this, three races were completed, each starting from a barge moored a mile above Teddington Lock.

Henry Jeffs of the National Swimming Club won the quarter mile, GH Vize of the London Swimming Club took the half mile, while his fellow club member William Adams – described by the Pall Mall Gazette as a 'very beautiful side-swimmer' – won the mile, in which, reported the Illustrated London News, he beat 'formidable antagonists with the utmost ease'.

All three winners, it will be noted, were from London, as were most of the other contestants, representing the Serpentine Swimming Club and the German Gymnastic Society. But the NOA could still claim the event to have been a national one, as there had also been entries from Southampton, Brighton and Liverpool.

»

Edward Stanford's 1862 map of Crystal Palace Park shows the cricket ground where the 1866 NOA Games were staged, on the park's eastern edge, bordering Penge New Road (since renamed Crystal Palace Park Road). This area remains as public open space, whereas the adjoining Great Fountains would, in 1895, be drained and the southern basin converted into the massive turf bowl where FA Cup Finals were staged until 1914, and where the present day athletics stadium was laid out in the 1960s.

>> As at Liverpool, each winner won a silver medal, the gold being reserved for the Games' overall top performer. Second and third placed swimmers won bronze medals.

There was one unfortunate incident on the night. One of the bronze medallists, C Nurse from Brighton, who had finished third in the half mile, found himself the first person to be disqualified by the NOA. This followed accusations that he was a professional.

If Teddington Lock was a relatively modest location, day two of the first National Olympian Games took place the following afternoon twelve miles to the east, in what was, at the time, arguably the most spectacular and grandiose leisure attraction ever built in Britain.

Crystal Palace Park, of course, took its name from Joseph Paxton's giant glass and iron construction that had originally housed the Great Exhibition in Hyde Park in 1851. Since being rebuilt at Sydenham in 1854, the Palace had been filled with exotic plants, sculptures, and courts themed around classical and medieval civilizations and their artefacts. Millions of daytrippers were drawn to its programme of events, which included firework displays, brass band contests, musical and dramatic entertainments.

In the surrounding grounds the Crystal Palace Company laid out a park that they hoped would rival Versailles. There were two huge fountains, formal and informal promenades, gardens, woods, a lake, geological

formations and Benjamin Waterhouse Hawkins' hugely popular sculptures of dinosaurs.

In other parts of the park there were areas for sport and recreation. These consisted of a boating lake, two archery grounds and, at the park's eastern edge, a cricket ground. It was on this picturesque expanse that the NOA staged the second day of their inaugural games, on Wednesday, August 1 1866.

In the *Daily News* the event was described as 'The Great Gymnastic Gathering'. The *Morning Post* carried the billing, 'First Great Gathering of the National Olympian Association'. For weeks tickets had been on sale from the German Gymnasium, ranging from one shilling for general admission to the park up to five shillings for a reserved seat and a place at the post-Games banquet.

But would the spoiling efforts of the AAC pay off? Not a bit of it. A crowd of around 10,000 spectators turned up, drawn in by the NOA's promise of a day of 'Athletic Exercises and Competitive Sports without parallel'.

According to an glowing report in The *Penny Illustrated Paper*, 'one of the prettiest sights imaginable' was the 'roped arena... surrounded as it was by admiring spectators, while the grassy interior was gay with the gold, red and black striped flags of the Germans...'

Accompanied by the 'enlivening strains' of the band of the Coldstream Guards, the proceedings began with a procession of 'athlete gymnasts' who, 'clad simply in black and red striped shirts, or in closely-fitting white jerseys and white trousers... went through their evolutions with limbs almost as unhampered as though they were in their birthday suits only.'

Also catching the eye of The *Penny Illustrated Paper* was 'a turbaned gentleman attired in the garb of a Turk' whom he supposed to 'represent the East'. This of course was John Hulley, or to give him his full title, as the reporter put it sarcastically, 'the Gym – wait a minute, I'll spell it directly – the Gymnasiarch of Liverpool'.

The contests themselves were similar to those seen at Wenlock and Liverpool.

Foot races were run over various distances of up to two miles. There were hurdle races and a fearsome half mile steeplechase that with 20 hurdles, four ditches and two barriers, one nine feet high and the other eleven and a half feet high, was more akin to an assault course.

The throwing events included putting the 36 pound shot and throwing the 'spear' (or javelin) for accuracy at a target shaped like a man. For the jumpers there were high running leaps, long running leaps, high standing leaps and pole leaps, while combat sports included boxing and wrestling – both 'catch-as-catch-can' and Westmorland style – plus sabre v. bayonet fights.

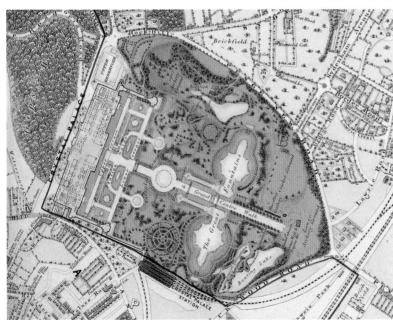

Keen for the Olympian movement to be associated with the military, the NOA also staged a competition for army and navy personnel, and a race for Volunteers dressed in combat clothing while carrying their weapons.

As with the swimming the previous evening, London competitors dominated at Crystal Palace, with two members of the German Gymnastic Society – Hugo Landsberger, known to his pals as 'Baby', and HW Brooke, whom we encountered at Much Wenlock (see page 42) – finishing level on points for the accolade of top performer overall, for which the prize was the gold medal. In the end, however, as reported in *The Penny Illustrated Paper*, 'the young Briton' amicably stood aside to let the 'tough Teuton' take the honour.

Significantly, there also appeared among the winners a number of AAC members who clearly chose to ignore the boycott of NOA events. Among them was W Rye of King's College, who won the mile, albeit only after the first placed runner had been disqualifed, having been accused of professionalism. Whether or not he was professional, the accused athlete certainly was persistent, for he turned out to be the same C Nurse from Brighton who had been exposed at Teddington the night before. In fact Nurse also won the two mile race at Crystal Palace, before being disqualified a third time, thereby allowing Humphreys of Southampton to take the silver medal.

Humphreys was one of the few competitors from outside London. Others were from Liverpool, Norwich and Winchester. Another was from Bristol. Eighteen years old, he won the 440 yard hurdles in a time of one minute and ten seconds. But rather more noteworthy is that during the same week this young athlete had been playing cricket for England, in a match against Surrey at the Oval, where he had managed an innings of 224 not out. His captain had then allowed him to nip down to Crystal Palace, five miles to the south, to compete in the hurdles.

The name of this precocious talent? WG Grace.

Grace was the recipient of one of 120 medals, art prizes, trophies, certificates and pocket watches given out that evening during a ceremony presided over by William Penny Brookes, who inevitably used the opportunity to make a speech. In this, Brookes set out the case for what had recently become known as the philosophy of 'muscular Christianity' (a term coined in response to the writings of Charles Kingsley, who was known to have been much impressed by the Liverpool Gymnasium).

'It has often been a matter of surprise to me,' said Brookes on that August evening in 1866, 'that we who bestow... so much care and attention on the development of the bodies of the lower animals designed for our use, should be so regardless of the means which are »

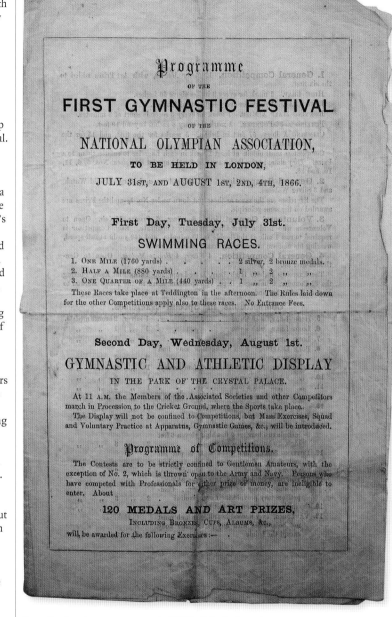

From the London Metropolitan Archives, this is the cover of the programme issued for the NOA's inaugural games in 1866. Note that apart from certain events for Army and Navy entrants, entry was for 'Gentlemen Amateurs' only.

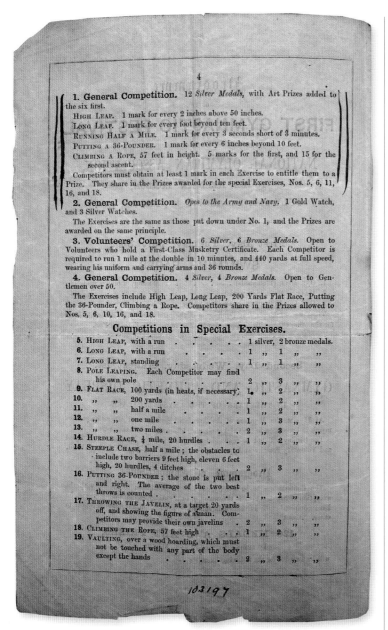

4

1. General Competition. 12 *Silver Medals*, with Art Prizes added to the six first.

HIGH LEAP. 1 mark for every 2 inches above 50 inches.
LONG LEAP. 1 mark for every foot beyond ten feet.
RUNNING HALF A MILE. 1 mark for every 3 seconds short of 3 minutes.
PUTTING A 36-POUNDER. 1 mark for every 6 inches beyond 10 feet.
CLIMBING A ROPE, 57 feet in height. 5 marks for the first, and 15 for the second ascent.

Competitors must obtain at least 1 mark in each Exercise to entitle them to a Prize. They share in the Prizes awarded for the special Exercises, Nos. 5, 6, 11, 16, and 18.

2. General Competition. *Open to the Army and Navy.* 1 Gold Watch, and 3 Silver Watches.

The Exercises are the same as those put down under No. 1, and the Prizes are awarded on the same principle.

3. Volunteers' Competition. 6 *Silver*, 6 *Bronze Medals.* Open to Volunteers who hold a First-Class Musketry Certificate. Each Competitor is required to run 1 mile at the double in 10 minutes, and 440 yards at full speed, wearing his uniform and carrying arms and 36 rounds.

4. General Competition. 4 *Silver*, 4 *Bronze Medals.* Open to Gentlemen over 50.

The Exercises include High Leap, Long Leap, 200 Yards Flat Race, Putting the 36-Pounder, Climbing a Rope. Competitors share in the Prizes allowed to Nos. 5, 6, 10, 16, and 18.

Competitions in Special Exercises.

5. HIGH LEAP, with a run	1 silver, 2 bronze medals.
6. LONG LEAP, with a run	1 „ 1 „ „
7. LONG LEAP, standing	1 „ 1 „ „
8. POLE LEAPING. Each Competitor may find his own pole	2 „ 3 „ „
9. FLAT RACE, 100 yards (in heats, if necessary)	1 „ 2 „ „
10. „ „ 200 yards	1 „ 2 „ „
11. „ „ half a mile	1 „ 2 „ „
12. „ „ one mile	1 „ 3 „ „
13. „ „ two miles	2 „ 3 „ „
14. HURDLE RACE, ¼ mile, 20 hurdles	1 „ 2 „ „
15. STEEPLE CHASE, half a mile; the obstacles to include two barriers 9 feet high, eleven 6 feet high, 20 hurdles, 4 ditches	2 „ 3 „ „
16. PUTTING 36-POUNDER; the stone is put left and right. The average of the two best throws is counted	1 „ 2 „ „
17. THROWING THE JAVELIN, at a target 20 yards off, and showing the figure of a man. Competitors may provide their own javelins	2 „ 3 „ „
18. CLIMBING THE ROPE, 57 feet high	1 „ 2 „ „
19. VAULTING, over a wood hoarding, which must not be touched with any part of the body except the hands	2 „ 3 „ „

103197

Another page from the programme for the 1866 NOA Games. As may be seen, although cash prizes were strictly taboo in NOA circles, the prizes for the General Competition for Army and Navy entrants were gold and silver pocket watches.

» calculated to promote the health, the symmetry, and the strength of our own bodies.'

'I rejoice,' he went on, 'that we have in this country many Christian ministers who believe, and who rightly believe, that the Gospel of Christ, whilst intended to fit us for a better and happier world, was never meant to make us gloomy in the present one – who think that we show our gratitude to the Almighty better by the cultivation than by the neglect of the faculties with which He has so beneficently endowed us.'

Robert Dover could hardly have put it better.

And just to make it clear that the NOA's ambitions were not confined to London, nor to this single event, nor even necessarily to 'gentlemen amateurs', Brookes urged the government to help develop the 'stirling qualities of the Anglo-Saxon race' by supporting the promotion of physical education.

He concluded with a rallying call to all Olympians.

'I congratulate you… on the success of which has attended this movement wherever it has been introduced – a success the rapidity of which is the more remarkable when we consider the length of time usually required in a free country to change the current of opinion, or to convert the people to a new idea… If our institutions… like our native oaks, are slow in their growth, like our oaks, too, they take the deeper root.'

The speeches over and the medals awarded, the evening ended in great style, with a banquet, a spectacular fountain display, a torch lit procession through the park, and entertainment provided by Crystal Palace's resident Italian gymnast, Signor Ethardo.

On the next afternoon, Thursday August 2, the NOA Games were reconvened at a third location, the German Gymnasium. But before describing the day's events, some explanation is necessary of how this building, originally known as *Die Turnhalle*, came into being.

Ernst Ravenstein established the German Gymnastic Society (GGS) in London in 1861. Yet while many of its original members were indeed from the German community, the name referred as much to the type of gymnastics as to its origins (in the same way that we refer to 'American' or 'Australian Rules' football).

German, or Turner-style gymnastics had emerged in various German states during the Napoleonic Wars.

Designed to build strength, courage and teamwork, they consisted mainly of drills and exercises, using ropes, vaults, dumb-bells and so on, combined with martial sports such as fencing. (In contrast, Swedish gymnastics, which was to become popular in Britain during the late 19th century, concentrated more on movement, agility and stretching.)

So successful was the GGS that in 1864 it set about building its own headquarters, just as Hulley and Melly had opted to do in Liverpool. Although not finished at the time, the building was first opened to members in January 1865, and appeared to be mostly complete when featured in *The Builder*, in May 1866 (*see following page*).

As research by Frank Galligan has shown, by then German members were outnumbered at least two to one by the British, with a wide range of other nationalities also represented, including French, Dutch, Belgian, Spanish, Italian, Russian and Latin Americans. But whatever their nationality, noted *The Builder*, 'the mercantile class preponderates'. Crucially, the GGS also welcomed women, as users of the Gymnasium if not actually as full members.

In short, here was a building of a type not seen before in London, used by a remarkably diverse group of individuals. (As such, it will be featured in more detail in our forthcoming study, *Played in London*.)

Small wonder then that some of the conservative figures in the AAC viewed the German Gymnasium and Ernst Ravenstein with some suspicion. But not the likes of Hulley and Brookes. And so it was that the third day of the inaugural NOA gathering took place in this, the capital's newest, state-of-the-art sporting establishment.

According to the last page of the programme, not shown here, the schedule started at midday – given that there had been a banquet the night before – with a Gymnastic Congress. At this the NOA's rules were discussed and sites for the 1867 Games proposed. In the evening there followed a two hour Gymnastic Display which, as described in *The Penny Illustrated Paper* finished with a smiling 'plucky Teuton' leaping from a 36 feet high cross beam onto a 'canvas sheet held firmly by a score of trusty comrades' (*see page 75*).

Ravenstein then delivered yet another speech on the benefits of physical education, after which, according to the programme, a competition for 'gymnastic songs... popular in style' was held, perhaps in the Gymnasium's refreshment room. For as *The Penny Illustrated* report concluded, the GGS was as much about 'promoting sociability at the *kneipe*... as physical education in the gymnasium'.

Accordingly, after a day of rest on the Friday, on the Saturday the NOA officials, members and friends headed down to Dorking for a picnic on Leith Hill.

The NOA, said Brookes during the course of the celebration, had brought together all of 'the athletic societies of the country' into 'one grand body', and as a result, the organisers now looked forward to the Games, as intended, being staged in other cities. »

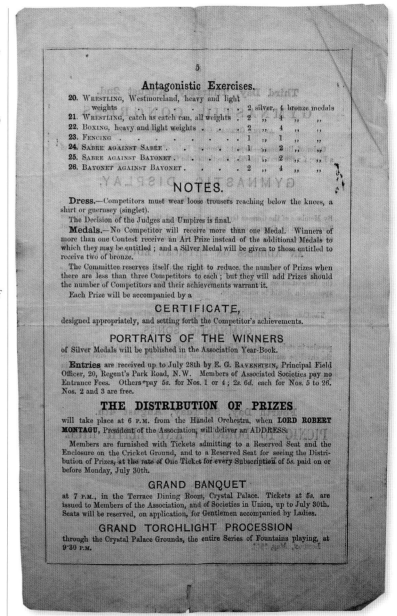

A further page from the 1866 programme reveals much about the social conventions that prevailed amongst those who campaigned for physical education. This was rational recreation, but with tasteful entertainment in its wake.

THE GERMAN GYMNASIUM, ST. PANCRAS ROAD, LONDON.——Mr. E. Grüning, Architect.

▲ Restored in 2005 as part of the King's Cross Central development, the Grade II listed **German Gymnasium** sits between King's Cross and St Pancras International stations and was designed by Edward Gruning to a brief set out by Ernst Ravenstein. Opened in January 1865 but not completed until the following year, the building was dominated by the **main hall** (illustrated above in *The Builder* of May 19 1866), measuring 120 x 80 feet and surrounded by viewing galleries. This hall has since been sub-divided by the addition of a mezzanine floor, and the building's length cut by some 30m at the front.

》 Southampton, Norwich, Bristol, Liverpool and Birmingham were all named as possible venues.

But was Brookes' optimism misplaced? According to the athletics historian Peter Lovesey (*see* Links), the AAC had already become the more powerful body by mid 1866. It had numerous subscribers at three guineas each. It had opened its own gymnasium in a building off the Strand and had taken over the management of the Beaufort House athletic ground in west London. WG Grace's cameo notwithstanding, Lovesey dismisses the NOA's athletics programme at Crystal Palace as 'unremarkable'.

The underlying issue, moreover, had not gone away. As Lovesey writes, to the elite amateurs in the capital, 'the prospect of athletics (being) controlled from anywhere but London was unthinkable...'

The second NOA Games, Birmingham 1867

By the 1860s, although its population was rapidly approaching the magnitude of Liverpool and Manchester, in sporting terms the city of Birmingham had yet to make its mark.

It offered the NOA fertile ground, nevertheless. The Birmingham Athletic Club had formed in 1866, and in the emerging middle class suburb of Edgbaston, where the BAC's grounds lay, on Portland Road, there were some interesting developments in the air. In around 1859 or 1860, in the back garden of an Edgbaston villa, the first trials had taken place of a game that would eventually evolve into lawn tennis. This would lead to several tennis clubs forming in the Edgbaston area during the 1870s. The area's renown would be further enhanced by the arrival of Warwickshire County Cricket Club in 1886.

For the NOA back in 1867 the appeal was obvious. Birmingham was accessible by rail from London, Liverpool, Manchester and from Brookes' home in Much Wenlock. Birmingham athletes had often competed at Wenlock, while Clement Davies, Honorary Secretary of the BAC, had joined the NOA's committee.

But there was a cloud on the horizon. Not least, as the debate intensified over how amateurism should be defined – a debate that had been brought to the fore by the disqualification of Nurse during the previous year's NOA Games – more athletes opted to toe the AAC line and not risk entering the NOA's 1867 Games.

This was because the hardline attitude of the AAC stated that not only could no athlete be considered an amateur if he had ever competed for money, but nor could he be considered amateur if he had raced, knowingly or not, against any other athlete who had ever competed for money. In other words, one could be guilty merely by association. And just to make doubly sure of keeping out professionals, in 1867 the AAC also barred from participation any 'mechanic, artisan or labourer'.

This draconian stance was all very well in the exclusive circles in which AAC members operated. But for the likes of Hulley and Brookes this was taking matters too far. In fact, it was too much also for the IOC which, when it formed in 1894, adopted a more pragmatic stance.

In 1867 it was the battle over amateurism that would start to whittle away at the NOA's standing.

The Association's second Games took place over three days, from Tuesday, June 25 to Friday, June 27.

On the opening day, proceedings began in true Wenlock style with the athletes, accompanied by the band of the Warwickshire Rifle Corps, processing to the Birmingham Athletic Club's headquarters at Portland Road. Compared with Crystal Palace Park, Birmingham's Festival Grounds, as they were called, were hardly developed, and lay in the less leafy part of Edgbaston, close to a prison and a workhouse. (The site is now occupied by George Dixon School.)

The Wenlock influence continued with tilting at the ring, that favourite of William Penny Brookes, making its national Olympian debut. In a repeat of the previous year, there was also a 'General Competition', in effect a pentathlon, involving events for jumping, throwing, running and climbing.

Some of the entrants' names were familiar from the year before, such as Hugo Landsberger from the German Gymnasium. As well as London, competitors came from Birmingham, Gloucester, Norwich, Liverpool, Leeds, Bristol, Newcastle and, despite the AAC's warnings, from the universities of Oxford and Cambridge.

For boys aged under 16 there were races ranging from a 50 yard sack race to a half mile run, and competitions for throwing and leaping.

In the evening, the Games moved to the city centre. Birmingham's Town Hall, a splendid edifice completed in 1834 and modelled on the Temple of Castor and Pollux in Rome (and still extant today) provided a suitably classical setting for the gymnastic competition.

On the Wednesday, Portland Road hosted the rest of the athletics programme, plus wrestling, then it was back to the Town Hall in the evening for the fencing, boxing, broadsword and sabre v. bayonet competitions.

The final day saw the swimming competition. Unlike the 1866 Games, where the swimmers had braved the River Thames, the 1867 event was held indoors, also in the city centre, at the Kent Street Baths (opened in 1851). There was then a cricket match at Portland Road.

To conclude matters, the Town Hall hosted the prize-giving and an 'Olympian Ball' in the evening, complete »

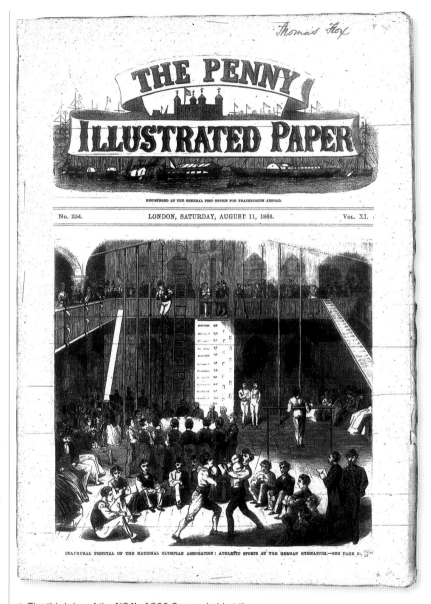

▲ The third day of the NOA's 1866 Games, held at the **German Gymnasium**, made front page news. Here the artist has depicted several events which in reality took place separately. Ernst Ravenstein stands on the far right, next to Charles Westhall, a reporter from *Bell's Life*, who acted as a judge for the boxing. Note the 'plucky Teuton' dropping from a high beam for the evening's finale.

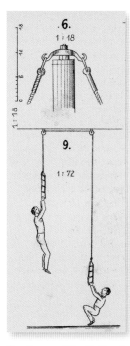

One legacy of the National Olympian Association was that John Hulley and Ernst Ravenstein co-wrote two detailed manuals in 1867; *The Gymnasium and its Fittings: Being an Illustrated Description of Gymnastic Apparatus, Covered and Open-Air Gymnasia* (from which this diagram is taken) and *A Handbook of Gymnastics and Athletics*.

》 with speeches by Brookes and Ravenstein on the now familiar themes of physical education and the benefits of Olympianism to the nation.

John Hulley, incidentally, was otherwise engaged that evening, for somehow the organisers of the Liverpool Olympic Festival had decided to start their own 1867 event that same night (*see pages 63–64*).

If this diary clash suggests a lack of forward planning, or even possible rifts within the NOA leadership, there were to be more problems in store for the NOA over the ensuing months. The Birmingham Games had, in truth, not attracted the finest athletes. Nor had the tilting at the ring competition helped to give the impression of a forward looking organisation.

There then followed a major blow in 1868 when the NOA failed to persuade any club or organisation in the city of Manchester to act as host of the third Games. This was despite the city's strong athletic culture, and the fact that many a Mancunian athlete had participated in previous Liverpool Festivals and both NOA Games.

The National Olympian Games, 1868–1883

Manchester's rebuff was a bitter pill to swallow, and so there was no doubt a deep sense of disappointment when the third annual NOA Games ended up not in any of the major cities, as had been the intention, but in the Shropshire town of Wellington.

Wellington, it will be recalled from Chapter Four, had already staged the 1861 Shropshire Olympian Games, in a field at the foot of Wrekin hill, just south of the town and about ten miles from Much Wenlock. This was again chosen as the site for the 1868 NOA Games.

There was sufficient interest for the Birmingham newspapers to send reporters, and for the Great Western Railway to lay on a special train from Birmingham Snow Hill to Wellington. But in truth, these third Games, held over two days on August 25–26 1868, were regional rather than national.

They followed the now familiar pattern. The competitors assembled in the Market Place at midday and processed to the Wrekin, with the mounted tilters at the head of the parade. (Clearly Dr Brookes continued to hold sway.) According to the *Birmingham Daily Post* the field 'presented a very gay aspect', with its flags and decorations, while the fine weather helped to attract a crowd of about 3,500. Clouds on the second day cut this down to 2,500.

Various sports that were popular locally appeared on the programme, such as quoits and bowling. There was also a brass band competition. The 'event of the day' was, however, the 'tilting over hurdles', won by a Wenlock

rider. He took home a trophy worth 15 guineas and a laurel wreath presented by a Miss Charlton. The runner-up won a mounted hunting whip.

Otherwise, apart from an accident in the 150 yard hurdles, in which a competitor broke his leg, the two days went well, and were concluded with a dinner at the Wrekin Hotel, followed, at Wellington's Town Hall, by the seemingly obligatory lecture by William Penny Brookes on physical education.

As for the range of entries, some came from the Athenaeum Gymnastic Club in Manchester and the GGS in London. But the majority were Midlands men, from Birmingham, Shrewsbury, Wenlock, Ketley and Wellington itself.

It was as if the NOA was having to resign itself to a peripheral role, while in London, the AAC went from strength to strength, and in March 1869 opened its very own, purpose-built athletics ground at Lillie Bridge.

Ominously, there would be no fourth consecutive NOA Games that year, nor indeed for the next four years, until, with John Hulley now in poor health, Brookes returned doggedly to the helm and relaunched the NOA in 1874.

As before, the Wenlock doctor intended that the Association be 'a centre of union for the many gymnastic, athletic, Olympian, and other similar societies springing up in the United Kingdom'. But rather than focus on competitive athletics and gymnastics – an area now dominated by the AAC – the emphasis was more on the promotion of physical education to the wider masses, the training of teachers and the endowment of every school with a gymnasium.

To help further these aims Brookes assembled a group of titled patrons and council members, including Lord John Manners, General Sir Percy Herbert and Thomas Hughes, the Rugby-educated lawyer and social reformer who had done so much to promote muscular Christianity with his popular novel of 1857, *Tom Brown's School Days*. The organisation also had a new president, the MP for South Shropshire, the Earl of Bradford.

Hughes apart, however, none of these men were of any great national standing, at least not in sporting circles.

The relaunched NOA held its first Games on May 25–26 1874 on Linden Field, Much Wenlock (the location a clear indication of Brookes' overriding influence but also of the Association's inherent lack of standing).

As was Brookes' inclination, there was a competition for the best essay, this time on the subject of 'physical education with special reference to our national elementary schools'. Significantly, in view of how the NOA had shunned such prizes during its early incarnation, the winner of this competition was offered a prize 'to the value of £20'. But then throughout his life Brookes never appeared to see any conflict between such prizes and the wider argument surrounding amateurism. Not only that, he went further by programming an extra half-mile race especially for 'labouring' men, an approach that would have horrified anyone in the AAC.

Almost inevitably tilting at the ring was reintroduced, while Brookes also made sure that all winners were crowned with laurel wreaths and given silver medals, 'a custom borrowed from the Olympian Games of old Hellas', as the *Western Mail* put it.

Clearly buoyed by the success of the 1874 games on his home turf, in January 1875 Brookes returned to Manchester to plead once again for the city to provide a venue for the next NOA Games. He even got as far as addressing the public at a special meeting held in the Mayor's parlour at the Town Hall.

But, as in 1868, his appeal fell on deaf ears, and so, once again, the good doctor was forced to fall back on his allies in Shropshire.

Shrewsbury staged the fifth NOA Games in August 1877, at the same venue as for the Shropshire Olympian Games in 1864, The Quarry. As in 1864, the weather was unkind, so much so that a thunderbolt struck the field and floored some spectators, though with no serious consequences. Also fortunately, the fireworks stored nearby for the evening's entertainments were spared.

As well as the usual athletics and gymnastics, the 1877 NOA Games included rowing on the River Severn. The tilting at the ring attracted six competitors, with, according to one report, Much Wenlock's reigning champion, J Webster of Stanway, throwing down his glove to challenge the others, and the 'loveliest lady' in the crowd presenting the eventual winner, W Braithwaite of Droitwich, with a laurel wreath.

Another highlight was that the winner of the pentathlon, as the 'General Competition' was now officially called, was awarded with a silver trophy donated by no less a figure than King George of Greece. This, as noted in Chapter Four, had been sent via the Greek ambassador in London, whom Brookes had befriended. Given in honour of the 40th anniversary of Victoria's accession, the trophy was also a belated thankyou for the Wenlock medal Brookes had donated to the Athens Olympics organised in 1859 (*see page 46*).

Not that this link with the Olympic homeland assisted Brookes in any way, for the 1877 NOA Games at Shrewsbury were followed by a break of six years. While in London the newly renamed Amateur Athletic Association, the successor to the AAC, continued to consolidate its rule over English athletics, not even the

small market town of Ludlow, which Brookes approached in 1882, was prepared to find the £800 required to stage another NOA Games. The NOA itself, Brookes admitted at this point, was 'without any funds at all'.

And so to the final, ignominious sixth NOA Games, of which almost nothing is known, other than it took place during the summer of 1883 in the Shropshire village of Hadley, ten miles north of Much Wenlock.

The dream of creating a national Olympian movement was over, at least during Brookes' lifetime.

Numerous explanations can be found for this failure, starting with the strength and greater spending power of the London athletics establishment and the suspicions of its leaders towards provincial administrators and towards Ernst Ravenstein and the GGS. Nor did the ongoing conflict over differing interpretations of amateurism help the NOA's cause.

To which we might add that surely no competition that featured tilting at the ring as its main event ever stood a chance of becoming nationally significant in the burgeoning sporting culture of Victorian Britain.

But as we stated at the outset, this failure should not blind us to the noble intentions or the good sense of the NOA's founding principles. For apart from nurturing the notion of a national Olympian movement, the NOA's ambition of promoting physical education was eventually taken up by a new body, the National Physical Recreation Society (NPRS), which Brookes founded in 1886. Among its supporters were the MP Herbert Gladstone (son of the Liberal Prime Minister), the Earl of Meath, Lord Charles Beresford, Lord Kinnaird (a leading light in the Football Association) and Alexander Alexander, once of the Liverpool Gymnasium, now of the German Gymnasium.

In turn, the NPRS was one of the bodies that helped to form the British Olympic Association in 1905, thereby providing yet another link between Brookes, the NOA and the modern Olympic Games.

One of the oddest and most inaccessible plaques to feature in our story is this one in Much Wenlock. For some reason situated half way up the side of a railway bridge, now disused, on Sheinton Street, the text states, as it continues around the corner: 'The fourth festival of the National Olympian Association was held in Linden Field, May 25th and 26th 1874. The Right Honourable Earl of Bradford, President'.

For those unable to read the fading lettering, a newer plaque has been helpfully placed below.

Chapter Seven

Morpeth Olympic Games

Arguably one of the least known corners of Britain's Olympic heritage lies in Northumberland, where two streets, Olympia Gardens and Olympia Hill, commemorate the field where Morpeth's Olympic Games and its forerunners were staged between 1870 and 1895. Three other venues were used before the games ended in 1958.

When the House of Commons sat in May 1953 to debate whether certain sports could or should be excluded from a proposed rise in Entertainment Duty, the Labour MP Robert Taylor pleaded the case for athletics.

In doing so, from his own constituency he cited a sporting event which the previous year had celebrated its 71st anniversary. Yet as recorded in *The Times* on May 20, the mere mention of 'the Morpeth Olympic Games' elicited laughter around the chamber.

An Olympic Games in a small, if charming county town in Northumberland? For over seventy years?

Was the Right Honourable gentleman making it up? And if not, how come this was the first time most of the assembled MPs had ever heard of it?

The answer is simple. Morpeth does not form, and has never formed part of the history of the Olympic movement because, during the 88 years that its Games ran, between 1870 and 1958, albeit not every year, it was an event which unashamedly sought to attract professionals.

There was in Morpeth no Robert Dover to lend the town's Olympics any philosophical or historical substance, no William Penny Brookes to promote them as part of a Christian movement, no John Hulley to argue their role in popularising physical recreation.

Nor is there any evidence that the Morpeth promoters ever sought links with the National Olympian Association, or, despite the prominence at Morpeth of wrestling – a sport so integral to the ancient Olympics – that they ever attempted to link their own efforts with those of the Greeks.

Instead, Morpeth's Games were run predominantly by local business interests for the benefit of the town, and were largely aimed at working men and working class sportsmen. A decade before the formation of the International Olympic Committee, the Morpeth promoters adopted the title 'Olympic' purely because it added value and status to their endeavours.

And because they could.

Such an association would of course be anathema to Pierre de Coubertin and his cohorts. To them, any hint of professionalism sullied the very name and ethos of the Olympian ideal. But to the flat-capped, Woodbine puffing colliery workers who flocked to Morpeth's Olympics, laurel wreaths and the principles of amateurism counted

for nothing. Hence, the Morpeth Olympic Games are the exception that proves the rule; excluded from the official narrative precisely because they did not conform to the received, purist version of Olympic history.

Sport in 19th century Northumberland

Straddling a bend on the River Wansbeck, the county town of Morpeth lies 14 miles north of Newcastle upon Tyne and 50 miles south of the Scottish border. In a 1920 guidebook to Northumberland, Peter Anderson Graham noted that it was not a town 'associated with any events of historical importance'.

This seems a little harsh. Morpeth Castle saw action during the Civil War, in 1644. For centuries its imposing prison gatehouse had, according to Graham, struck 'terror to the horsecopers, muggers and other gangrels who were credited with the thefts and burnings which constituted the more ordinary forms of crime in North Northumberland'. Morpeth's main street is dominated by a town hall designed by no less an architect than Sir John Vanbrugh, in 1714. At St Mary's, the former parish church, lies the grave of the suffragette Emily Davison, fatally injured by King George V's horse when she ran onto the track at Epsom on Derby Day in 1913. The town was also the birthplace of the 16th century botanist William Turner and the pioneering 19th century railway engineer John Rastrick.

By the early 1870s, when the Games began, Morpeth was a regional centre of some 5,000 inhabitants, served by two railway lines and with over 50 collieries, quarries and brickworks operating within a five mile radius.

Sporting life in the town was dominated, as in the rest of Northumberland, by traditional sports such as wrestling (Cumberland or Westmorland-style), potshare bowling (in which contestants had to throw a small heavy ball the furthest distance along a roped-off course), and by those other favourites of the mining community, quoits, pigeon racing, rabbit coursing and dog racing. Professional running, known then as 'pedestrianism', was also well entrenched in the north east.

In other words, these were sports that, in contrast to team games, pitted one man or one animal against another in a trial of strength, stamina or skill. Moreover, all were sports in which gambling played a central role.

As the region's population grew, so too did these activities become more popular and, in time, more organised. Where before working men had been content to issue and organise challenge matches amongst themselves, usually on public open land, by the 1870s, as historians such as Alan Metcalfe (*see Links*) have shown, commercial interests, particularly publicans, had started to intervene.

Across the north east, enclosed sports grounds charging an entrance fee were opened. Promoters also, crucially, introduced a system of handicapping, so that gamblers could bet on a wider pool of runners of differing abilities (human and canine). Skilled handicappers worked out each runner's chance of winning a race. The best runners then started at the regular starting line, with those rated slower given staggered starts further along the course. This made the outcome of a race less predictable than if everyone started at the same line, and greatly added interest for gamblers and athletes alike.

Sporting contests also became an integral part of the region's annual 'gala' days. These were days on which local mining communities would gather to show off their prowess with displays of prize blooms and vegetables, or in brass band and choir competitions. Adding sport to the mix was an obvious extension, bringing in spectators from across the county and beyond, and creating a calendar of gala days – in effect, a circuit – that, taking in the likes of Newcastle, Durham, Blyth and Ashington, helped to raise the level of competition and, in the process, offer rich pickings for the best performers.

Morpeth Olympic Games 1870–95

Unlike at Much Wenlock and Liverpool, Morpeth's annual Games had been running for several years before they assumed the title 'Olympic'.

The first reports of their existence appeared in the *Morpeth Herald* in September 1870. Staged on the Old Brewery Field, just north of the town centre (*see right*), they featured 'a capital programme of sport, embracing wrestling, pedestrianism and other popular athletic exercises'. The field's slope allowed most spectators to watch from the northern end, looking down towards Howard Terrace.

The reports suggest that the Games were by then an annual event, and that in 1870 they made a profit. But no reports in 1871 or 1872 have been found, and when the Games re-emerged at the Old Brewery Field in August 1873 they were under new jurisdiction, that of a 30 year old wheelwright and former wrestler, Edmund Dobson.

As the *Morpeth Herald* suggests, not only were most contestants in it for the prize money, but they were also »

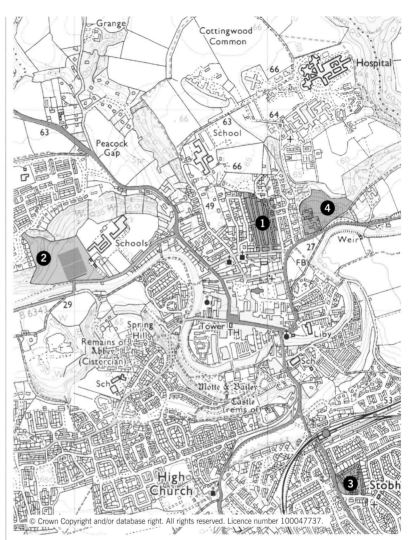

Four venues were used to stage the Morpeth Olympics:

1. **Old Brewery Field** site of Games 1870–95 (now housing, including Olympia Gardens / Olympia Hill)
2. **Grange House Field, Mitford Road** site of Games 1896–1914 and 1946–58 (now Morpeth RFC and Morpeth Harriers AC)
3. **Old Cricket Field, Stobhill** site of Games 1919–20 (now housing, including Boundary Drive / The Covers)
4. **Mount Haggs Field** site of Games 1921–39 (part remains open space)

» able to supplement their winnings with side bets. For example one entrant in 1873, D Anderson, pocketed an accumulated total of 23s from the high leap, the long leap and the pole leap, and from a side bet of 10s wagered on another pole leap after the main competition had ended. This, it should be noted, was at a time when a typical miner's weekly wage in the Northumberland coalfields stood at around 20s.

In the wrestling, regarded as the chief event of the Games (*as explained opposite*), the prize of Dobson's old championship belt and £2 in cash went to the reigning Northumberland champion, J Potts of Wooler, a small town 30 miles north of Morpeth. Two other wrestling contestants had come further, from Brampton in Westmorland, 60 miles away. There were also 50 entrants for the quoits.

Indeed so packed was the August 1873 programme that the final of the main athletics event, the 150 yard handicap sprint, had to be held over until the Monday (Sunday racing then being taboo). Thomas Garvie, an attendant at the County Lunatic Asylum, won by just six inches, having started the race seven yards further back from the man he beat (a distance determined by the handicapper).

'Next year,' commented the *Morpeth Herald*, 'it is hoped the arrangements for carrying out the sport will be better, and the prizes larger, for there is really a good opening for a grand annual athletic gathering at Morpeth'.

This hope was well placed. By the time of the Games in August 1876 Dobson had established a committee to run the day's events, with himself appointed as secretary and chief wrestling umpire. There was now a 'commodious stand' for local worthies, while the list of patrons grew each year. In 1879 it included bankers, doctors and military men. Mr Stanley, a watchmaker and jeweller, supplied the silver trophies and displayed them in his shop on Bridge Street during the preceding week. Competitors, meanwhile, had to register their interest

at the Newcastle Hotel on Bridge Street or at the Black and Grey Inn on Newgate Street. In the all-important wrestling there were three weight categories: the lightest being for local men who had lived within five miles of Morpeth for at least one year, the two heavier classes being 'open to the world'.

Officially, betting was banned from the Old Brewery Field. In practice, as we saw in 1873, the ban was virtually unenforceable. But even without a wager, entrants could still profit more handsomely at Morpeth than at most other local Games. In 1879 the total prize money stood at £55, of which £7 was to be shared by the first three runners in the 120 yards. This compared with £2 for the equivalent race at Beddington in the same week.

It was presumably for this reason that by 1879 Dobson and his Committee were describing their event as the 'Great' Games at Morpeth, and why by August 1882, the word 'Olympic' started to appear in advertisements and reports in the *Morpeth Herald* (*below left*), as in 'the Olympic Games at Morpeth' and the 'Morpeth Olympic Games'.

This of course ties in with the growing interest in all matters Olympian, resulting from the German excavations of the original site in Greece, begun in 1875 (*see Chapter Two*). But it also suggests that the promoters were keen to press Morpeth's status as one of the leading professional meetings in northern England.

This status was to be further enhanced over the remaining years of the century. In 1882 the *Morpeth Herald* reported that the Old Brewery Field – which was rented to the Games Committee by Councillor Thomas Miller – had been 'literally besieged with visitors', many of them arriving on excursion trains provided by the North Eastern Railway Company. A gate of 3,500 spectators was said to have earned the organisers £700.

Fifty six wrestlers from across the northern counties entered the 10 and 11 stone classes alone.

In 1887 the Morpeth Sports Committee was reported to have spent 'a large sum of money' levelling the running track. But this outlay was soon repaid, for by 1895 the total attendance had risen to an estimated 15,000. At a time when the town of Morpeth's population stood at around 5,200 (according to the 1891 census), this represented good business.

Undoubtedly one of the chief attractions was the calibre of the entrants, drawn by the ever rising prize money. By 1895, it had reached £176. This pot, moreover, derived from an increasingly eclectic group of patrons, amongst whom were Lord Decies – a great supporter of wrestling – Father William Davey, of St Robert's Roman Catholic Church, and Dr Macdowell of the County Lunatic Asylum.

THE OLYMPIC GAMES.

" When Greater meets Great,
Then comes the tug of War."

The Eleventh ANNUAL GATHERING of the
Athletes of the World.

MORPETH WRESTLING, &c., will be held on
Saturday, August 26th, 1882.
For particulars see future Advertisement.

Morpeth Olympic Games 1896–1914

In April 1896, while the first Olympic Games of the modern era were being staged in Athens, the members of the Morpeth Sports Committee, still led by Edmund Dobson, were also busy preparing for a new era.

Following the sale of the Old Brewery Field for housing – built on streets named appropriately Olympia Gardens and Olympia Hill (*see page 78*) – a new site had been secured to the west of the town. This was a field immediately west of Grange House, where Mitford Road spanned the River Wansbeck at Lowford Bridge. On the southern bank of the river lay the ruins of Newminster Abbey, a Cistercian house founded in 1137 by monks from Fountains Abbey.

Surrounded by over 20 acres of open space and bordered by woodland, Grange House Field was already in use for local football and cricket matches, had staged various circuses and agricultural shows, and in 1887 had been the site of Morpeth's Golden Jubilee celebrations for Queen Victoria.

Compared with the marble grandeur of Athens' newly restored stadium, this was hardly a venue to elicit lofty thoughts of Olympianism. Yet the Morpeth Sports Committee not only clung to the title 'Olympic', but, as seen on the right, when advertising their own Games for that August, their tone appeared almost defiant.

The 1896 Games, they announced with obvious pride and perhaps an eye to Athens, were the 25th in the series. (That tells us that they considered the 1870 Games to have been the first, and the 1873 Games the second.)

In addition, while that same year in an article on the Athens Olympics in *The Century Magazine* (*see Links*) Pierre de Coubertin described professionalism in sport as a 'threatening evil' that needed to be eradicated, Morpeth made great play of the fact that their total pot of £180 was 'The Largest Sum for One Afternoon in England'.

As listed in the lower part of the advertisement (not shown), the largest single pot on offer at the Games was £43 10s, to be shared among the placed runners in the 120 yard handicap foot race, the climax of the day's programme. Entrants to this and all the other athletic events were required to wear long drawers and guernseys, and were warned that any attempt to hoodwink a handicapper would lead to instant disqualification.

Total prize money in the wrestling, meanwhile, ranged from £6 for the 'ten and a half stone and under' category for local wrestlers, up to £24 for the 'fourteen stone men and under'. There was also a ten shillings prize for the wrestler wearing the 'neatest costume'.

Despite showery weather on the day – a seemingly common characteristic at Morpeth over the years – the

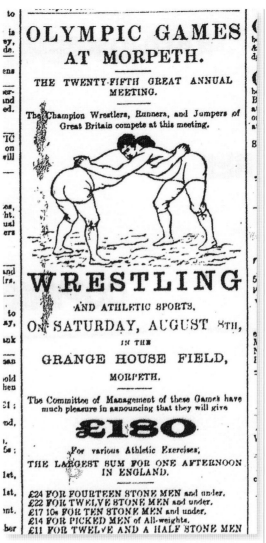

OLYMPIC GAMES AT MORPETH.

THE TWENTY-FIFTH GREAT ANNUAL MEETING.

The Champion Wrestlers, Runners, and Jumpers of Great Britain compete at this meeting.

WRESTLING

AND ATHLETIC SPORTS.

On SATURDAY, AUGUST 8TH,

IN THE

GRANGE HOUSE FIELD,

MORPETH.

The Committee of Management of these Games have much pleasure in announcing that they will give

£180

For various Athletic Exercises;

THE LARGEST SUM FOR ONE AFTERNOON IN ENGLAND.

£24 FOR FOURTEEN STONE MEN and under.
£22 FOR TWELVE STONE MEN and under.
£17 10s FOR TEN STONE MEN and under.
£14 FOR PICKED MEN of All-weights.
£11 FOR TWELVE AND A HALF STONE MEN

Committee's reward for amassing this pot of £180 was an equally impressive crowd of 10,000 spectators. Most of them, it would seem, gathered at the top end of the Grange House Field where, as at the Old Brewery Field, there was a clearer view of the 'capital running track' (marked out on the turf). Entrance to the field cost sixpence, with an extra sixpence for a seat by the wrestling ring, and one shilling for a seat in the temporary, but 'substantial grandstand'.

While in Athens four months earlier a surprisingly slight German gymnast called Carl Schuhmann

Boasting 'the largest sum for one afternoon in England' this advert from the *Morpeth Herald* of July 11 1896 depicts a scene that would have been instantly familiar to the ancient Greeks.

Known as Cumberland or Westmorland wrestling, this style, still practiced in the north of England today, requires contestants to maintain the holds as seen, with each man resting his chin on the other's shoulder. The first to floor his opponent wins the bout.

Other forms of wrestling, such as the 'catch-as-catch can' style favoured in Lancashire, also contested at Morpeth, were more free-form and often ended up with both men tussling on the ground.

At the Olympic Games in Athens earlier that year, Greco-Roman wrestling was the only style on the programme. This form, developed in the 19th century in imitation of classic styles, involved more throws than the northern English versions, and only minimal contact below the waist.

One of the few artefacts to have survived from the Morpeth Games is this 1897 trophy, won by the wrestler Jack Little (*above*) and now in the keeping of his grandson, John Little.

Described in one unsourced newspaper from c.1914 as a publican at the Crown and Anchor Inn on Scotch Street, Carlisle, Jack Little (1864–1935) fought his first bout as an 18 year old at the Barony Races at Burgh-by-Sands. Apart from Morpeth he won honours at various weights in Newcastle, Sunderland, Grasmere, Keswick, Penrith, Bridge of Allan, Luss, Belfast and Wood Green, London.

》 won the gold medal in the Greco-Roman wrestling competition (for which there had been no weight categories), in the heaviest, fourteen stone category of the wrestling at Morpeth, J Robinson of Cockermouth justified his 200 mile round trip by taking home the winner's prize of five pounds, the equivalent of over a month's wages for a working man.

There was further interest in the contest reserved for local wrestlers, particularly as several of them had been training at a new wrestling school set up on Bridge Street, in the centre of Morpeth.

Morpeth's 1896 Olympics were also marked by the introduction of a tug-of-war contest, worth £2 10s, won by a team from the Newcastle Police, and by the award of a special gold medal to RD Dickinson of Windermere, who managed to beat by one inch the professional pole leaping record of 11′2″. It is a mark of the quality of the competition at Morpeth that in the same event at Athens, the gold medal had been won, by an American – albeit an amateur – with a leap of 3.3m, or just under 10′10″.

Seemingly undaunted by the spread of Olympianism elsewhere, and even by the staging of the London Games in 1908, the Morpeth Olympics continued to flourish until the First World War, with only one setback. This occurred in 1911 when Grange House Field was flooded, causing the Games to be cancelled. Yet they returned in style the following year, and for the first time were extended to two days, the Saturday and Monday of the August Bank Holiday weekend. 'This year,' trilled the *Morpeth Herald*, 'has seen a revival of Morpeth's great athletic carnival, and such a revival as almost ensures a fresh spell of prosperity for the premier sports of the North.'

John Gray, a landscape gardener, had done a splendid job in preparing the field for the sports. Half price entry was introduced for women and boys. But most significantly of all, for the first time in the event's history bookmakers were officially allowed to set up on Grange House Field on a first come, first served basis, an invitation that led to them being 'present in strong force'.

That the Committee had backed down on this suggests that in previous years the bookies had simply camped out in adjacent fields or on the road, whereas at least if they set up their pitch on the main field they were paying rent.

To help fill the programme and make the Bank Holiday Monday more entertaining, new events for 1912 included a half mile bicycle handicap, an obstacle race, a 'bolster and bar' contest and a pony race. Each one, as ever, attracted a cash prize. The total pot for the elite athletics event, the 120 yard handicap, meanwhile, now stood at a handsome £55, worth over £21,000 in today's terms, if comparing average earnings over the interim. 》

This rare image, one of the few original photographs found of the Morpeth Olympic Games, shows the final stage of the 100 yard handicap at Mount Haggs Field, on a typically wet August Bank Holiday Monday, some time during the mid 1920s. It shows just how rudimentary was the set up, despite the relatively rich rewards on offer and the fact that there were plenty of purpose-built athletics tracks available elsewhere.

A major factor behind the success of the Games was the Morpeth Sports Committee, posing here in 1928 (*below left*).

Several men served the Committee for decades, among them members of long established Morpeth families. President Bob Arrowsmith sits in the centre of the middle row. His son Arthur is at the front (*second from right*). At the back stand the Charlton brothers; Jack (*third from left*) and Harry (*far right*). The family of Fred Rutherford (*second from left, back row*) still own a department store in Morpeth.

» So attractive had Morpeth become to professional runners that at the August 1914 Games – for which the total pot was now £250 – 224 runners entered the 120 yard handicap, necessitating 32 heats. Only 3,000 spectators were there to see the final, however. The following day Britain declared war on Germany.

Morpeth Olympic Games 1919–1958

Grange House Field was no longer available when the Committee reconvened in 1919 and, in the words of the *Morpeth Herald*, 'began work in earnest to uphold the name that Morpeth Sports has borne in the North for years'.

But if the new venue, the Old Cricket Field at Stobhill, was inferior to Grange House, the Committee made a virtue of necessity by stressing its proximity to the railway station. They also had to announce a smaller pot of prize money, down to £100, and impose a limit on the number of events, so that the whole fixture passed off in one afternoon. Meanwhile, owing to the introduction of an Amusement Tax in 1916, admission fees rose to eight pence for women and children, and one shilling for men.

Yet the public rallied, and a crowd of 5,000 attended, with 225 runners entering the prime event, the 100 yard handicap (reduced from its pre-war distance of 120 yards). For this the prize pot stood at £45, a total that, despite the ongoing post-war economic crisis, rose to £75 the following year. Indeed, as the Northumberland historian Fred Moffat has noted (*see Links*), from then until the Second World War the Morpeth 100 yard race became the region's prime handicap, eclipsing all others.

From the *Evening World* newspaper on August 4 1930, published in Newcastle, the cartoonist 'Spot' celebrates yet another Morpeth Olympics caught out by adverse weather conditions over the August Bank Holiday. But while the rain was sufficient for punters to complain about watered down beer, it did not prevent *al fresco* boxing from making its Morpeth debut.

The "Aquatic" Sports—By Spot.

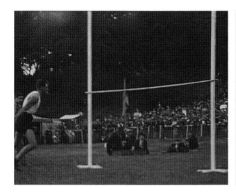
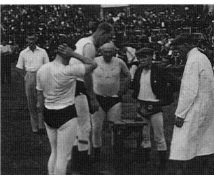

In 1921 the Committee relocated the Games to its fourth site which, coincidentally, like its predecessors before the First World War, had a natural slope that proved ideal for viewing (*as seen on page 83 and above right*).

Known as Mount Haggs Field, but also called locally Mount Hag Field, or Easter Field, this new venue lay to the north of the town within the grounds of the Northumberland County Lunatic Asylum. Built in 1859, this was a classic Victorian asylum, discreetly shielded from the town by woodland. In 1921 it housed 386 male and 282 female inmates in a building originally designed for 200. Over the years a number of the staff had been involved with the Olympics, as patrons or competitors.

The Morpeth Olympics proved remarkably robust during the difficult years of the 1920s. In its first year at Mount Haggs, by which time it was back to a two day programme, the total pot stood at £300. Over the ensuing years this would rise on occasions to £350, a considerable incentive to working men during the Depression.

The Games' status was also elevated by the decision to give the Cumberland and Westmorland wrestling events at Morpeth the title of 'world championships'. True, there were few, if any contestants from outside the northern counties, and there were now just two weight categories. But the billing of 'world championships' at least added a little extra lustre to the occasion.

The introduction of boxing, meanwhile, brought in contestants from a wider region, and proved popular with the crowds (and no doubt the bookies too). One of the best known boxers to have fought at Morpeth during this period was the flyweight, George Stockings from Bethnal Green. Better known as 'Kid Socks', in 1933, nearing the end of his career, he was erroneously billed as having 'met and defeated more champions than any boxer in the world', only to lose at Morpeth that year to George Marsden from Nottingham, one of several Midlands flyweights to appear at Mount Haggs during the 1930s.

Considering how basic conditions were at Morpeth, at a time when boxers and athletes were accustomed to purpose-built stadiums and running tracks – Stockings, for example, had fought at the Albert Hall only a few years earlier – it seems extraordinary that an event so rooted in the 19th century should have survived at all. And yet the Morpeth Olympics appeared to be in good shape when once again war with Germany intervened.

Indeed, the Games bounced back after the Second World War with a spring that demonstrated just how strongly they had become established. With Alderman Sanderson now in the chair, on November 30 1945 the Morpeth Sports Committee reconvened at the Queen's Head Hotel and started planning for the Games to recommence the following August.

Mount Haggs Field was no longer available but, with the help of the Town Clerk, Sanderson was able to secure the use of Grange House Field once again, at a token rent of £20 a year. The field had been turned over to agricultural use during the war, and as a result would present several problems over the ensuing years, not least poor drainage and the fact that cows were grazing on it.

But this was post war Britain and in a spirit of make do and mend, the Committee members dug out and dusted down all the mothballed equipment. The neighbouring Ashington Sports Committee lent Morpeth its small grandstand in return for a share of the takings. The prevailing sense of optimism might also be judged from the decision to rename the Grange House Field as the 'Morpeth Sports Stadium'.

Nor was this optimism misplaced. The two day programme in August 1946 attracted a total gate of around 8,600 and yielded record receipts, a scenario that would be repeated all over Britain during the immediate post-war years as sports grounds, cinemas, amusement parks and seaside resorts cashed in on the public's thirst for entertainment after the privations of war. »

These grainy images are from a 16mm film of the Morpeth Olympics shot in 1933 by Tom Temple, a market gardener and film enthusiast whose footage of Morpeth life is available on a DVD called *A Portrait of Morpeth Through The Ages* (see *Links*).

In the centre, wrestlers are weighed in, one of them enjoying a last puff on a cigarette before his bout. Above, the wrestlers grapple in true Cumberland style in front of the crowds.

One Morpeth regular was Penrith high jumper N Watson, seen on the left. No mattress or sandpit was there to cushion his fall, and, as was his trademark, Watson carried on smoking as he jumped.

For its part the Morpeth Sports Committee returned to its usual haunts at the Queen's Head and the George and Dragon, where members granted themselves 'one round of liquid refreshment' from petty cash after each meeting. For the Games themselves, Mackay Brothers of Bridge Street provided the printing. From Newgate Street, the confectioner Louis Bertorelli supplied ice creams while Ralph Main, a cycle maker who dabbled with electronics, supplied the loudspeakers. Committee member Rangdale Rutherford, who owned Morpeth's department store (which still exists), displayed the medals and trophies in his windows on Bridge Street.

Thus all looked set for the Morpeth Olympics to maintain its status as one of the prime sporting events on the Northumberland calendar for many years to come.

Not even the return of the IOC's Olympics to London in July 1948 could blunt local enthusiasm, although the *Morpeth Herald* did express regret that the dates of the two Olympics had coincided. 'August Bank Holiday has passed for another year and with its passing another page in the long history of the Morpeth Olympic Games has been completed. In some respects it was rather unfortunate that the "Great Olympic Games" in London should clash, as in many respects really fine individual performances on the banks of the Wansbeck last weekend were dwarfed by the knowledge that at Wembley the cream of the amateur world was accomplishing stupendous feats under the very best of conditions'.

But, for the Morpeth Games the cream was about to turn sour. In 1953 its accounts posted a loss, forcing the Committee to sell some of the shares it had bought in the Northumbria Permanent Benefit Building Society.

The *Morpeth Herald* of August 6 1948 celebrates the victory of T Little (no relation to Jack Little) in the World Championship of the Cumberland and Westmorland Wrestling challenge. By coincidence the previous day at the other 1948 Olympics, the finals of the Greco-Roman wrestling had taken place at the Empress Hall in London, in front of rather fewer spectators, it would appear, than were recorded at Morpeth.

WORLD CHAMPIONSHIP AT MORPETH

Mr. T. Little, of Carlisle, winner of the Cumberland and Westmorland challenge cup for the all weights wrestling championship of the world, receiving the cup from Mr. J. Dunn, president of the Games, with Alderman R. Elliott looking on.

There were several reasons for this decline.

Firstly, and most importantly, by the early 1950s the post war boom in attendances at all sports events, great and small, had run its course, with the public now gaining access to a growing range of leisure pursuits and distractions that would steadily transform the entire social and cultural life of the nation.

In a vain attempt to halt this decline in interest, the Committee repeatedly approached local rail and bus companies to lay on excursions, from places such as Edinburgh, Carlisle and Newcastle. In the old days, the companies did not need to be asked.

Secondly, the prize money on offer from the Morpeth Sports Committee no longer appeared sufficient to attract professional athletes, who had plenty of better appointed meetings to choose from. In 1950, for example, the Committee had been able to attact an American sprinter, Barney Ewell, who had just turned professional after winning a gold medal and two silvers at the London Olympics. At Morpeth he lost in the heats.

Yet in 1951 the Scottish sprint champion, Eric Cummings, refused the £60 appearance fee he had been offered by Morpeth. The following year an American athlete, Lloyd LaBeach, gave the same response. Apart from the money, the poorly drained track must have been a deterrent.

Thirdly, there was the ongoing burden of Entertainment Tax, the subject of the Parliamentary debate mentioned at the start of this chapter. For many small sporting organisations this extra tax was a particularly onerous burden.

Fourthly, when approached by outside interests offering to bring new activities to the Morpeth Olympics, the Committee members, most of them advanced in age, proved resistant to change. In 1950 they turned down an offer to stage hound trailing – the sport of laying a scent over open ground for hounds to chase after. They also refused William Murphy of North Shields permission to set up a funfair. Then in 1953 they enlisted the help of the police to stop 'the owners of dart boards from carrying on their business on the Games Field'.

The final ignomiffy occurred at the 1958 Games when only 800 spectators turned up.

Worn out by their efforts, on April 10 1959 the Morpeth Sports Committee met for the last time at the Town Hall.

After a brief discussion, 'it was unanimously resolved that the two day meeting at the August Bank Holiday week-end be discontinued'.

After 77 Games, the Morpeth Olympics were no more.

There was one short-lived revival. In June 1985 a retired policemen turned athletics historian, Fred Moffat, whom we encountered earlier, staged the Morpeth Olympic Games Commemoration Handicaps, as part of a Family Fun and Fitness Day, sponsored by the Health Education Council. In the best tradition of the Games, runners from across the region turned out for the 110 metre and 200 metre races on Morpeth Common, chasing prizes from £30 to £250. However, the event was not repeated.

That is not to say that there will never be another annual athletics or wrestling event in Morpeth. After all, as we have seen, both Robert Dover's Cotswold Olimpicks and the Much Wenlock Olympian Games endured periods in abeyance before enjoying a subsequent revival.

But there would be one major obstacle should a revival in Morpeth ever be contemplated.

When the Committee adopted the title 'Olympic' in the early 1880s there were no legal impediments to prevent this. Today, whatever Morpeth's historical record, there is no way that the International Olympic Committee would countenance such an event labelling itself as 'Olympic'.

Even then, whatever alternative title might be adopted, the IOC and the BOA would never acknowledge the Morpeth Olympics as they have, in recent years, learned to look upon the Cotswold and Wenlock Games as part of the British back story to the Olympics.

The issue, of course, remains that of professionalism. Even though the IOC has embraced professionalism and commercialism since the 1980s, it considers its origins to be purely amateur. As a result, those professional wrestlers and athletes who competed at Morpeth will never form part of the official history.

But that does not mean Morpeth should be denied its place in our story. The Games there were an open celebration of working men's strengths and skills. Their organisers were transparent about professionalism. At a time when amateur sport was plagued by a culture of illegal payments and inflated expenses, a culture that became known as 'shamateurism', the Morpeth Olympic Games, for all their small town scale and simplicity, exhibited a real integrity.

Three years before the final curtain fell, the programme for the 1955 Morpeth Olympic Games shows the familiar range of sports scheduled over two days, with £430 in prize money on offer. Seven of the committee members listed in 1955 appear also in the group photograph taken in 1928 (see page 83).

OFFICIAL PROGRAMME
MORPETH OLYMPIC GAMES
(74th Meeting)
30th JULY & 1st AUGUST, 1955
in the
MORPETH SPORTS FIELD
Mitford Road, Morpeth, Northumberland

President: J. B. Nicholson, Esq.
Vice-Presidents: Ald. W. S. Sanderson, Ald. R. Elliott, Messrs J. T. Charlton, H. P. Charlton, A. Arrowsmith, W. Shiel, A. W. L. Davy and S. Rutherford.
Committee: Ald. R. Elliott, Messrs J. T. Charlton, W. Wright, Jas. Nicholson, John B. Nicholson, Stanley Rutherford, N. Wylie, A. Armstrong, John Wright, Jas. Ed. Nicholson and R. Arrowsmith.
Secretary: Mr. James Nicholson, 2 St. Mary's Field, Morpeth.
Treasurer: Mr. A. W. L. Davy.
Handicappers: Messrs T. and I. Blackburn, 24 Second Avenue, Blyth.
Starter: Mr. K. Blackburn, Bedlington. **Marksmen:** Messrs Jack and James Brown.

SATURDAY, 30th JULY (Commence 2-15 p.m.)
£25 HALF-MILE FOOT HANDICAP.—1st, £15; 2nd, £4; £6 divided amongst other Finalists.
£130 110 YARDS FOOT HANDICAP (Heats only).—1st, £85 and Morpeth Gold Medal, winner also to hold Berwick Memorial Cup for 12 months; 2nd, £10; 3rd, 4th and 5th, £5 each; £20 divided amongst Heat-winners who compete on Monday and take no prize in the final.
£15 220 YARDS (Non-Penalty) FOOT HANDICAP—1st, £10; 2nd, £3; 3rd, £2.
£10 FELL RACE (about half a mile).—1st, £5; 2nd, £3; 3rd, £2. (Entries taken on field.)

MONDAY, 1st AUGUST (Commence 1 o'clock prompt)
£130 110 YARDS FOOT HANDICAP (Ties and Final)
£25 HALF-MILE FOOT HANDICAP.—Prize Money same as Saturday.
£50 80 YARDS FOOT HANDICAP.—1st Prize. £40; 2nd, £7; 3rd, 4th and 5th, £1 each. In addition, Medal for first.
£30 CUMBERLAND & WESTMORLAND WRESTLING (Same as Saturday).
£10 POLE LEAP.—1st, £5; 2nd, £3; 3rd, £2. There must be at least two bona-fide competitors for this event. and to qualify for prize-money ten feet must be cleared.
£5 HIGH LEAP.—1st, £3-10-0; 2nd, £1; 3rd, 10/-.

ADMISSION TO FIELD EACH DAY: ADULTS 2/6, CHILDREN 1/-
Bookmakers' Stands 12/6 each day (includes Number Men). Cars 5/-
RING SEATS 1/-
SATURDAY: Gates open 1 o'clock.   Commence 2-15.
MONDAY: Gates open 12 o'clock.   Commence 1 p.m.
Refreshments: Liquor Tent:
Luncheons, Teas and Light Refreshments   R. EDGAR & Co
by OLIVERS (Morpeth) Ltd.   Morpeth

J. & J. S. MacKay, Morpeth

Chapter Eight

Coubertin and the British

Born in Paris in 1863 – his father a painter, his mother a musician – Pierre de Coubertin, seen here at the age of 23, was no mean sportsman in his youth. Apart from rowing, boxing, fencing and horse riding he won the French pistol shooting championship seven times and played a lead role in the establishment of rugby in France. His family's aristocratic pedigree went back to at least the 16th century, hence his use of the title 'Baron'.

The French aristocrat Baron Pierre de Coubertin is celebrated as the founder of the modern Olympic Games, and rightly so. It was Coubertin who founded the International Olympic Committee (IOC) in 1894, which, two years later, under his leadership, organised the first Olympics of the modern era, in Athens.

But as we have seen, Coubertin was not the first person to consider reviving the Olympics. Nor was he the first to base his philosophy of sport on a romanticised interpretation of the ancient Games.

The Cotswold Olimpicks, Much Wenlock's Olympian Games, Liverpool's Olympic Festivals and the National Olympian Games all had in common the same characteristic; that is, they were shaped by what the historian Eric Hobsbawm has called 'invented tradition'. Each was a reimagining rather than an actual revival of the ancient Games.

Nevertheless taken together, by the 1880s, with the exception of Morpeth – where, as we saw in the previous chapter, the title 'Olympic' was adopted for opportunistic rather than for ideological reasons – the various British games and their promoters did their best to foster a basic understanding of what practices and concepts, ancient and modern, were conveyed by the words Olympic and Olympian.

The likes of Brookes, Hulley and Ravenstein were not alone in seeking to reinvent Olympian ideals. In the 1880s and 1890s the journalist John Astley Cooper proposed a cultural and athletic festival to unite the English-speaking peoples of the world under the banner of the 'Pan-Britannic Gathering' or the 'Anglo-Saxon Olympiad'. In August 1887, *The Times* likened the first Eisteddfod to be held in London to an 'Olympian Games of a purely intellectual character'. As we saw in Chapter Two, the use of Olympia-related terms was by then familiar, in cultural as well as in sporting circles.

But equally, as outlined in Chapter Six, the efforts of the NOA notwithstanding, there was no consensus behind this trend. In the sporting context there were regional variations. There were also conflicting views as to how professionalism might or might not be accommodated within a modern Olympic culture. Not least, the NOA's attempts to establish a national Olympian games in Britain had, by 1883, resulted in failure.

Yet as the saying goes, failure can be a good teacher, and no-one learned more from what he saw of conditions and circumstances in Britain than Coubertin.

Naturally he took ideas from other quarters, most notably from Greece, the USA and his native France. Influenced by late 19th century classicism, Coubertin was fascinated by what he called in 1890 'the mysterious influence that the Greek civilisation has continuously exerted over humanity throughout the ages'.

This influence was felt in many areas of public life in late 19th century Europe and America. Artists like John Waterhouse in England and Gustave Moreau in France drew their inspiration from Greek legends, while the architecture of art galleries, museums and government buildings in cities as diverse as Washington DC, Paris, Berlin, London and Manchester unashamedly echoed ancient Greek motifs. Coubertin's Olympic project was very much part of this wider cultural movement.

As well as his love of the classics, Coubertin was a committed internationalist, a stance that barely gained currency in Britain, even though Brookes had been an advocate. Moreover, while internationalism did not always chime with Britain's imperial outlook, during the second half of the 19th century Anglo-French relations improved considerably, as the two countries gradually moved towards an informal alliance, the *Entente Cordiale*, signed in 1904.

It was in this setting that cultural contacts between Britain and France steadily grew. French opera, ballet, music, art, architectural styles and literature all found devoted adherents in Britain, thereby helping to pave the way for Coubertin, with his aristocratic credentials and his love for all things English, to embark upon a new era of cross-Channel co-operation in the field of sport and physical education.

After the staging of the first IOC Games in 1896 Coubertin wrote, 'The Olympic Games which recently took place in Athens were modern in character, not only because of their programmes, which substituted bicycle races for chariot races and fencing for the brutalities of pugilism, but because in their origin and regulations they were international and universal, and consequently adapted to the conditions in which athletics have developed to the present day.'

We might question just how 'universal' was an event that excluded women, but what is significant here is Coubertin's claim that his Olympic Games were of their time, that they were 'modern in character'.

In this chapter we look at just how much of that character derived from Britain, and how, in time, Coubertin would himself come to 'invent' and nurture an Olympic narrative of his own.

Coubertin and the public school ethos

It all started with *Tom Brown's School Days*. As noted in Chapter Six, its author, Thomas Hughes, went on to join the National Olympian Association and show support for the work of William Penny Brookes. But it was through his novel that Hughes was to wield the greatest influence.

Published in 1857 but based on Hughes' years as a pupil at Rugby School during the 1830s – when Thomas Arnold had famously served as headmaster – the novel turned Tom Brown into the Harry Potter of his day, with Rugby School taking centre stage as Hogwarts, and football, played Rugby-style, portrayed as its Quidditch. Less magical perhaps, but to boys of the period no less alluring. Here, seemingly, was an education conducted on the playing fields, where fresh air and masculine competition combined to inculcate the values of loyalty, discipline, bravery, and ultimately, duty; duty to one's captain, to the school, to the nation and to the Empire.

Of course the novel presented a romanticised view, as contrived in parts as the often-quoted myth that would later emerge of how a Rugby pupil called William Webb Ellis had, in 1823, 'invented' the game of rugby by picking up the ball and running with it, 'with a fine disregard for the rules of football...'

That aside, *Tom Brown's School Days* was unquestionably a winning yarn, and one which, according to Coubertin's biographer, John MacAloon (*see Links*), became 'like a bible' to the young French aristocrat after he came across it, serialised in a French publication *Journal de la Jeunesse* in 1875. Aged twelve at the time, in common with many boys of his age, Coubertin was captivated.

From *Tom Brown's School Days* the French youth next turned to a more up-to-date work of reference, Hippolyte Taine's *Notes sur l'Angleterre*, published in 1872.

'Nearly all the amusements are of an athletic cast...' Coubertin would read in a passage on the English passion for horses and rough sport, a passion shown by both males and females. 'Like that of the greyhound and the racehorse; they need muscular exertion and the rigours of the open air to put their blood in circulation.'

Thus there formed in the adolescent Coubertin's mind a vision of a robust, thrusting and confident England,

TOM'S FIRST EXPLOIT AT FOOTBALL.   P. 113

made wealthy from industry, and strong from that cultivation of 'muscle and mind'. How different it must have seemed to the troubled France in which he was growing up, humbled during the recent conflict with its mighty Prussian neighbour, by the defeat of Napoleon III and ultimately by the fall of Paris in January 1871.

Possessing both the means and the contacts to experience England at first hand, Coubertin first crossed the Channel in 1883, when, aged only 20, he stayed with friends at the Jesuit-run Beaumont College near Windsor. (One report suggests that he may have come earlier, in 1881, but this has never been substantiated.)

As Olympic historian Don Anthony has shown in his painstaking reconstruction of Coubertin's numerous visits to Britain throughout his lifetime, it was on this first trip that the Frenchman made perhaps his most important visit, a pilgrimage to Rugby School. He also took in Harrow and Eton, plus the universities of both Oxford and Cambridge.   »

From the first illustrated edition of *Tom Brown's School Days*, published by Macmillan in 1869, artist Arthur Hughes (no relation to the author Thomas) depicts young Tom's first bruising encounter on the football field.

'Stand back, give him air,' cries Brooke, one of the older boys, and then, feeling Tom's limbs, adds 'No bones broken,' as Tom comes to and sits up.

'Who is he?' asks Brooke. 'Oh it's Brown, he's a new boy,' replies another. 'Well,' says Brooke, 'he is a plucky youngster and will make a player.'

(Note that a strikingly similar scenario was enacted at Hogwarts when JK Rowling's hero, Harry Potter, played his first game of Quidditch.)

Brown, it will be seen, is pictured in his day clothes. This is because junior boys were expected to join in as general football fodder.

Note also that the generic term 'football' remained in use, this being before the formation of the Rugby Football Union in 1871 formally broke the links with 'soccer'.

▲ It was during one of his trips to **Rugby School** in the 1880s that Coubertin, in his own words, experienced something of an epiphany. 'In the twilight, alone in the great gothic chapel at Rugby, my eyes fixed on the funeral slab on which, without epitaph, the great name of **Thomas Arnold** was inscribed, I dreamed that I saw before me the cornerstone of the British Empire'.

Arnold himself (*left*), and for sure many of his contemporaries, would have baulked at such a claim. While it is true that as Rugby's headmaster from 1828–41 Arnold introduced various reforms, he was only one of several modernisers. Moreover, an intensely devout man with a deep love of the classics, he was no great advocate of sport. Rather, he helped to create an environment in which sport was allowed to flourish under other teachers.

Nevertheless, after his death in 1842 Arnold evolved into one of the century's most revered cult figures.

Addressing an audience in Athens in November 1894, for example, Coubertin described him as 'the greatest educator of modern times who, more than any other Englishman, is responsible for the current prosperity... of his country'. In a speech of 1929 he said, 'Arnold made the muscles the most thoroughly educated, meticulous, and constant servants in the formation of character... Soon, the cornerstone of the British empire had been laid'.

》 Further trips are thought to have followed between 1884–86, and in 1888 he visited again, taking in the Regatta at Henley. By this time it would appear that Coubertin had visited numerous other schools and colleges, such as Winchester, Wellington, Marlborough, Charterhouse, Cooper's Hill, Westminster and Christ's Hospital. He also crossed the Atlantic to see how the English public school system had been adapted in the United States.

This interest was not merely personal. On yet another visit to England in 1889, for example, he travelled as a representative of the French government, tasked with finding out how the French educational system might benefit from English practices.

Coubertin's English lessons

Over the course of several trips during the 1880s, during which he combined observations of everyday school life with formal meetings with teachers and pupils, Coubertin came to the firm conclusion that the British educational system was indeed superior to that of the French.

Whereas in French schools, he noted in 1887, pupils received mere instruction, 'the ultimate goal of teachers in England is to make men and to get them to teach themselves thereafter'. He described sport as 'the most noteworthy aspect of English education', stressing that the educational value of team games such as rugby, football and cricket was 'physical, moral, and social, all at the same time'.

In the short term, Coubertin's enthusiasm for school sports simply fed into his recommendations for educational reform back in France. But it was not only the way that English schoolboys learnt to 'play the game' that so impressed the Frenchman. He was also full of admiration for the way that, even after they left school and university, young Englishmen continued to enjoy sport at a competitive level, and to use their leadership skills to help administer and improve those sports.

What he saw during his first visit to the Henley Regatta in 1888 was to leave a particularly lasting impression, and not only because rowing was one of his passions.

Held annually since 1839, and given its Royal charter in 1851 when Prince Albert became its patron, the Henley Regatta had the reputation then, as now, of being one of the highlights of the English summer 'season'.

It was also a bastion of amateurism. While on other stretches of the Thames, in London, and on the River Tyne in Newcastle, professional boatmen would regularly compete for large sums in front of huge crowds, the gentlemen in charge of Henley adopted an exceptionally stern stance against any semblance of professionalism.

They determined in 1879 that no individual would be allowed to enter Henley events if he had ever rowed for money, or indeed had ever competed against any other rower who had competed for money. This ban, moreover, included anyone who had competed for money in *any* form of athletic exercise. Even stricter than that, Henley also excluded all working boatmen, and even those who simply earned a wage as a 'mechanic, artisan or labourer'.

This ruling, which also applied in amateur athletic circles, was to survive at Henley until 1937, and amounted to arguably the strictest interpretation of amateurism imaginable. Not only did it seek to exclude professionals, it also set out to exclude an entire social class.

Dedicated as he was to the amateur sport, Coubertin, it has to be said, never quite embraced this hardline stance. Although he did not endorse the idea of people making money from sport, he had no problem with the Olympics becoming a forum in which the classes could mix. In this respect, his concept of amateurism was influenced more by William Penny Brookes than by the elite at Henley.

Coubertin was to learn another vital lesson at Henley, however, and that concerned the actual organisation of the Regatta (what was then a three day event, compared with five today). In particular he was drawn to the Henley committee's structure of 'three concentric circles'.

In the centre of these three circles, wrote Coubertin in his 1932 autobiography *Olympic Memoirs* (see Links), lay the 'nucleus'. This included the members of the management committee and other club officials whose involvement with rowing spanned the whole year. These were the men who knew the rules (largely because they had drawn them up), knew how to organise and manage an event, and were able to provide leadership and expertise.

Next came what Coubertin called the 'nursery'. These were the enthusiastic, up-and-coming individuals who could learn from members of the 'nucleus' and eventually step into their role. Amongst this group were the stewards at Henley, who acted as the interface between the management committee, the oarsmen and the spectators.

Finally came the outer ring of the circle, called by Coubertin the 'façade'. This consisted of individuals who were sympathetic towards the sport and who also occupied positions of power and influence. Coubertin described them as men of 'varying degrees of usefulness', whose presence would 'add prestige' to the organisation.

As he explained in his memoirs, it was the Henley model that Coubertin adopted as the blueprint for the constitution of the IOC, based on a committee made up of leaders, activists, patrons and networkers, and one that was 'permanent in its principle and stable in its composition'.

It is a legacy that essentially survives at the IOC until the present day, although it underwent various reforms after the Salt Lake City bidding scandal of 1995.

But it was not only the structure at Henley that impressed Coubertin. He also noted how certain individuals took on roles within the rowing hierarchy. Rather than being nominated and voted into position along democratic or representative principles, at Henley it was more a matter of who you knew and what you could offer. As a member of an aristocratic family, Coubertin would have been expected to endorse such a set up. He disliked what he described in 1925 as the 'electoral chaos' of democratically chosen committees. *Noblesse oblige* and the expectation that a gentleman would do his duty – whether by rolling up his sleeves, donating funds or attending committee meetings – constituted, in his view, and those of the circles in which he mixed, the best way to get things done.

Coubertin and the 1889 Paris Congress
Eleven months after his first visit to the Henley Regatta, Coubertin was involved in organising a gathering that, indirectly at least, was to have a crucial impact on shaping the future of the modern Olympic movement. »

From the collection of Balliol College, Oxford, this view of Henley in 1897 shows the kind of scene that had so impressed Coubertin on his first visit, nine years earlier. In 1893 he returned with a French crew and in 1907 awarded the Regatta an IOC honour known as the Olympic Cup (*see page 98*).

From *The Times* of May 28 1889, this is the circular that caught the attention of William Penny Brookes, thereby leading to the Frenchman's first visit to the Wenlock Olympian Games in October 1890.

It was this visit that is seen by some historians (but not all) as the point at which Coubertin's ambitions evolved from an interest purely in physical education to the wider ambition of reviving the Olympics.

On the opposite page are reproduced extracts from *The Times'* editorial that appeared on the same day as the circular.

The language and tone tell us much about how the English elite regarded the French, and about the cultural environment in which Coubertin was operating as he crossed back and forth across the Channel.

Of the Congress itself we know little. But for being the means through which Coubertin met Brookes it must surely rank as one of the most important events in international sporting history.

CONGRESS OF ATHLETIC EDUCATION IN PARIS.

À MONSIEUR LE RÉDACTEUR DU TIMES.

Monsieur,—J'ai l'honneur de vous communiquer la lettre ci-jointe qui a été adressée par la Commission d'Organisation de notre Congrès aux Directeurs des Écoles et Universités d'Angleterre, d'Amérique, et d'Australie.

Je vous serai bien reconnaissant de la reproduire dans votre journal.

Notre Congrès se tiendra du 15 au 23 Juin, à Paris ; les séances auront lieu à l'École des Ponts et Chaussées et alterneront avec des concours d'equitation, d'escrime, de gymnastique, de natation, de courses à pied, etc. Je vous en adresserai le programme détaillé, si vous le désirez.

Veuillez agréer, Monsieur, l'expression de mes sentiments très distingués,

PIERRE DE COUBERTIN, Secrétaire du 20, Rue Oudinot. Congrès.

République Française.
Exposition Universelle de 1889.
Congress for Studying the Aims and Advantages of Athletic Education.
Paris, January, 1889.

Sir,—During the Exhibition of 1889, in the month of June, a Congress will be held in Paris for studying the aims and advantages of athletic sports and games and their physical, moral, and social effects on education. We greatly hope that you will be able to attend the Congress, and give us on this most important question such information as your experience in educational matters will suggest. At all events, we hope you will be kind enough to write and send us an answer to the following questions.

With anticipated thanks, we remain, Sir,
Very faithfully yours,
JULES SIMON, Ex-Prime Minister, Member of the Senate and of the French Academy.
DR. BROUARDEL, Member of the Medical Academy.
MOREL, Director of Secondary Instruction.
H. DE VILLENEUVE.
PIERRE DE COUBERTIN.

1. What are the games played in your school or University ? (If local games, please to give the chief rules.)
2. How many hours do the boys play a day ?—a week ?
3. What about riding—gymnastics—fencing—military drill—rowing—bicycling ?
4. Are the boys allowed to form sporting associations ?
5. Have they a Debating Society and of what kind ?
6. Do you believe in athletic games improving companionship ?—morality ?—temper ?—work ?
7. What are the subscriptions, extra fees......paid for the games and sports ?
Nota.—Detailed accounts, books, pamphlets, school-papers will be received with gratitude.
All information to be sent to M. Pierre de Coubertin, 20, Rue Oudinot, Paris.

Staged in June 1889 at the much respected *École Nationale des Ponts et Chaussées*, this was a Congress for Studying the Aims and Advantages of Athletic Education, held as part of that year's *Exposition Universelle* in Paris. (The French may have lagged behind their neighbours in certain respects, but they led the way when it came to staging international exhibitions and congresses.)

However, it was not so much the Congress that had an impact, as a circular sent by Coubertin to the heads of various schools, colleges and universities in England, the USA and Australia, inviting them either to attend the Congress or to fill in a questionnaire concerning sport and physical education at their particular institutions.

Crucially, either one of these circulars, or a similar notice – placed in *The Times* on May 28 1889, and accompanied by a lengthy editorial (*see left and opposite*) – caught the eye of a certain doctor in Shropshire.

By this time, although the Wenlock Olympian Games remained in fine fettle, William Penny Brookes' dream of a National Olympian Association had all but faded, and he was now focusing his efforts on the National Physical Recreation Society which he had helped to found three years earlier, in 1886 (*see page 77*).

Brookes duly sent Coubertin a copy of the speech that he had made at Crystal Palace during the 1866 NOA Games. In this speech, as we have noted (*see pages 71-72*), Brookes spoke at length about the importance of physical education and the need for government support, a subject already dear to Coubertin's heart.

But just as importantly, Brookes finished his address with a rallying call to all British Olympians, stressing his conviction that the NOA's Games would, in time, become 'spectacles more brilliant and imposing, contests more varied and exciting... than any of the like yet recorded in the pages of history'.

Over the years Coubertin was to amass a considerable volume of articles and speeches of his own, while also entering into correspondence with an impressive array of politicians, educationalists and sporting figures.

In that respect he found a true kindred spirit in the indefatigable Brookes, even though, when the doctor sent him the speech, he was aged 80 and Coubertin only 26. Nevertheless, reading Brookes' stirring words during that summer of 1889 was a revelation to the Frenchman.

Not only had Coubertin found himself another friend across the Channel, but a new *cause célèbre* to boot.

Coubertin goes to Much Wenlock
Pierre de Coubertin, it should be added, was not Brookes' first foreign correspondent. Nor, it may be recalled, was he the first to read Brookes' suggestion that an »

extract from *The Times*, May 28 1889

Among the many congresses to be held in connexion with the Paris Exhibition is one upon the subject of athletic education, and its promoters have issued a curious circular to heads of English schools and seminaries... In effect, M. Jules Simon and his co-signatories appeal to us to help them in introducing outdoor exercises to French youth.

That the French should thus officially, as it were, express a desire to become our disciples in the matter of manly sports is exceedingly flattering to our national vanity. Hitherto it has been left to individual Frenchmen to pay high compliments to our habits of physical exertion. M. Taine is so enthusiastic about us that we are overwhelmed. Another observer, "Max O'Rell," also praises us, but takes care that we shall not be unduly elated. He admits that the Englishman, in the heyday of his youth, is a splendid animal, but he is also constrained to record that this same athlete soon becomes beefy and bloated. Whether the qualified or the unqualified compliment is the truer, we think we may fairly boast that a little imitation of ourselves in the cultivation of physical games would immensely improve the morale of French schoolboys and young men, as well as their bodily aptitude.

It is possible that we cherish illusions about the tastes of the typical French youth, just as the typical English youth certainly remains a mystery to French people. At all events, a belief prevails in the country that French youths devote little or none of their leisure to developing their bodily activity, but give it up to indolence and its brood of bad habits. This belief is supported by what is a matter of common observation, that English boys sent by their parents to France – or Germany, for the matter of that – to finish their education generally return with their moral tone distinctly lowered. We could hardly expect our neighbours to admit all this, but they are beginning to own freely that there is an ugly lacuna in the training given at their schools. Only the other day the President of the Republic, in opening a gymnastic club, commented upon the deficiency of French physical education. Now the circular before us acknowledges the same thing with semi-official force.

The questions put in the circular testify in a singular degree to the refreshing innocence of Frenchmen upon the subject of our field sports. The framers of the circular have a clear conviction that our field sports are capital institutions, but what they are, how are they are managed, and what is the terminology appropriate to them they have but the very mistiest idea. The headmaster or don is first asked to enumerate the games played in his school or University. In a parenthesis, he is requested, if they are 'local games', to give the 'chief rules'. Strange as the phrase 'local games' may appear, we had our 'local' period once, when every school had its own peculiar game or code of rules. Probably the French, so far as they have any school-games at all, are in the same stage of development. But although Eton, Harrow and Winchester may each play football in their own way, we advise M. Jules Simon and his colleagues not to bother themselves even with the 'chief rules' of such survivals, but to begin work upon the codes of the Marylebone Cricket Club, the Rugby Union, and the Football Association.

The next interrogatory is 'How many hours do the boys play a day? – a week?' Then follows a question apparently intended to exhaust the games and exercises known or conceived of in France. 'What about riding, gymnastics, fencing, military drill, rowing, bicycling?' One would have thought that a Frenchman who had ever visited England, or who had set eyes on an English newspaper, would have included cricket and football. The four exercises which first occur to the questioner are, of course, more or less directly connected with military training. From this point of view they are not sports at all in our sense of the word. In an average school not one of the whole half-dozen exercises is practised at all – rowing being confined to those schools which are situated upon a suitable river, and the gymnasium being regarded as a penal place whither few boys resort except under stress of weather.

The circular goes on to inquire whether the boys are allowed to form 'sporting associations?'. Of course, the term 'sporting', which sounds so drolly to English ears, means nothing that the most anxious mother could object to. We despair of getting the French to understand the difference between 'sport' and 'sporting', on the one hand, and 'sports' on the other. We are not sure that the confusion of the two terms has not done a good deal to retard the progress of physical games among the French, whose Anglo-mania has taken the superficial form of devotion to 'sport', without cultivating that taste for 'sports' without which the mere sporting-man is a somewhat despicable character.

'Have the boys a debating society, and of what kind?' A debating society is not, or ought not to be, an arena for bodily prowess; but, no doubt, what is in the mind of the questioner is that the same spontaneity which originates physical contests is also the parent of contests of mental and oral agility.

This circular, which was intended to be very much in earnest, reads drolly enough to those for whose eyes it is meant... but it may also indicate a deeper misconception... Frenchmen find it very difficult to get away from the idea that education, whatever its form, must be imposed upon boys by the authorities.

If the framers of the circular entertain this belief, the first thing to do is to disabuse themselves of it.

No real love of manly sport can be implanted in the schoolboy's breast by force of authority. What physical education there is to be found in French schools is official, because it is of a kind which has military efficiency for its object.

In our enthusiasm for our own national sports, it would be folly to underrate the exercises in which the French are proficient – military gymnastics, and, above all, the art of fence. The last is a pastime which is almost extinct in England, partly because it is not an outdoor sport, and partly because we are not duellists; but we do not disparage its value as a training for the eye, the muscles, and the bearing. For every amusement that is at all martial in character the French have a born aptitude.

When this has been said, we fear that the French schoolboy has never given any sign of a temperament which would take a pleasure in games which involve personal exertion and inculcate voluntary habits of discipline. Not a year passes, we suppose, but many hundreds of French boys come over to England to be educated, and English boys are sent in at least equal numbers to France. Yet the English taste for outdoor sports has never obtained any permanent footing in France, and we do not believe that a congress of gentlemen at Paris will succeed in changing the nature of the young Frenchman.

Boys, we are sorry to say, are not in the habit of regulating their conduct according to the views of congresses. But we hope it will be otherwise, and that the boys of English public schools will have the credit of converting the pupils of French lycées to a more healthy view of the pleasures of life.

» international Olympic games be staged. As noted by the historian David Young (*see Links*) Brookes had already put forward that same idea to John Gennadius, a Greek diplomat in London, as early as 1876.

Coubertin proved a rather more enthusiastic respondent, however. Whether or not at this stage he had ever heard of the Wenlock Olympian Games, or indeed any of the English festivals or events, is unknown. But Brookes was patently much taken by his letters, for within a few months of their first exchange he not only invited the Frenchman to Much Wenlock, but also arranged for a special Olympian Games to be staged in Coubertin's honour, in October 1890.

That the doctor was able to make this offer, despite the annual Games having already taken place, as usual, in July of that year, and that he was also able to persuade his fellow townsmen that the effort would be worthwhile, gives a clear indication of just how great an impact Coubertin's letters must have had on Brookes.

But it surely was worth the effort, for as the Frenchman would report shortly afterwards in the December 1890 edition of *La Revue Athlétique* – a magazine he had recently founded – he was very much taken with Much Wenlock. Indeed some historians have argued that his visit was no less of an epiphany than had been his first visit to Rugby School, several years earlier. Or, furthermore, that it was from this moment onward that Coubertin started to consider the idea of reviving the ancient Games.

From his description of the Wenlock railway station – 'a delightful cottage surrounded by flowers and banks of greenery' – to his admiration of the octogenarian doctor,

Coubertin's enthusiasm appeared boundless, almost as if Brookes were the living incarnation of Thomas Arnold and Linden Field was Olympia itself.

The sports on show at Wenlock also impressed him, even the old-fashioned spectacle of tilting at the ring. These sports, wrote Coubertin, were 'based on the principles of the past, which are as true and noble today as they once were in the gymnasiums of Athens'.

He was similarly enamoured with the ceremonial aspect of the Games, the opening procession and a triumphal arch which had been erected over the entrance to Linden Field and decorated with a personal message of greeting. In all his visits to Britain during the previous seven years it is unlikely that Coubertin had ever received such a welcome, or such press coverage (in the local Shropshire newspapers at least). There would be one other appeal to his vanity when Brookes invited Coubertin to plant an oak tree at Linden Field.

It would be tempting to infer from this that Brookes somehow knew that the Frenchman's visit represented, like the acorn in the ground, a new beginning; the start of something big. But in truth all visiting dignitaries to the Wenlock Games were invited to plant trees.

It is nevertheless noteworthy that on the original plaque created to commemorate the planting ceremony (*see page 52*), Coubertin's title of Baron was used, whereas, for example in the circular published for the 1889 Congress (*page 92*) he signed himself simply as Monsieur. Whether this was owing to Dr Brookes' penchant for titles, or to Coubertin's personal preferences, we cannot say. But the Frenchman certainly found himself accommodated in rather less than aristocratic surrounds at the Raven Arms in Wenlock, where after the Games he was entertained at a ball, again held in his honour.

Of course at the time, no-one present can possibly have imagined the impact on international sporting history that Coubertin's visit, or his relationship with Brookes, were to have. Or that Coubertin's oak would become a place of pilgrimage, or that some 120 years later, a sapling grown from an acorn from that oak would be planted in east London, in an Olympic Park where the capital was preparing to stage its third modern Olympiad.

But the facts speak for themselves.

At Much Wenlock, Coubertin met a group of civic-minded men who every year volunteered their services to run a long established multi-sport event, embellished with ceremonies and traditions, and given the title 'Olympian' out of genuine respect for ancient Greek sport and culture. Coubertin described his Wenlock experience as 'a story enveloped by a veil of poetry, fragrant with the scent of antiquity'.

Presented to the Wenlock Olympian Society by Pierre de Coubertin as a token of his appreciation for their hospitality in October 1890, this medal was awarded to one of the winners of the tilting at the ring competition during the following year's Wenlock Olympian Games. It is now on display in the Wenlock Museum (*see Chapter Four*).

Coubertin takes up the baton

As we noted in Chapter Four, and as has been quoted on many an occasion, Coubertin wrote in that December 1890 report of his visit, 'The fact that the Olympic Games, which modern Greece has been unable to restore, are being revived today is due not to a Hellene, but to Dr WP Brookes. He is the one who began them forty years ago.'

That, at least, is what he wrote at the time. Another, much later version of events has it that Coubertin had already been considering a revival of the Olympics before meeting Brookes, hence in his subsequent writings he played down the British connection, to the point of virtually writing Brookes out of the story altogether.

Only by close reading of the available sources (see Links) will readers be able to draw their own conclusion.

In the current context we will confine ourselves to a brief summary of what happened next, and a reminder of how else the British contributed to the formation of the IOC in 1894 and to the staging of the first modern Olympics two years later.

Certainly Coubertin maintained his links with Brookes, and Britain, throughout the ensuing years. Indeed in 1891 he was made an Honorary Member of the Wenlock Olympian Society. But as Coubertin was to discover, and as Brookes knew only too well, few people at that stage supported the idea of reviving the Olympics. Most notably when Coubertin first proposed the idea publicly, in a speech at the Sorbonne in Paris in November 1892, apart from general applause he found few backers.

Far more effective during this period were Coubertin's efforts to promote French rugby (see right).

Brookes by this stage was too infirm to leave Wenlock, but he continued to encourage Coubertin in his letters, and wrote also to his contacts in Greece to urge them to support Coubertin's efforts.

These efforts finally came to head in 1894. In January of that year Coubertin announced plans to hold an International Congress on Sport at the Sorbonne in June. On the agenda was a discussion on the 'possibility of restoring the Olympic Games'. In February, en route to the United States, Coubertin returned to England, where he attended a reception at the London Sports Club, hosted by a well known man-of-the-turf, Sir John Astley. Astley's involvement suggests that for all Coubertin's espousal of amateurism, he would gladly deal with gambling interests if they could in any way help his Olympic cause.

The following May the Wenlock Olympian Society again conveyed their support for Coubertin, and suggested that his proposed organisation for reviving the Olympics adopt a Greek or Latin motto (as had the Liverpool Olympic Festival and the NOA). »

Presented to the London club Rosslyn Park on the occasion of their match against Stade Français in Paris on April 18 1892 – the first time a British rugby club had played on the Continent – this exquisitely crafted silver piece, just 32cm tall, symbolises the *entente cordiale* by representing oak and laurel leaves growing from a single stem.

Mindful of what he had witnessed in England, Coubertin was determined that the French should take up rugby. A month earlier he had refereed the nation's first rugby championship final, and in 1890 had organised the first French school championships. During the 1880s he is said to have been an active player himself, in the Bois de Boulogne.

Although it did not feature in the 1896 Games, rugby was included in four of the first seven Olympics, until dropped from the 1928 Games following Coubertin's retirement. However, after a 92 year gap, the sport will return to the Games in 2016.

The moustache had grown, as had his international standing. This was Pierre de Coubertin posing in that all important year of 1896. In addition to the Games in Athens, he was appointed as the second President of the IOC (following on from Demetrios Vikelas), a position he would retain for 29 years, until 1925. It was also in 1896 that Coubertin appeared to overlook the contribution of one of his old friends...

》 Finally, the breakthrough came on June 23 1894, when at the Sorbonne Congress, Coubertin announced the formation, at last, of the International Olympic Committee.

Of its first thirteen members, only two nations had more than one representative. France had two, including Coubertin, as did Britain, represented by Oliver 'Dick' Russell, the 2nd Baron Ampthill (a dashing rower and steward at Henley who was active in foreign affairs and diplomacy), and Charles Herbert, the Honorary Secretary of the Amateur Athletic Association.

Coubertin later described Herbert as one of 'an immovable trinity' at the core of the IOC – echoing the 'nucleus' of administrators he had encountered at Henley – along with himself and the American, William Sloane, a history professor at the University of Princeton. As well as nominally representing Great Britain and the Empire, Herbert brought to the table unmatched experience in the running of athletics meetings, at a time when the annual AAA Championships were the foremost in the world.

Meanwhile eight British and British-based luminaries were accorded honorary membership of the IOC.

First and foremost, for his rank alone (if not his personal habits) was the heir to the throne, Edward, the Prince of Wales, a notorious playboy who loved gambling, horse racing and golf. He was joined by his soulmate, Sir John Astley, known to all in the horse racing world as 'The Mate', by Lord Aberdare (an advocate of higher education) and by Lord Dufferin (the British Ambassador in Paris who had facilitated the first Association football matches between English and French clubs).

From the House of Commons there was the Liberal politician and tennis player AJ Balfour, and from Cambridge University the archaeologist Charles Waldstein, who was also Director of the American School of Classical Studies in Athens.

The seventh honorary British member was Hodgson Pratt, a Francophile peace campaigner who was active in the Co-operative Movement and promoted sport and poetry festivals for international students.

Last but not least, honorary membership of the IOC was also accorded to William Penny Brookes, with whom Coubertin had remained in contact but who, having broken his leg, had been unable to attend the Congress.

Amongst other delegates from the British Isles who attended there were also several prominent members of the sporting world, representing such bodies as the International Cycling Association (whose headquarters were in London), the National Cyclists' Union, the National Skating Association, the London Rowing Club, the London Polytechnic Club and both the Scottish and the Irish Amateur Athletic Associations.

What this list tells us is not only that the British played an active role in supporting the IOC, but also that Coubertin himself was an assiduous networker who well understood the need to get on board men of influence and rank. As his biographer John MacAloon put it, Coubertin had a 'habit of barging in on the famous who (had) something, even remotely, to do with his projects'.

One such man was the Paris-based Greek businessman and writer Demetrios Vikelas, who had lived in London between 1852 and 1874, where he had taking up fencing, rowing and horse riding. Appointed as the IOC's first president, it was Vikelas who persuaded the organisation to stage the first Games in Athens in 1896, rather than in Paris in 1900, as Coubertin had envisaged.

This tight deadline of less than two years placed the Greeks in a challenging position. It also required Coubertin to continue his charm offensive in order to make sure that a respectable number of accomplished athletes would attend the Games.

In the interim, as cruel fate would have it, William Penny Brookes died, in December 1895, just four months short of the Athens Games, thereby robbing the doctor of the chance to witness his cherished dream come to fruition. For his part Coubertin paid fulsome tribute to his aged friend and mentor, whom he called one of the 'most hearty supporters' of the Olympic project.

All seemingly heartfelt, and yet as we hinted earlier, within months, bizarrely and inexplicably, Coubertin appeared to have changed his tune significantly.

Olympic historian David Young has shown in his analysis of Coubertin's evolving philosophy (*see Links*), that this process first revealed itself in the Frenchman's introduction to the *Official Report* of the Athens Games. In this, Coubertin acknowledged that the name 'Olympic Games' had not 'entirely fallen into disuse'. But he made no mention of any British games, of Wenlock or even of Brookes, preferring instead to mention the staging of the Revolutionary Olympic Games in France in the late 18th century and various 'local sports' held in Greek villages.

Later that year, in November, in an article entitled 'The Olympic Games of 1896', published in the New York illustrated monthly, *The Century Magazine*, Coubertin again omitted any references either to Brookes or to the Wenlock Olympian Games.

Within less than a year of his death, it would seem, Brookes' contribution had been all but airbrushed out of the emerging, official Olympic narrative.

Added to which, Coubertin's correspondence with the Wenlock Olympian Society also seems to have stopped abruptly once Brookes had died. 》

▶ Magnificent though it was and with a capacity of around 60,000 spectators, the Panathenaic Stadium in Athens was quite unsuited to the requirements of modern athletics. Typical of ancient stadia in its U-shaped configuration – Olympia was the same – the stadium's marble core dated from the fourth century BC. For centuries it had lain in ruins before being excavated and partially rebuilt by the businessman Evangelis Zappas for the Greek revival Games of 1870 and 1875. After this, as stated in the IOC's *Official Report* for 1896, the site returned to being 'a mere wilderness... its slopes overgrown with thorns and brambles, its ground covered by a mass of broken stones'.

A second phase of refurbishment for 1896 then restored its former glory, even if the track dimensions were unlike any most visiting athletes had ever seen.

To assist the Greeks in preparing the track and its infield (which was sand, rather than turf), Charles Perry from the London Athletic Club, then based at Stamford Bridge, was asked to assist. As seen here in 1896, the result was a track of about 330m, shorter than the standard 440 yard British tracks of the time, and with tighter curves.

Perry also helped coach members of the elite Athens Athletic Club in English styles of running and jumping – which many apparently resisted – and once the Olympics started, acted as a timekeeper. Perry went on to lay the Olympic tracks at London in 1908, Stockholm in 1912 and Antwerp in 1920.

Yet despite the involvement of Perry, and indeed a number of other British individuals active in supporting Coubertin, it would be wrong to overstress Britain's participation in 1896. After all, it would be another nine years before the formation of the British Olympic Association and as yet there was no concept of an official British team. However several athletes from Britain or with British connections did make an impression.

Britain's first gold medallist, for example, was the 22 year old weightlifter **Launceston Elliot** (*right*). Born in India to a Scottish family, Elliot had moved to Essex and trained in London under the well known body builder Eugen Sandow. An indication of the informality of this first modern Olympics is that Elliot also had a go, albeit unsuccessfully, in the 100m sprint, in the wrestling and in the rope climbing event.

Similarly, the London-born Australian runner Edwin Flack, who won both the 800 and 1500m races, played in the lawn tennis tournament and made a brave attempt at the marathon, despite having never run further than ten miles before. He collapsed while in the lead, two miles before the end. Meanwhile Edward Battell, who competed in three cycle races, coming third in the 87 kilometre road

race, was a servant at the British Embassy in Athens.

Watching Battell in the crowd was an Oxford-educated Irish lawyer John Pius Boland, who, although on holiday at the time, was invited to enter the lawn tennis singles tournament, which he won, despite playing in ordinary street shoes. He also won the doubles, partnering a German. Boland's recently discovered diary of 1896 (*see Links*) offers a fascinating insight into the character of the Games, and of how poorly Britain was represented.

Finally, there was the plucky George Robertson. Having studied Classics at Oxford and won the University's Gaisford Prize for composing Greek verse in 1894, Robertson travelled to Athens in order to throw the hammer, a discipline for which he had recently gained a Blue at Oxford. To his dismay, however, there was no hammer throwing at Athens, so instead he had a go at lawn tennis, the discus and putting the shot. Poor George. His discus throw of 25.2m is still one of the shortest ever recorded at Olympic level. And yet still he triumphed, for during the closing ceremony, in front of the Greek king and the assembled crowd, he was invited to recite an Olympian ode of his own composition.

In the words of the *Official Report*, 'In this ode, written in Ancient Greek in Pindarian meter, the poet gave vent to the most noble sentiments, which only an ardent love of Ancient Greece could have inspired him.

'The King lent a most attentive ear to the recital of those beautiful verses, and the audience cheered heartily.'

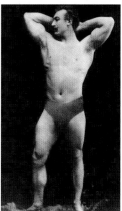

COMITÉ INTERNATIONAL OLYMPIQUE

La Coupe Olympique

créée par le Baron Pierre de COUBERTIN,

rénovateur des Jeux Olympiques de l'ÈRE MODERNE,

a été attribuée pour l'année *1915*

à *Rugby School England*

LE PRÉSIDENT DU C. I. O.

Pierre de Coubertin

One of the many honours to emanate from the IOC is the Olympic Cup, awarded on an annual basis since 1906 to the individual, institution or association deemed to have made the most positive contribution to the Olympic movement.

This is the certificate held by Rugby School, awarded the trophy in 1915. Other British recipients have been the Henley Regatta, in 1907, the National Playing Fields Association in 1931, and the Central Council of Physical Recreation in 1948.

▲ Further recognition of Britain's contribution to the Olympic movement was the unveiling by **Lord Coe** (*centre*), of a plaque at **Rugby School**, in April 2009. On the left is Michael Fowle, the then Chair of the Governors. On the right is the school's Head Master, Patrick Derham.

The plaque reads, 'Within these grounds and in the works of Thomas Arnold, Pierre de Coubertin (1863–1937), creator of the modern Olympic movement, found inspiration for his vision to improve education through sport, a vision which gave rise to the modern Olympic Games.' To this is added a quote from Coubertin: 'It was to Arnold that we turned, more or less consciously, for inspiration.'

Unveiling the plaque, Lord Coe said, 'It is very important, as we go towards 2012, that we understand our own history.' As already noted, Arnold may well have baulked at being remembered in this way. Yet as both a historian and as a teacher, he would surely have been delighted to have proved such an inspiration to so many.

>> For historians this sudden and apparently ungracious *volte-face* has been the cause of much speculation. Certainly Coubertin remained pro-British in all his dealings and continued to visit London on a regular basis. The IOC happily held their Congress in London in 1904, when they were guests at an official banquet staged by the Lord Mayor of London at the Mansion House. Coubertin gave a lecture on sport and international understanding at the Society of Arts. The Worshipful Company of Fishmongers also hosted a dinner for the IOC, and did so again at the time of the 1908 Olympics in London. Coubertin returned the compliment by awarding the Company an Olympic Medal.

Nor was there any lack of British involvement in the IOC. On the contrary, after 1894 several more Olympic evangelists emerged from British sporting circles; men such as the Reverend Robert Courcy de Laffan, headmaster of Cheltenham College, who represented the Headmaster's Conference at the IOC's meeting in Le Havre in 1897, and Theodore Cook, a leading journalist on *The Field*.

Another recruit was William Grenfell (created Baron Desborough in 1905), who would go on to be one of the founders of the British Olympic Association in 1905 and the chief organiser of the 1908 Olympics.

So there can be no question of any fundamental antagonism between Coubertin, the IOC and the British.

Nevertheless, given the age and status of this new generation of British Olympians, it is understandable that few of them would have upbraided Coubertin for his omission of Brookes, Much Wenlock and all the other British games from the official record. After all, it was partly Brookes' lack of status and that of his fellow campaigners during the 1860s and 1870s that had caused their efforts to fail.

At the same time, without Brookes, there was no-one of sufficient status from Wenlock to press the town's case or to re-open contacts with the IOC, which was now far more concerned with international matters than with a parochial sports meeting in Shropshire.

As a result, Much Wenlock continued to fade from the record. When Coubertin published an account of the Olympic revival in 1909 (*see Links*), he simply wrote of an 'English doctor, from another age, who had made his little village into a metropolis of popular sports'.

Fortunately, as noted in Chapter Four, this long felt historical slight has since been addressed, starting with the work of Olympic historian Don Anthony at the time of Birmingham's bid for the 1992 Games. This led to the attendance of IOC and BOA representatives at the 100th Wenlock Olympian Games, in 1986, an event also attended by Coubertin's great nephew, Geoffroy de Navacelle. One of Coubertin's successors as IOC president, Juan Antonio Samaranch, then further restored Wenlock's place in the official history by visiting the town in 1994 as part of the IOC's centenary celebrations, and by paying tribute to Brookes at his grave.

Coubertin's legacy

Before we move on from Coubertin and turn our attention to the London Olympics of 1908, it is important to consider Coubertin's own legacy in Britain.

Firstly, as has been often noted, as well as travelling around the country extensively from 1883 onwards, Coubertin conducted a wide ranging correspondence with a number of British politicians, educationalists and sporting figures. His letters to Brookes, for example, were pasted onto the pages of the Wenlock Olympian Society's minute book, where they remain today as a touching reminder of their relationship. 'You were kind enough to send me your photograph', Coubertin wrote to Brookes in August 1890. 'I beg to return mine regretting that I have not a better one for it gives the idea of one much taller & stronger than I am.'

Other examples of Coubertin's correspondence can be seen in the archives of the Royal Geographical Society – with whom he discussed Britain's Everest Expedition of 1922 – and in Lord Desborough's private papers, held at the Centre for Buckinghamshire Studies.

In addition, Coubertin's writings and speeches were voluminous. For historians, these writings have provided a rich source of material, and in 2000 were published by the IOC in a single volume (see Links).

Secondly, just as many British individuals and institutions left their own mark on Coubertin's thinking, so his constant networking would leave its mark on British Olympians. Where the likes of Brookes, Hulley and Ravenstein had failed to gather around them a body of movers and shakers who could deliver the dream of an Olympic revival, Coubertin managed to assemble a coterie of individuals who would go on to form the British Olympic Association in May 1905, and to organise the first London Games in 1908.

Coubertin's legacy continues to be felt as London prepares itself to host the 2012 Olympics.

In Much Wenlock, the William Brookes School is Britain's first accredited 'Coubertin School', part of a global network of around 50 schools which place particular emphasis on the study of Olympism and offer students the opportunity of taking part in international, Olympic-themed educational events.

For university students, the International Pierre de

Coubertin Committee runs the Coubertin Olympic Award, an international essay competition, while the IOC's Pierre de Coubertin Prize, launched in 2008, rewards advanced research. Fittingly, its inaugural winner was Dikaia Chatziefstathiou, a Greek-born sports sociologist who studied at Loughborough University and, at the time of the award, was teaching at Canterbury Christ Church University. This mix of Greek heritage and English education appeared to offer the perfect combination for an award designed to keep Coubertin's legacy alive.

For this legacy can hardly be overestimated.

As an outsider, Coubertin was able to evaluate what he regarded as the most successful elements of the British educational and social system, yet not be encumbered by the factionalism that so plagued the governance of British sport. Thus where earlier British interpretations of Olympianism had been content to remain localised, or had floundered in the face of apathy, Coubertin proved able to develop the idea on an international scale.

As a result, it could be argued that, rather than seeing the IOC's Olympic Games as a revival of the ancient games, or even as a fin-de-siècle innovation, they were instead a natural evolution of an Olympian movement that had already been emerging in Victorian Britain.

It was Coubertin who recognised this, and who gave it meaning in the modern world.

Throughout his final years Pierre de Coubertin hardly ceased to promote Olympism. After 1908 we know of only one visit to Britain, for a dinner at the Hotel Dieudonné in London in November 1913.

After war broke out, he moved the IOC office from Paris to Lausanne, in neutral Switzerland. Once there he worked hard to ensure that the 1920 Games took place, in Antwerp. He then oversaw the first Winter Olympics in Chamonix in early 1924, followed by that year's Summer Games in his beloved Paris.

Shortly after he stood down from the IOC presidency, but carried on writing, lecturing and broadcasting. His last Games were those at Berlin in 1936. The following year, aged 74, he died in Geneva.

According to his wishes he was buried in Lausanne and his heart interred in a memorial built at Olympia.

As for his family, neither of his children married, so it has been left to his grand nephew, Geoffroy de Navacelle, and Geoffroy's son, Antoine, to keep the Coubertin flame burning in the public realm.

Chapter Nine

London Olympic Games 1908

In the absence of a national sports museum, artefacts relating to the 1908 Olympics are to be found scattered amongst dozens of public and private collections. This badge is thought to be from the swimming costume of John 'Rob' Derbyshire, a member of the victorious 4×200 metre freestyle relay team. The badge is held by the Amateur Swimming Association, the governing body which oversaw the swimming, diving and water polo tournaments.

During the run up to the 2012 Olympics and Paralympics in London, considerable emphasis was placed on securing the legacy of the Games; of not just laying on 28 days of sport, but of leaving behind tangible benefits across the nation and particularly for the host community in east London, in terms of sporting and recreational facilities, urban regeneration, housing, employment and educational opportunities.

This commitment to legacy formed a crucial part of a London bid that had been first considered by the British Olympic Association in 1997, before it was formally submitted to the International Olympic Committee in 2003. Two more years passed before London won the vote on July 6 2005.

The 2012 bid was thus in the planning stage for around eight years, allowing a further seven years for construction and preparation; a total gestation period of fifteen years.

The 1908 Games in London, by comparison, were planned and prepared for in just under two years. Given this timescale, small wonder that the idea of a planned legacy did not come up for discussion.

Nevertheless, despite the hurried nature of the preparations, it is not mere jingoism to state that the 1908 Games were the first recognisably modern Olympics, or that they were a success overall (albeit with important reservations), or that a number of the conventions and practices that we now take for granted sprang from innovations made in 1908.

In this chapter, therefore, rather than retell the story of the Games – a story well told in a number of other excellent sources (see Links) – we will focus on the question of what, apart from hosting and participating in the Games, the British achieved in 1908 that would leave a lasting impression on the Olympics, as they evolved into the 20th century and beyond.

We will also seek out those tangible reminders of the 1908 Games; the buildings, places, artefacts and commemorations that, in lieu of any planned legacy, and in the absence of a national sports museum, have somehow survived for over a century.

But before embarking on that trail, it is worth explaining how the 1908 Games came to be in London in the first place.

As previous chapters have recounted, between the demise of the ancient Games in the fourth century AD and the staging of the first modern Games in 1896, a greater number and variety of events bearing the name Olympic, or its variants, had taken place in Britain than in any other country. After 1896 – the continuance of the Games at Wenlock and Morpeth notwithstanding – this heritage mattered little to most members of the IOC, even if Pierre de Coubertin did clearly retain an affection for Britain.

To a large extent it also mattered little to the British, for there already existed in the country a thriving and deep rooted athletic culture which, at best, paid little heed to events overseas, and at worst remained openly hostile to the Olympic movement. As The Times put it in 1896, 'One cannot but deplore the fact that, while the Olympic games were advertised in every village in France, a comparatively slender effort was made to attract the attention of the English athletic world.'

As to where the modern Olympics might be staged, almost from the beginning there arose differences within the IOC. At the founding meeting of the IOC in 1894, Coubertin announced that the first modern Olympics would take place in Paris in 1900. Greek members responded by offering to make Athens ready by 1896.

Then, when the 1900 Games were held in Paris, they were beset by problems. Most of all they were overshadowed by the Exposition Universelle that dominated the French capital that year. In addition, the sporting programme was too long, extending from May 14 until October 28, compared to the ten days of the 1896 Games. Meanwhile, certain of the venues were unsuitable. For example, with its currents and mud, the River Seine was hardly ideal for the swimming races, while the running track in the Bois de Boulogne was uneven.

Coubertin later acknowledged that these Games had been held 'under seriously deficient circumstances'.

In the aftermath of this debacle both Coubertin and the Greeks felt that in order to strengthen the Olympic movement and maintain its links with the motherland, an extra series of 'Intercalated Games' should be held in the middle of each Olympiad, to be hosted always in Athens.

Whilst this somewhat ambitious proposal was being discussed, the Games of the Third Olympiad were staged, in the American city of St Louis in 1904.

In his introduction to the *Official Report* of the 1896 Olympics, Coubertin had proposed that the Games be held 'in every large capital of the world in turn'.

Not only was St Louis not a capital, it had not been the IOC's original choice. Instead, Chicago had been selected (again, not a capital). But when the organisers of a world fair in St Louis realised that a Chicago Olympics would clash with their own efforts, they muscled in on the act. Despite what had occurred in Paris, in 1904 the Olympics were therefore once again destined to become the adjunct of an exhibition, this time the Louisiana Purchase Exposition.

Also echoing Paris, the sporting programme at St Louis was spread out between May and October.

As for the Games' global appeal, although athletes from twelve countries appeared, of the 651 participants, 575 were from the USA and Canada, hardly the celebration of internationalism that the IOC had sought. In fact Coubertin did not even attend the 1904 Games, scathingly describing them in his autobiography *Olympic Memoirs* (*see Links*) as 'completely lacking in attraction'.

With the IOC project now in danger of petering out, the Greeks, as planned, staged their first Intercalated Games, held once again at the Panathenaic Stadium in Athens, from April 22 to May 2 1906. As it transpired these turned out to be the only Intercalated Games ever staged, but they are worth noting all the same because they did a great deal to put the Olympic movement back on track and, in the process, saw the introduction of some key practices that have since become the norm.

Most important of all, the 1906 Intercalated Games were the first to require that athletes register via their national Olympic associations, rather than entering as individuals. In the years that followed the formation of the IOC in 1894, twelve national associations had affiliated. One of them was the British Olympic Association, formed in May 1905 at a meeting held in the Houses of Parliament. (Of course there had been a National Olympian Association in England as early as 1865. But this was long since defunct.)

With offices in Victoria Street, Westminster, the BOA's first Honorary Secretary was, as we learnt in the previous chapter, the Reverend Robert Stuart de Courcy Laffan, a former Headmaster of Cheltenham College who had served as a member of the IOC since 1897 and was a close associate of Coubertin. The structure of the BOA, Coubertin would later write, offered a model that many other national Olympic associations had followed to good effect.

The 1906 Intercalated Games were also the first at which an opening ceremony was staged as a distinct and separate event; an event at which, again for the first time, all the athletes marched into the stadium behind their national flags. Another innovation was the practice of raising national flags to salute each victor.

But while the 1906 Games were generally deemed to have been a success, as they were taking place doubts were mounting that the Games of the Fourth Olympiad, scheduled for 1908, would take place at all.

The German Olympic Association had been the first to express an interest in 1908, putting forward Berlin as the potential host. But when doubts were raised as to whether the German government and the Berlin authorities would back the idea, the Italians offered Rome instead. Much to Coubertin's frustration, however, rival factions in Rome started to quarrel over who would do what, until, with barely two years to go, and just as the Intercalated Games were about to start, Mount Vesuvius in southern Italy erupted, causing the deaths of over 200 people. Officially this was the reason given for Rome pulling out as host city, but in truth the IOC was by then already looking for a white knight.

And in the arch enthusiast Willie Grenfell, 1st Baron Desborough, Chairman of the British Olympic Association, they found one.

London takes up the challenge

Lord Desborough, of all people, did not need to be told of the seriousness of Mount Vesuvius' eruption. En route to the Intercalated Games in Athens in Lord Howard de Walden's yacht, along with fellow members of the British fencing team, he had seen for himself some of the devastation while anchored in the Bay of Naples. So while in a wave of sympathy the Italians were able to withdraw gracefully from their commitment, to the relief of the IOC, Desborough leapt into action.

Firstly he obtained royal approval for his plan from Edward VII, who also in Athens for the Intercalated Olympics whilst on a visit to his brother-in-law, King George of Greece. Edward was by then already well aware of the IOC. Indeed in June 1904, shortly before the ill-fated St Louis Games, the king had hosted a reception at Windsor Castle for IOC members, who were also that week treated to a drinks party with the Prince of Wales at Marlborough House and a banquet with the Lord Mayor of London. So the IOC hardly needed persuading that London could put on a decent show.

Edward made only one stipulation. On no account, he told Desborough, should public money be expended on the 1908 Games. But for Desborough this was not a »

As Dover was to the Cotswold Olimpicks and Brookes to Much Wenlock, so was Lord Desborough to the 1908 Olympics in London.

Born William Grenfell in 1855 and educated at Harrow and Oxford, the genial 'Willie' was a genuine all rounder.

Apart from fencing at the Intercalated Olympics he climbed the Matterhorn, swam across Niagara Falls and rowed the Channel. After spells as an MP he was a founding member of the BOA and held high office also at the MCC, the Lawn Tennis Association and at Henley. He died in 1945, aged 90.

» problem. He felt sure that London's network of elite private sports clubs, the likes of the Hurlingham, the Queen's Club and the All England Club at Wimbledon, were bound to rally round. (He himself was president of the Bath Club, in central London.) Desborough was similarly confident that the BOA would win over the governing bodies needed to run an Olympics. After all, the British had been organising sporting events for decades, as Coubertin himself was well able to attest. In August 1906 the IOC therefore accepted Desborough's offer with enthusiasm.

Planning commenced in November.

First a sub-group, the British Olympic Council (BOC), was set up to manage the project (the equivalent of the modern day London Organising Committee of the Olympic Games, or LOCOG). As Desborough put it in an open letter to the British press, published on November 27, 'As this country has been the cradle of so many forms of athletic sport, it is absolutely essential that the Olympic Games, if they are held in England, should be carried out in a manner worthy of a great athletic nation'.

That meant, for a start, making sure that the Games would not clash with any existing events, especially after the Royal Yacht Squadron turned down the BOC's request to stage the yachting at its Isle of Wight headquarters. The club, the BOC were informed, would be otherwise engaged with Cowes Week.

The sensitivities surrounding scheduling may also be deduced from the BOC's pointed announcement that 'the Games will be held in July, *after* Henley Regatta and *after* the AAA Championships'.

On the thornier issue of an Olympic Stadium, it appears from Desborough's letter to the press in November 1906 that the BOC was already in talks with an unnamed body offering to provide a stadium holding 100,000 spectators, at no cost to the BOA. Desborough also felt able to promise that, 'As far as possible, all the competitions, including swimming, archery, fencing, wrestling, &c., will be held on the same site in which the amphitheatre for the track-athletics and cycling will be erected.'

But where would this ambitious, multi-purpose stadium be built? There were two obvious candidates. These were Crystal Palace, the venue for FA Cup Finals (and of course the NOA Games of 1866), and Stamford Bridge, the former home of the London Athletic Club which, the previous year, had been taken over and expanded by Chelsea Football Club.

In fact, the answer came from an entirely unexpected source, for as fortune would have it, London was gearing up for a major international exhibition of its own, also in 1908. Supported jointly by the governments of France and Great Britain as evidence of their recently signed *Entente Cordiale*, and designed to foster commercial and cultural ties at a time of growing German industrial and military muscle, the Franco-British Exhibition promised to be the largest single attraction ever seen in the capital.

Even better, the site on which it was to be constructed, as had already been announced in July 1906 – covering 140 acres of brickfields and farmland in Shepherd's Bush – had more than enough space for a stadium, being eight times larger than the site of the 1851 Great Exhibition. Indeed, some sources have suggested that the exhibition organisers were already considering building a stadium when they learnt of the BOC's search for a venue.

The exhibition company struck a hard bargain, all the same. In return for financing the stadium's construction they demanded from the BOC a swingeing 75 per cent of all receipts. But that suited Desborough fine. It meant that he could keep his pledge to avoid recourse to public funding and, in any case, the stadium was not expected to remain standing after the exhibition closed.

No mention of legacy in those days. Or of the fact that after the Paris and St Louis Games, Pierre de Coubertin had gone on record to say that never again would an Olympics be held in conjunction with an exhibition. But with so little time left and with the offer of a stadium on the table, this was a deal that suited everyone.

The Franco-British Exhibition

In common with the 1924 Empire Exhibition at Wembley, the 1951 Festival of Britain, the Millennium Dome and the 2012 Olympic Park at Stratford, the Franco-British »

The 'Great Stadium' as envisaged in early 1908, complete with towers, extensive cladding and only very limited spectator cover. Earlier designs showed an even more elaborate ceremonial spectator entrance in the near corner. Owing to time and cost constraints, the final design was rather simpler, at least compared with the ornate exhibition buildings erected alongside.

Stadium · THE GREAT WHITE CITY, LONDON

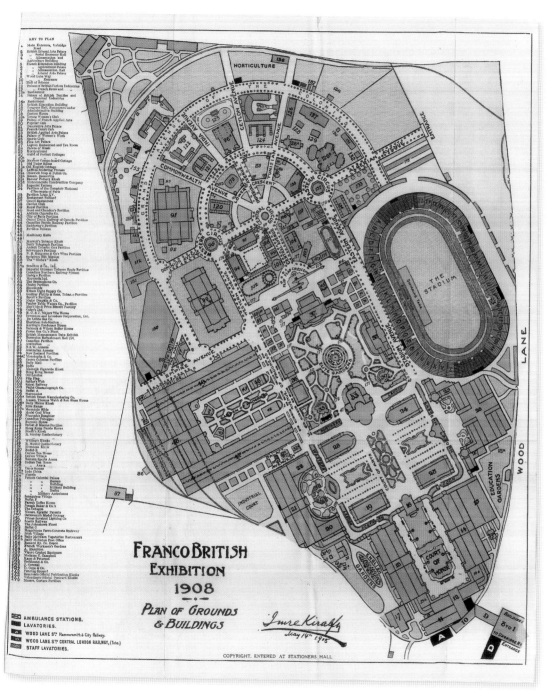

FRANCO BRITISH
EXHIBITION
1908
—•—
PLAN OF GROUNDS
& BUILDINGS

Imre Kiralfy
May 14th 1908

COPYRIGHT. ENTERED AT STATIONERS HALL

▬ AMBULANCE STATIONS.
▬ LAVATORIES.
Ⓐ WOOD LANE STⁿ Hammersmith & City Railway.
Ⓓ WOOD LANE STⁿ CENTRAL LONDON RAILWAY, (Tube).
▨ STAFF LAVATORIES.

This official exhibition map is from the collection of Bob Wilcock of the Society of Olympic Collectors.

Among the attractions listed were halls for fine arts, science, education, agriculture, textiles and industry. There were show cottages, mocked-up Irish and Senegalese villages, French cafés, stalls showcasing gramophones and electric lighting, a scenic railway and, in the centre (just above the Grand Restaurant, shown as building 37), the celebrated Flip Flap.

Every element was intended to be temporary, so it is ironic that one of the least sophisticated structures, the stadium, survived until 1985.

Apart from the name White City, still applied to the area, no traces of the exhibition survive. True, Wood Lane station, which closed in 1959, reopened on an adjacent site in 2008. Otherwise, the D-shaped Avenue of the Colonies is now sliced through by Westway, while the south east corner was redeveloped as BBC TV Centre in 1960.

The remaining areas are now mainly residential, with Hammersmith Park occupying the south west corner. Loftus Road, the home of Queen's Park Rangers FC, occupies the area where the words Franco British Exhibition 1908 appear.

›› Exhibition of 1908 was a colossal enterprise that helped to transform the urban fabric of London.

The details are well recorded elsewhere, but in brief, the design and construction of the site was masterminded by a Hungarian showman, Imre Kiralfy, who had earlier made his reputation by staging extravaganzas in New York, at Earls Court and at Olympia (where he had famously recreated a Venetian waterscape).

Construction started in January 1907, and over the next 18 months an amazing transformation of the brickfields took place. Working with architects from Britain and France, and with a labour force of up to 12,000 men, Kiralfy oversaw the creation of 120 temporary steel-framed exhibition buildings and 20 pavilions, each decked with fibrous plaster cladding in a variety of faux oriental and neo-baroque styles, and painted in brilliant white, hence the exhibition site earning the nickname 'White City'. (It was not the first White City, however. A section of the World's Columbian Exposition in Chicago in 1893 had been similarly named.)

One noteworthy aspect of White City was its transport links. The main access point was Shepherd's Bush station on the Central Line, where an elaborate gateway, or *Porte Monumentale*, channelled visitors into a winding, overhead walkway leading to the south east corner of the exhibition site. This walkway intersected what is now the site of the Westfield Shopping Centre.

A second station on the Central Line was opened on Wood Lane itself, plus a third, also on Wood Lane, served by the Metropolitan Railway. (The current White City tube station was a later development, in 1947.)

All three stations were certainly needed. Between the official opening by Edward VII on May 14 1908 and the exhibition's closure on October 31, some 8.4 million visitors passed through the turnstiles, including 130,000 on a single day at the end of August. One of the most popular attractions was the Flip Flap, for which 1.1 million people paid 6d to be lifted 200 feet into the air in carriages attached to two, crane-like gantries.

The Great Stadium

Although the 1908 Games were the fourth Olympics of the modern era, they were the first to be staged in a stadium built especially for the Games, thereby setting a precedent followed at all but six of the Summer Games held since.

Its construction, by the Hammersmith-based contractors George Wimpey, was, by modern standards, exceptionally rapid. Watched by a Mr Metaxas from the

Viewed in around late May 1908, from a balloon looking north towards Wormwood Scrubs, the 'White City' or 'Great' Stadium – never officially titled the Olympic Stadium – was arguably the most advanced multi-purpose stadium in the world at the time. Unlike the original designs there were no towers or any external cladding. For this reason the stadium was variously decried for its lack of architectural pretension or admired for its unfussy functionalism. Certainly the provision of stand roofs proved wise given the wet summer that was to follow.

For an internal view, see inside the front cover flap.

The Stadium, FRANCO-BRITISH EXHIBITION.

Imperial Sports Club, Franco-British Exhibition, London, 1908

From the collection of Jack Murray of the Society of Olympic Collectors, this postcard shows the Imperial Sports Club, built as a meeting point for IOC dignitaries attending the Games. The building (on the right, just beyond the bridge) was typical of the lavish, some thought vulgar 'wedding cake' style of the Franco-British exhibition, and was linked to the adjacent stadium (just visible in the distance beyond the 'Eastern Lagoon') by a VIP entrance. It also had its own private garage. Non IOC individuals were eligible to join, but only if, in the words of *The Times*, they were members of 'first class West End clubs'.

The spot from which this shot was taken is now a community centre on White City Close, just north of BBC TV Centre.

Greek Embassy, Lord and Lady Desborough ceremonially fixed the first steel stanchion on August 2 1907. Nine months later the stadium was opened, on the same day as the exhibition.

Known at the time as 'The Stadium' or 'The Great Stadium', the structure appears now to have been fairly basic. Certainly the final version was much less grand than its designer, the engineer John James Webster, had envisaged, even though its construction costs rose from the original estimate of £44,000 to some £60,000.

On the other hand, it was designed only for the duration of the exhibition. So there was no discussion of who might use it after 1908, even though it was palpably superior in form to every other stadium or sports ground in London at the time, was much more accessible, and was larger than all of them other than Crystal Palace (which was otherwise hardly more than a turf bowl with three basic timber stands). In their *Official Report* of the 1908 Games, the BOA put the stadium's capacity as 70,000, of which 17,000 seats were under cover. (Other sources gave totals of 80,000 and even 93,000, but then capacities of this era were notoriously inexact.)

To put it another way, the *Official Report* continued, 'The containing walls of the Stadium... are large enough in extent to enclose seven buildings each the size of the Albert Hall.' Souvenir postcards, meanwhile, showed how either of the two giant Cunard liners of the day, the *Lusitania* or the *Mauretania*, might also fit within the structure, which measured 1,001 feet from end to end.

To put all of this into context, in 1908 only three other stadiums in the world were of comparable size and modernity, all three being in Glasgow (namely Hampden Park, Ibrox Park and Celtic Park). Discounting the relatively primitive Crystal Palace, as far as purpose-built English stadiums were concerned, Stamford Bridge had managed to accommodate 67,000 for a football match in 1906. However, all but 7,000 of those were standing on open terracing formed on banks of earth. In fact, not until Old Trafford was built by Manchester United in 1910 would the Great Stadium at White City be rivalled in either size or technical sophistication.

This modernity was matched by the attention paid to the staging of test events in the run up to the Games.

Firstly, despite work still continuing on the structure, on May 14, the day that the Franco-British exhibition was officially opened, The Prince of Wales, the French Ambassador and Lord Desborough watched a display of gymnastics, swimming, diving and athletics put on by ≫

One of the key figures at the 1908 Olympics was the Reverend Robert Stuart de Courcy Laffan, secretary of the BOA and Rector of St Stephen, Walbrook, in the City of London.

An unlikely figure in the world of sport, Laffan – previously the headmaster of Cheltenham College – first made an impression on Coubertin at a meeting in Le Havre in 1897, at which he gave a stirring yet impromptu speech on the moral benefits of sport, in perfect French.

Thereafter he became in effect Coubertin's man in London, loyally serving the BOA and IOC until his death in 1927. There is a simple memorial to him at St Stephen.

》 the Polytechnic Harriers and the Finchley Harriers. In a sign of what was to come, it rained throughout the day.

On May 26 there followed the official opening of the stadium, conducted jointly by Edward VII and Armand Fallières, the President of France. This was accompanied by various displays by the Polytechnic Harriers, whose Honorary Secretary, Jack Andrew, had been tasked with the all important role of organising the track and field events at the Olympics. The stadium's facilities were further tested in late May and early June by the holding of Olympic trials by the Amateur Athletic Association and the Amateur Swimming Association, and on July 4 by the staging of the AAA's annual championships, watched by a crowd of 22,000.

The stadium was not alone in being put to the test. The BOA was itself entering unknown territory by staging a major international event; a challenge for which, for all his panache and contacts in high society, Desborough had few practical credentials. Nor did his right hand man, Robert de Courcy Laffan (see left). A third unlikely amateur with a major role to play was William Henry. Born in Poland and best known as a swimmer – he won a bronze at the 1906 Games at the age of 47 – Henry had co-founded what would later be called the Royal Life Saving Society in 1891. Apart from helping to design the diving platform, Henry was for some reason given the role of Stadium Director. So onerous did this task become that he resigned a fortnight before the Games started, and was only cajoled back by the promise of further assistance.

One of Henry's tasks was to plan the use of a network of 38 changing and committee rooms under the stands, each one being designated to a particular nation or sport, or to a group of nations or sports. Planning who went where must have presented a real headache. For example Italy, Russia and Belgium were grouped together in one room, with Hungary, Greece and Switzerland next door. The 30 or so female participants, meanwhile, had to make do with just one room to themselves.

But what really presented William Henry and Jack Andrew with their greatest operational challenge was the intention to stage so many different events within the one arena, as promised by Desborough from the outset.

In order to achieve this, the BOC consulted with all the relevant governing bodies to ensure that their particular discipline would be properly accommodated.

Which brings us to the first major lesson learned in 1908, concerning the athletics track. For while British athletics operated under the imperial system, the IOC had always worked in metric measurements.

True, at the time there were no set standards in any country. During the 19th century British running tracks

had varied considerably in length, although by 1908, at venues such as Stamford Bridge and Belle Vue in Manchester, 440 yards was becoming the norm; that is, four laps to a mile, and with room in the infield for a full size football pitch.

At White City, however, the BOC called not only for a running track and a full size football pitch, but also for a cycling track around the outside and a swimming pool to be located within the infield.

Such a combination had never been tried before.

At Athens in 1896 and 1906, for example, the swimming had taken place in the sea at Piraeus. In Paris in 1900, as noted earlier, the swimming and water polo were held in the River Seine, pollution, currents and all. Four years later St Louis had used an artificial lake which doubled up as a cattle dip; hardly conducive to good water quality, as several queasy swimmers found to their cost.

So the stadium pool at White City, despite being hardly more than a rectangular hole in the ground, with raised edges, actually represented a significant advance, in the Olympic context at least.

Its effect on the geometry of the stadium was less welcome, however. Instead of a more standard 440 yard track, Charles Perry – the specialist from Stamford Bridge who had also worked on the 1896 track – was forced to lay a track measuring 1,760 feet per lap (or three laps to the mile), the length used also at St Louis. But this still did not accord with the IOC's preference for metric distances and so required continual compromises to be made by both runners and officials. (Not that this impasse made any difference. At Stockholm in 1912 the track measured an even more eccentric 384.1 metres.)

The elongated shape of the track also meant that viewing distances for spectators were far beyond what would be deemed acceptable by modern standards.

A further inconsistency was that while the running track was measured in feet, the pool was built to metric standards, the first time this had happened in Britain. It measured 100m long (twice the length of a modern Olympic pool) and 15m wide. Yet for some reason the depth was expressed in imperial units; that is, ranging from 4 feet 6 inches at each end to 12 feet 6 inches in the centre, where the diving platform was located.

As for the cycle track, this was laid out under the directions of the National Cyclists' Union, and measured 660 yards to the lap with banked curves and a concrete surface. The grass infield, meanwhile, had room for another track, used for hurdle races and the steeplechase, as well as all the usual jumping and throwing events – the shot put, the hammer, the discus (freestyle and classical) and the javelin (freestyle and centre hold). 》

The Daily Mirror

THE MORNINQ JOURNAL WITH THE SECOND LARGEST NET SALE.

No. 1,469. | Registered at the G. P. O. as a Newspaper. | TUESDAY, JULY 14, 1908. | One Halfpenny.

THE KING OPENS THE OLYMPIC GAMES: PROCESSION OF WORLD'S FINEST ATHLETES IN THE STADIUM.

Though the brilliance of the scene in the Stadium yesterday afternoon, when the King opened the Olympic Games, was greatly impaired by the unfavourable weather, the ceremony was still striking and impressive. Among the many royalties with the King and Queen in the royal box were the Prince and Princess of Wales, the Crown Prince and Princess of Greece, and the Crown Prince and Princess of Sweden. Lord Des-borough presented the foreign delegates to his Majesty, whom he then invited to declare the fourth Olympiad open. After the King had formally opened the Games the competitors paraded past their Majesties. (1) Making the best of it. (2) Danish lady gymnasts. (3) The King acknowledges the cheering—(A) The Queen, (B) Prince of Wales, (C) Duke of Connaught. (4) Start of the march-past.

As on the opening day of the Franco-British Exhibition four weeks earlier, heavy rain marred the opening ceremony of the 1908 Games on July 13. That, and the fact that it was held on a Monday afternoon explain why the stadium was only half full. Still, spirits were lifted by the presence of Edward VII and Queen Alexandra, and by 'Danish lady gymnasts' performing in ankle-revealing outfits.

Following the precedent set at Athens in 1906, the competitors marched into the stadium behind their national flags. However the USA contingent, which included several Irish-Americans, refused to lower their flag as they passed the royal box. Although little was said at the time, this slight and other perceived injustices became a cause of considerable friction between the British and American teams.

The *Daily Mirror*, incidentally, was one of several companies to advertise in the stadium, a practice banned by the IOC at later Games.

▲ British athletics officials were accustomed to running several events on the same day in the same venue, but the Olympic programme offered a formidable organisational challenge nevertheless, and that was before the differences between imperial and metric measurements were taken into account. Seen above, on days when clearly the weather and the events on offer were not to the public's taste, are the high jump and the steeplechase, both held within the infield. Note the official with the megaphone, this being in the days before electronic public address systems came into use.

» The infield was also used for archery, tug-of-war, gymnastics, football, hockey, lacrosse and rugby and, on a temporary platform, wrestling.

Given how much of the layout had been dictated by the presence of the swimming pool, it is worth asking whether the effort was worthwhile.

Almost certainly for those entering the aquatic sports, being able to perform in the same arena as the athletes, and on occasions in front of sizeable crowds, must have been a novel experience. But there were drawbacks.

Firstly the water was unheated. For the likes of Henry Taylor from Chadderton and Jack Jarvis from Leicester (*see opposite*), having learnt to swim in their local canals, this presented no problem. But the summer of 1908 was a truly miserable one, and one story, not corroborated, has it that the British 4 x 200m relay team only won the gold after one of their Hungarian opponents was struck down by hypothermia.

Secondly, no provision was made for the water to be either filtered or changed during the course of the twelve day programme, with predictable consequences for its quality. The great irony of this was that at the time Britain led the world in the provision of public swimming baths, and within a two mile radius of the stadium lay several state of the art heated indoor pools.

Still, the proximity and temperature of the pool was said to have been appreciated by some athletes on the few occasions when the sun did shine. But not so, it has also been claimed, by players in the hockey, football and rugby tournaments which took place two months after the main programme, in October, during which balls occasionally had to be retrieved from the water.

Whether true or not, one legacy of the 1908 Games was that the experiment of siting a competition pool within the main stadium was never again repeated.

Magnitude and management

Apart from being the first Olympics to be staged in a purpose-built stadium, the 1908 London Games were also noteworthy for the sheer number of events included in the programme, and for the way each event was organised and regulated by British officials, sometimes with unfortunate consequences.

In brief, the Games consisted of 109 events featuring 24 different sporting disciplines, involving 2,023 athletes from 23 nations. This not only made the 1908 Games the largest Olympics to date, but also the largest international sports gathering ever staged. As such, its organisation had to be of the highest order.

In terms of scheduling, the programme was divided into two distinct sections, summer and winter.

The summer programme began with a racquets tournament at the Queen's Club in West Kensington on April 27, and ended on August 29 with the motorboating on Southampton Water. Within that summer period the main events in the Great Stadium ran from July 13–25.

There was then a seven week break before the 'winter' programme – another new feature in 1908 – took place in October. This consisted of two days of ice skating at the Prince's Club in Knightsbridge and a one day boxing tournament at the Northampton Institute in Clerkenwell.

Meanwhile, back in the stadium, the football, rugby, lacrosse and hockey tournaments all took place over two weeks, starting on October 19, and ending with the hockey final on October 31, the day that the Franco-British Exhibition also came to a close.

(Although officially titled the 'Winter Games', these October events were not, it should be noted, considered as Winter Olympics in the modern sense. The first of these took place in 1924, at Chamonix in France.)

Thus the entire 1908 Games spanned a period of 188 days (compared with 15 days for the 2012 Olympic Games and 12 for the Paralympics). This was of course far too long, most especially for the public. Those who regarded the Olympics as only a passing curiosity, rather like the Flip Flap, could hardly engage with the full narrative, while those who were genuinely interested in sport had plenty of other distractions on the domestic front.

For entrants to some of the more minor tournaments held in venues other than the Great Stadium, moreover, there was also little sense of having taken part in an historic event. Nor could several of the events be even considered as international, given that only British individuals or teams had entered.

Overall, therefore, the 1908 Games proved to be too ambitious and too much geared towards homegrown sports and practices.

On the other hand, there could be no criticism that, as in Paris and St Louis, the Olympics had been lost in the midst of an exhibition. In truth, without the Franco-British Exhibition the Games may not have been deliverable, at least not without recourse to public expenditure. Yet without the Games, the exhibition would have enjoyed less of a focus.

That the crowds in the stadium had been smaller than expected, that the weather had been so unkind, and that certain events had been greeted with almost total apathy, was hardly the fault of the organisers. After all, these were only the fourth full Olympic Games, and everyone involved was still learning.

There were, nevertheless, some events that simply did not work. Motorboating, racquets and real tennis ›

One curiosity of the 1908 Games was the 10m diving tower, designed by William Henry to be lowered down with ropes and submerged inside the swimming pool when not in use – a process that, according to the *Official Report*, made a valuable contribution to 'the general amusement of spectators'.

It is interesting to note that whereas today's Olympic diving pools must be 5m deep to serve a 10m board, the maximum depth of the pool in 1908 was a mere 3.8m.

Seen at the poolside (*below left*), three of the British squad were (*left to right*) Rob Derbyshire from Manchester, Henry Taylor from Chadderton and Jack Jarvis from Leicester.

Derbyshire, who swam in four Olympics and whose badge from 1908 may be the one featured on page 100, later became the superintendent at Lime Grove Baths in Hammersmith, just up the road from White City.

Fate would be less kind to Henry Taylor, a winner of four Olympic golds, as noted on page 178.

CITY OF LONDON POLICE TEAM.
Who won the Tug-of-War Competition.
Back Row (left to right) : P.C.s. Barrett. Goodfellow. Hirons, Shepherd, Ireton, Mills.
Second Row : P. C. Humphreys, C. J. Duke (Captain), D. J. Moody (Asst. Sec. Athletic Section).
P.C. Merriman.
Sitting : P.C. Morse.

Photo by Venning, Hamerton.

▲ One rift of many to surface between the British and the Americans concerned the footwear worn by members of Britain's three **tug-of-war** teams, all of whom were policemen and who therefore competed in standard issue hobnail boots. These, the US teams felt, gave the British an unfair advantage. This is the victorious **City of London** team. The silver went to the Liverpool Police and the bronze to K Division of the Metropolitan Police.

Tug-of-war was not solely a British sport, but it was dropped after 1920. Also dropped in the 1920s, to be replaced by loudspeakers, was the **toastmaster**, a role that went back to the ancient Games. On the left is the 1908 '*megaphone* man' **William Knightsmith**, a popular character remembered also as the first in his profession to wear a scarlet coat in order to stand out from the crowd.

》 never appeared at the Olympics again, and some of the demonstration events, like bicycle polo, also failed to make an impact.

Other experiments, though, were successful. Hockey made its first Olympic appearance, as did women's gymnastics, albeit only as a demonstration event. And while the figure skating at the Prince's Club did not directly lead to a full-blown winter programme, it was still the first time that an ice-based sport had been included at an Olympic Games.

Rules and regulations

With their penchant for codification and control, and their much vaunted emphasis on the principles of 'fair play', the representatives of Britain's sports governing bodies saw in the 1908 Games a chance to show the world that their way was the best, and represented the truest and most honourable means of practising competitive sport.

A reflection of this is that within the *Official Report* of the Games, published in 1909, 212 of the 794 pages were taken up by the regulations of 21 different sports. A further 19 pages contained precise definitions of amateurism as laid out by various sporting bodies in five different countries. But while the entry for Belgium extended to just one sentence, those for the English, Scottish and Irish associations ran to eleven pages (and included, oddly, the regulations for golf and amateur billiards, neither of which were even Olympic sports).

In other words, here were the British laying down the law as they saw it to the rest of the sporting world. To most nations new to international sport, these guidelines were no doubt useful. But to others, they smacked of old fashioned British arrogance.

Nor did all the competing foreign associations approve of some of the British officials' methods. The US delegation in particular, led by James Sullivan, erupted on several occasions, most famously over the disqualification of an American runner in the 400m, and over the finale of the marathon (of which more later). Indeed, this festering distrust between the British and the Americans would inform all subsequent narratives on the 1908 Olympics, no less than a Russian linesman's call has come to be regarded as a seminal trope of the 1966 World Cup.

Naturally the organisers defended themselves robustly in the *Official Report*.

'It must be clear that the details of so complicated a programme could never have been carried out unless the executive power had been entrusted to these great governing Associations, which had already proved, at many previous International meetings, their competence to control such details. 》

◀ At a time when support for the suffragette movement was slowly building in Britain, the appearance of a record 37 female competitors at the 1908 Olympics prompted mixed reactions. As Pierre de Coubertin would later write in 1912, 'The feminine semi-Olympiad is impractical, uninteresting, ungainly and, I do not hesitate to add, improper. It is not in keeping with my concept of the Olympic Games… (which is) the solemn and periodic exaltation of male athleticism, based on internationalism, by means of fairness, in an artistic setting, with the applause of women as a reward.'

Fulfilling this last, subservient role perfectly in 1908 were Queen Alexandra, herself a regular presence in the stadium, and Lady Desborough, seen here next to her husband at the medals ceremony at Henley.

On the other hand there were female role models such as Lottie Dod, the five-time Wimbledon tennis champion, who won a silver medal in the archery (*below left*). Women also competed in the lawn tennis and the figure skating, while two women made history by racing on the water. Mrs Gorham accompanied her husband on *Quicksilver* in the motorboating, while the Duchess of Westminster sailed on her yacht *Sorais*.

Meanwhile, female gymnasts from Denmark, the London Polytechnic, the Northern Polytechnic Institute and the Yorkshire Amateur Gymnastic Association all put on demonstrations in the stadium. In the pool, there was another demonstration, of women's diving.

In fact, at a time of rising concern for the health of the population generally, in the *Official Report* of the Games the BOA directly contradicted Coubertin's sentiments, albeit for not entirely progressive reasons.

'The successful appearance of ladies in these competitions suggests the consideration that since one of the chief objects of the revived Olympic Games is the physical development and amelioration of the race, it appears illogical to adhere so far to classical tradition as to provide so few opportunities for the participation of a predominant partner in the process of race-production.'

Londoner Florence Syers, known as 'Madge', was one of the most inspirational female role models in Edwardian Britain, having become the first woman to enter the World Figure Skating Championships, in 1902. Seen here with husband Edgar at the Prince's Skating Club in Knightsbridge on October 29 1908, she came out of retirement to win gold in the ladies' single figure skating at the Olympics, followed in the afternoon by winning a bronze in the pairs, with Edgar.

Tragically, a heart complaint forced her back into retirement after 1908, and she died in 1917, aged just 35.

>> 'This principle of control was heartily approved of by Mr. James Sullivan, for instance, before the English Games began; and we are given to understand that on this principle similar meetings are managed in the United States, for which nation he was an official representative in London. The enormous amount of work done for the good of these Games by the officials in the governing Associations of the United Kingdom can hardly be estimated. It was continuous for over two years. It was given freely and ungrudgingly for the credit of this country, and for the assistance and proper treatment of our visitors. So large an area of sporting activities has never before been covered by officials of so much tried experience and special knowledge.

'Few greater tributes to the English love of fair play have ever been placed on record than the decision of the International Olympic Committee that the whole of the arrangements for judging these games should be placed in the hands of our great governing associations.'

Such an attitude was to yield a mixed legacy.

On the positive side, a tight definition of regulations was welcomed by the Olympic movement. Defined rules helped to clarify how different sports should be organised and judged, while the definitions of amateurism laid out in the *Official Report* helped the IOC to establish its role as a guardian of amateurism over the next 70 years.

However, the overbearing nature of some of the officials in London, and the dismissive manner in which the BOA dealt with complaints, led to a trail of bitter transatlantic correspondence over 'the battle of Shepherd's Bush'.

'Is the Britisher so perfect that he cannot err?' asked the American Gustavus Kirby in 1909. 'Is he going to be a "won't play" child because his games were found fault with?'

Certainly the IOC learnt from the altercations of 1908. At the next Games, at Stockholm in 1912, the appointment of officials was taken out of the hands of the hosts. Today's system of neutral judging was thus one of the unintended legacies of the first London Olympics.

A very British Olympics

Ask anyone who attended the Commonwealth Games in Manchester in 2002 and one of their abiding memories will be the rain. The same was also true in 1908. In that sense, the first London Olympics were a very British affair.

During the shooting competition at Bisley, from July 8–11, reported *The Sporting Life*, 'more miserable weather... it would be difficult to imagine'. There would be more rain during the opening ceremony on July 13, and still more over the ensuing weeks.

At Uxendon, near Wembley, the venue for the clay pigeon shooting, the host club had dug a trench so that marksmen would not be dazzled by the sunlight. In the event, the sky was so overcast that each clay had to be daubed with whitewash to make it more visible.

The motorboating also fell victim to what sounds, in the *Official Report*, like a typical August day at the English seaside: 'a strong gale was blowing from the south-west with constant downpours of rain'.

But there were other reasons why the 1908 Games may be considered quintessentially British. Not least, British participants dominated proceedings, just as the home-based athletes had in Paris in 1900 and at St Louis in 1904. As noted earlier, three British teams entered the tug-of-war. In the women's lawn tennis, all five entries in the singles were British. Only British men entered the racquets, the polo was a purely British and Irish affair, while the 12 metre class in sailing was contested by only two boats, both of them British; *Mouchette* from the Royal Mersey Yacht Club in Liverpool, and *Hera* from the Royal Clyde Yacht Club in Glasgow.

To save both crews having to sail down to the Solent, this last race took place on the River Clyde at Hunter's Quay, to the west of Glasgow, under the jurisdiction of the Clyde Corinthian Yacht Club.

Hardly a momentous event. But at least it extended the reach of the 1908 Olympics to Scotland.

But what of the public?

Crowds at the Great Stadium throughout the main Olympic fortnight were, on average, lower than hoped, particularly when compared with the numbers attending the Exhibition. Wet weather, high ticket prices and schedules that clashed with the working day were all cited as factors. Most embarrassing was the fourth day, July 16, a particularly damp and cold Thursday, when just 4,000 spectators rattled around in the stands. To put this in context, this was around half the number that the Morpeth Olympics attracted during the same period.

But attendances did pick up when ticket prices were reduced, and the final day, on which the much anticipated marathon was run, attracted a full house of around 80,000 (or more if some reports are to be believed).

One other indicator of public interest was the response to Lord Desborough's letter to the national press of June 20. He appealed for donations from the public in order to fund a series of social functions to which all visiting competitors and officials would be invited. At stake, he insinuated, was the British reputation for hospitality.

Within a week £10,000 was raised, mainly by the *Daily Mail*, the equivalent today of £570,000. The largest function was an official reception for 3,000 competitors hosted at the Grafton Galleries in Bond Street, on July 11, two days before the opening ceremony. The ceremony itself, meanwhile, was followed by a further reception for 800 Olympic guests, hosted by the Lord Mayor of London at Mansion House. Two days later, the Worshipful Company of Fishmongers entertained Coubertin and the IOC at their magnificent hall by the Thames, just as they had done in 1904. Busiest of all was the Holborn Restaurant on Kingsway, a recently completed thoroughfare which symbolised the resurgent London of the Edwardian era. This held no fewer than nine Olympic banquets between July 14 and October 31.

Small wonder that the *Daily Mirror* ran a cartoon strip showing overweight athletes struggling to get over hurdles and waddling around the track having gorged themselves on good old British hospitality.

And then there was the marathon. Surely there is no better way to characterise the Britishness of the 1908 Olympic Games than the fact that its enduring hero, even a century after the event, was an individual who, in the final analysis, was disqualified. By falling senseless during the last few yards of the marathon, albeit heroically in front of the Queen and 80,000 spectators, the little Italian Dorando Pietri won more admirers in Britain and a more secure place in history than every single one of the British athletes who won golds.

Finally, one of the most abiding British aspects of the 1908 Games, and one of the Games' most enduring legacies, concerns the awarding of medals.

Before 1908, there was no set system of prize giving at the Olympics. At Athens in 1896 there had been silver and bronze medals for those athletes placed first and second. Four years later in Paris, all competitors were simply given commemorative medals. At St Louis the only medals awarded were gold ones, for the winners, while at Athens in 1906 the organisers reverted to the 1896 model of silver and bronze.

Only in 1908, thanks to the BOC, was the prize system introduced that we are now so familiar with; that is, a gold medal for the winner, a silver for second and a bronze for third. Yet far from echoing ancient rituals, as is often thought, this tripartite system was in reality a practice that had been introduced four decades earlier at the Liverpool Olympic Festivals and at the Games of the National Olympian Association.

Needless to add, this system offered a useful showcase for the work of specialist British companies.

The 1908 medals were struck in the Birmingham works of the Bradford company Fattorini and Sons, and designed by a prominent Australian sculptor, Bertram Mackennal. Whether in gold, silver or bronze, each

measured just 34mm in diameter and had on its obverse side, as seen on the right, a naked male being crowned with a laurel wreath by two semi-clad women. This of course was a scene that had no historical basis, as women were denied entry at Olympia. But it certainly reflected the view held by Coubertin that women were subservient to men and should not themselves compete.

The intention was that Mackennal's design for the obverse would become standard for all Olympic medals, while the reverse, which in 1908 depicted St George slaying the dragon, would change every four years.

The same intention applied to the larger 'commemoration' medals. These were cast in four grades. Silver-gilt, silver and bronze commemoration medals were presented to officials, key individuals and to host clubs, such as the Hurlingham Club, which received the medal shown below to mark its staging of the polo. Meanwhile base metal commemoration medals were handed to every competitor, along with a lapel badge.

Also handed out were diplomas for prize winners and competitors. These were designed by Bernard Partridge, whose day job was as chief cartoonist for *Punch* magazine.

But while the designs for the 1908 medals and for the diplomas attracted much favourable comment, in one other artistic endeavour the BOC failed to deliver.

Pierre de Coubertin always held that the Olympics were not just about sport. He envisaged parallel competitions in fine art, architecture, literature and music, an echo of the intellectual and artistic competitions he had seen at Much Wenlock. However, none of the previous Olympic hosts had managed to deliver a cultural programme, and nor, in the event, did the BOC. The IOC asked them to include competitions for art and literature 'inspired by some athletic or sporting event'. But although the BOC did set this in train, they ran out of time and the competition never took place.

Shown actual size, this is one of only a handful of 1908 gold medals known to be held in the public realm. Awarded to a member of the Leander Rowing Club, winners of the eight oared final at Henley – a dramatic race watched by Coubertin and Desborough – the medal is now on display at the town's River and Rowing Museum.

Unlike present day Olympic golds, which are nearly twice the size but, ironically, made predominantly of silver, the 1908 medal is 15ct gold.

In 2008, a 1908 gold medal awarded to Charles Smith, a member of Great Britain's water polo team, along with his commemoration medal and lapel badge, was sold at auction for £4,200. A silver won by Arthur Cumming in the figure skating, fetched £3,500.

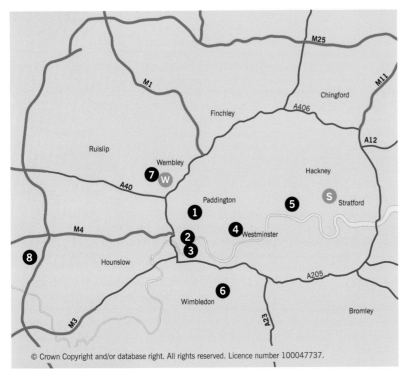

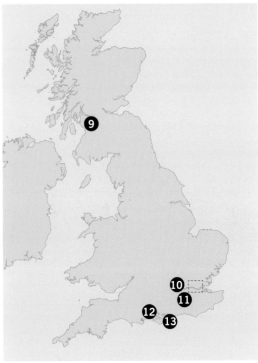

Turning now to the built legacy of the 1908 Games, as the map shows, west London was the main focus. For reference, W marks the site of Wembley Stadium (main venue for the 1948 Games) and S marks the site of the stadium at Stratford (main venue for the 2012 Games). Of seven London venues used in 1908, three remain in use for sporting activities. One other survival is Preston Road Station (*left*), opened by the Metropolitan Railway in July 1908 to provide access to the clay pigeon shooting range at Uxendon, albeit only as a 'request stop' (that is, passengers had to alert the driver in order to alight).

London locations in 1908

1. **Great Stadium, White City** *summer:* archery, athletics, cycling, diving, fencing, gymnastics, swimming, water polo; *winter:* football, hockey, lacrosse, rugby union (stadium demolished 1985, site now BBC Media Village)
2. **Queen's Club, West Kensington** indoor tennis, real tennis (*jeu de paume*), racquets (club still open)
3. **Hurlingham Club, Fulham** polo (club still open, but polo grounds now public park and housing)

4. **Prince's Skating Club, Knightsbridge** figure skating (club closed 1917, site now residential)
5. **Northampton Institute, Clerkenwell** boxing (now City University)
6. **All England Lawn Tennis and Croquet Club, Worple Road, Wimbledon** lawn tennis (site closed 1922, now school sports ground and ambulance station)
7. **Uxendon School Shooting Club** clay pigeon shooting (site now housing)
8. **Windsor Park** start of marathon

Non-London locations in 1908

9. **Royal Clyde Yacht Club, Hunter's Quay, Glasgow** yachting (12 metre class) (club merged with Northern Yacht Club in 1978, now based in Rhu)
10. **Henley, Oxfordshire** rowing (still in use for rowing)
11. **Bisley Camp, Surrey** shooting; rifle, pistol, and running deer (site still in use for shooting)
12. **Southampton Water, Hampshire** motorboating (based at Motor Yacht Club's launch)
13. **Royal Victoria Yacht Club, Ryde, Isle of Wight** yachting; 6, 7, and 8m classes (club still open)

◀ Viewed from the corner of **Spencer Street** and **St John Street**, shortly after it opened in 1896, the **Northampton Institute** in Clerkenwell – now part of **City University London** – is one of the three London venues from 1908 that remain extant, either wholly or partially.

Held on a single day, October 27, the Olympic **boxing** tournament was staged inside the Institute's **Great Hall** (*below left*). Each of the five weights contested resulted in gold medals for English boxers.

Quite why the Northampton Institute was chosen by the Amateur Boxing Association is unclear, for there were several larger and better appointed boxing venues in the capital and, as the *Official Report* noted, 'several halls of the size of that selected could easily have been filled with spectators eager to see the best amateur boxing yet exhibited in England.'

One explanation is that the choice was influenced by the presence at the Northampton Institute of an influential German gymnastics instructor, Rudolf Oberholzer, three of whose pupils entered the gymnastics, boxing and wrestling tournaments in 1908, and who went on to coach Britain's gymnastics team at the 1912 Olympics. It has also been suggested that the Institute's **swimming pool** and **gymnasium** were used during the Olympics for training purposes.

Today that pool, which occupied the far end of the single storey range seen on the left of the top photograph, remains in use as a computer area, with its cubicles converted into cupboards, while a five storey block built in the 1950s has replaced the adjoining gymnasium. As for the Great Hall, this remains in use for lectures, but with a much plainer roof, also constructed in the 1950s.

That apart, standing on the same street corner today the Northampton Institute, now listed Grade II and with its distinctive corner block and prominent clock tower unchanged, remains instantly recognisable.

As such, *Played in Britain* will return to the building and to its non Olympic sporting functions in our forthcoming study, *Played in London*.

◀ The second London venue from 1908 that remains in sporting use is the **Queen's Club** on **Palliser Road, West Kensington**, best known as the venue of an annual pre-Wimbledon lawn tennis tournament. Formed in 1886 as an exclusive multi-purpose sports club, the Palliser Road grounds hosted three Olympic competitions, all staged on indoor courts. These were for **real tennis**, referred to in the *Official Report* by its traditional French name of *jeu de paume*, for **rackets**, or racquets, and for **covered court tennis**, in effect lawn tennis played indoors.

Seen on this page is one of the two real tennis courts at Queen's, known as the **East Court** (*left and top right*).

This, and all the other courts used for the Olympic competitions remain in use, albeit with modern surfaces, yet their Olympic pedigree is barely acknowledged, and with good reason. Primarily this is because for the leading real tennis and rackets players of the day, the 1908 Olympics were hardly more than a distraction in the midst of an already well established calendar of domestic and international tournaments. Thus in the real tennis only two outsiders competed. Both were Americans, one of whom, Jay Gould, took the gold. In the rackets, only English players entered, and even then some of the best known individuals scratched. By contrast, several visiting players entered the court tennis tournament, in which three Swedes won bronze medals.

But in each discipline only a handful of spectators bothered to attend. In mitigation, it is true that, owing to the design of the courts, neither real tennis or rackets can be watched by significant numbers at any one time. Nevertheless, only 58 of the hundreds of tickets offered for sale across all three of the Olympic tournaments at the Queen's Club were taken up, raising less than £90 in receipts. As the *Official Report* later conceded in relation to real tennis, 'without any wish to minimise the beauty or importance of one of the best and oldest ball-games in the world... it is not quite suitable for future programmes in Olympic Games.'

The IOC agreed, and real tennis and rackets have not appeared at any Olympics since. Nor was indoor lawn tennis tried again, even though it has since become extremely popular on the wider tennis circuit.

As noted earlier, the outdoor lawn tennis competition of the 1908 Olympics was held at the **All England Lawn Tennis and Croquet Club** at **Wimbledon**. This was not the Church Road site we know today, which opened in 1922, but the club's original site on **Worple Road**.

Unlike the other racket sports, the lawn tennis attracted entries from a much wider pool of nine countries, although the women's singles was an all-UK affair, and, when the weather permitted, it drew reasonable crowds.

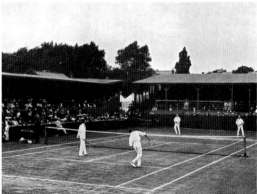

Seen above is action from the final of the men's doubles, in which **Reggie Doherty** and **George Hillyard** won the gold by beating their fellow Englishman **Major Josiah Ritchie** and the Irishman **James Cecil Parke**.

Centre Court had been rebuilt two years previously. Since 1922 the Worple Road site has been occupied by a sports ground for Wimbledon High School and by an ambulance station.

Once again, further details of both the Queen's Club and the All England Club will be found in *Played in London*, a future volume in the *Played in Britain* series.

▶ Of all the artefacts associated with the 1908 Olympics, this silver polo trophy, 70cm tall, is perhaps the most imposing. Held at the **Hurlingham Club**, on the banks of the River Thames at Fulham, it was awarded to Roehampton, the victors of a three-way tournament also involving teams from Hurlingham and Ireland.

The hosts had intended that the trophy be a **Perpetual Challenge Cup**, to be competed for at all 'international Olympiads'. But although polo did feature at the Games in 1920, 1924 and 1936, it would appear that the trophy did not leave London after 1908.

The polo ground where the matches took place is now Hurlingham Park, sold to the London County Council in 1951. However polo has since returned there, thanks to a new annual tournament initiated in June 2009.

Two other artefacts from the 1908 Games are a **starter pistol** and **stopwatch** used during the rowing tournament (*below*). Now part of the collection at the **River and Rowing Museum** in Henley, they are seen here in January 2010 as part of an exhibition entitled **Our Sporting Life**, the first of several such exhibitions organised in the run up to London 2012 (and beyond) by the Sports Heritage Network, a grouping of sport related museums, archives and collections around Britain (*see Links*).

▲ Barely noticed on the wall of a house called **Old Rowlands**, on the east side of **High Street, Eton**, by **Barnes Pool Bridge**, this distance marker – the first of 25 as shown on the route map – is the only tangible reminder of the route taken on Friday July 24 by the **1908 marathon**, one of the most celebrated Olympic races of all time.

Alas not one of the other 24 distance markers has survived, either in situ or, seemingly, in any collection.

As can be seen, on both the distance marker and on the route map there appears a diamond-shaped emblem. This was the symbol of the **Polytechnic Harriers**, an athletics club established in 1883 by students at the Royal Polytechnic Institute on Regent Street.

Under the leadership of Jack Andrew, the Harriers were asked by the BOC to organise the marathon because of their experience of staging long distance events, such as the London to Brighton race. The IOC's only requirement was that the race should be approximately 40 kilometres long (24.8 miles). Everything else was up to the Harriers.

Andrew chose Windsor as the starting point to give the race a historical flavour, ending up with a 26 mile route through the countryside, various towns and suburbs and ending at the stadium. Part of this route was then tested in April when the Harriers staged the British Olympic trial from Windsor to Wembley Park, a distance of 21 miles.

This map shows Andrew's original route. However, as will be explained, the final route was slightly different from this published version, both at its start and finish.

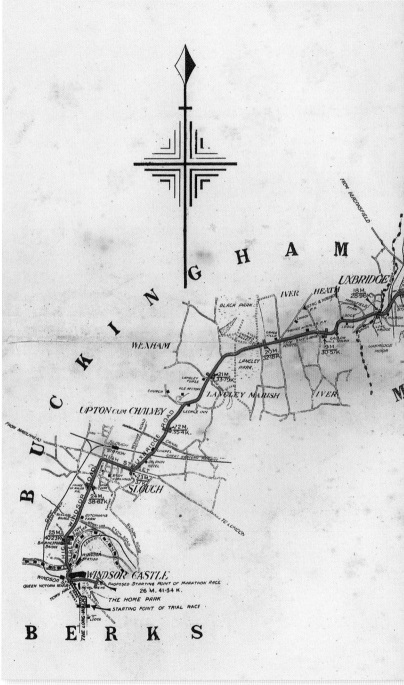

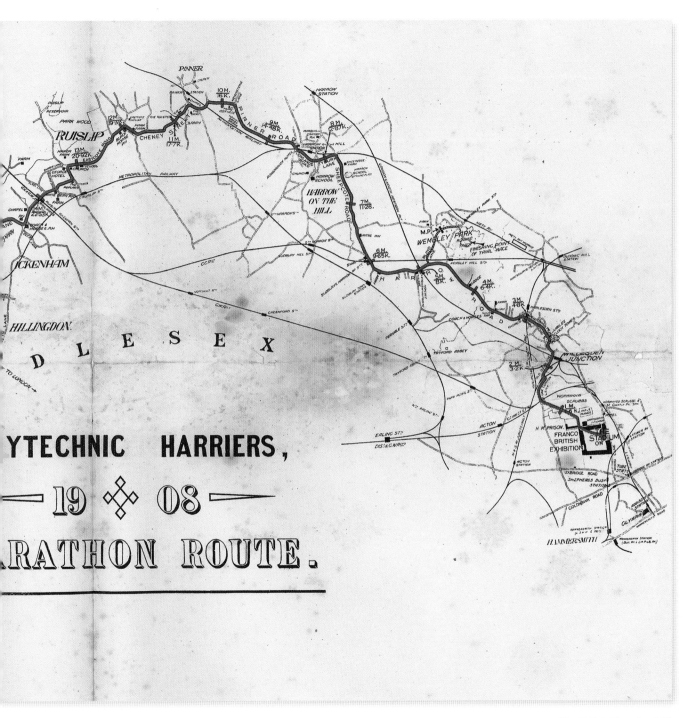

One indication of how highly the marathon ranks in the overall narrative of 1908 is the sheer volume of surviving artefacts, souvenirs and postcards relating to the race. Above is a steward's badge, originally belonging to John Brewer of the Polytechnic Harriers and now held by the University of Westminster (as 'the Poly' became in 1992).

SOUVENIR OF THE
MARATHON RACE
FROM WINDSOR CASTLE TO THE STADIUM,
SHEPHERD'S BUSH.
FRIDAY, JULY 24, 1908.

Fifty-seven picked Runners, representing Seventeen different nations, will start from Windsor Great Park at HALF-PAST TWO. The first man to enter the Stadium, after running once round the track will be acclaimed the victor in the greatest long-distance event in the history of the world.

The following time-table gives the approximate times at which the runners will pass different places on the course:—

		P.M.
Start	...	2.30
Slough	...	2.47
Uxbridge	...	3.20
Ruislip	...	3.50
Harrow	...	4.10
Wembley	...	4.30
Harlesden	...	4.45
Wormwood Scrubbs	...	4.54
The Stadium	...	5.5

A rocket or gun will be fired on reaching Willesden Junction, Wormwood Scrubbs, and on entering the Stadium.

The countries represented in the Race will be—

United Kingdom Canada
United States Australasia
Holland Sweden South Africa
Greece Finland Russia
Belgium Italy Germany
Austria Bohemia
Denmark.

In order that the competitors may not be impeded by traffic, a force of two thousand police will guard the course.

The public in the Stadium will not be kept in ignorance of the progress of the Race until the leader bursts into the arena for the final lap. Elaborate telephoning arrangements have been made, and the names and progress of the leading men will be shown every few minutes. The sports in the arena will be stopped and the track cleared when the approach of the runners is announced.

THIS great event in the Olympic Games is the Marathon Race on Friday, and which, without doubt, will arouse greater international interest than any other of the great struggles at the Stadium. They will be started at their 26¼ miles struggle from the East Terrace of Windsor Castle, and after traversing that portion of the terrace which overlooks the Great Park the runners will pass through the Sovereign's Gate and race through Windsor and Eton on their way to the Stadium.

The King has given permission for the general public to assemble within the Castle Gates at the start of the race, and for the school children to congregate within the Castle walls. The general public may occupy places on the grass between the guests' entrance and the St. Alban Street entrance to the Castle.

GRAND DISPLAY OF FIREWORKS. A HUGE SET PIECE SHOWING THE NAME OF THE WINNER AND COUNTRY HE REPRESENTS.

Printed and Published by Mrs. S. BURGESS, 14 Artillery Lane, Bishopsgate Street, London, E.C.

▲ In the 18th and early 19th centuries long distance races were a regular feature of London life. But the first **marathon** ever to be staged in the capital was in 1908, coming twelve years after the inaugural marathon at the 1896 Games in Athens.

This flimsy, faded **souvenir flier**, held in the collection of Hillingdon local studies library, is one of several similar designs put on sale before the big day. Printed by Mrs S Burgess of Artillery Lane, Bishopsgate, it states that two thousand police officers were to be on hand to ensure that the runners were not impeded, and that via 'elaborate telephoning arrangements' the crowd in the stadium was to be kept fully informed of the runners' progress.

Mrs Burgess was not alone in hoping to profit from the day. All along the route local businesses did their best to attract custom, while several pubs, such as the Crooked Billet at Iver Heath (which has since been rebuilt), and The George Hotel at Ruislip (which still exists), acted as official refreshment stations for the runners.

They were in for a busy day, for despite the rest of the Games being blighted by rain, on the day of the marathon temperatures reached 78 degrees F (26 degrees C).

▶ No barriers, no security, and seemingly very little cap-doffing deference on show as **Jack Beale** of the Polytechnic Harriers (wearing number 17) and **Arnost Nejedly** of Bohemia (18) – two of the 55 runners from 16 nations – saunter past Princess Mary, the Princess of Wales, and other members of the royal party on the East Lawn at Windsor Castle, shortly before the start of the 1908 marathon on Friday July 24. A more informal start to a major race can hardly be imagined.

Much has been written about how the 1908 marathon route came to be measured at 26 miles and 385 yards, an unlikely total that in 1921 was finally established as the set distance for all future marathons. As such, this single measurement is perhaps the most enduring legacy of all from the 1908 Games.

The most commonly expressed misconception is that the race should have been exactly 26 miles, and that the extra 385 yards were added purely to suit the royal family. Two stories have arisen to back that claim. The first is that the start of the race was moved from Windsor town centre to the grounds of Windsor Castle because Princess Mary wanted two of her sons (seen in the photograph) to have a closer view of the start. The second is that the finishing point of the race was relocated in order to line up with the royal box of the stadium.

Neither story is correct. Firstly, as stated earlier, at that time there was no official distance for the marathon, so it was never likely that the chosen route would be an exact total of 26 miles. The four previous Olympic marathons had ranged from 24.85 miles at Athens in 1896 to 26.01 miles in the Intercalated Games of 1906.

Secondly, research by Hugh Farey (*see Links*) has found no evidence of any royal request to move the start. Instead, states Farey, it was the Polytechnic Harriers who asked for the start to be relocated from Windsor town centre to the Castle, purely on logistical grounds.

As for the final entry to the stadium, it is true that this differed from the original route as published. But this was not to suit the royal family. Rather, it was because the entrance in the stadium closest to the royal box turned out to have been ramped, in order to make it easier for ladies to enter, and this ramp was felt to have been too difficult for tired runners to negotiate at the end of a gruelling race. Another entrance was therefore used.

Hence the final distance of 26 miles and 385 yards, arrived at by chance, with no intention on anyone's part that one day this odd total would be enshrined in the rules.

As for the route itself, its full length can still be negotiated on foot, although two motorways – the M4 and the M25 – cut through it, as does London Underground's Central Line near the site of the stadium. Town centre

redevelopments in Uxbridge and Harrow also require minor diversions. But some parts of the route, such as at Eton and Iver Heath, still look much as they did in 1908, while others, such as the junction of **The Avenue** and **Swakeleys Road**, **Ickenham** (*above*), are no longer leafy rural lanes but busy dual carriageways.

On stretches such as this, between pubs and larger junctions, only a sprinkling of onlookers gathered. But as those runners who managed to stay the course approached the outer suburbs of London, the crowds, and the excitement grew...

Nine miles gone and a cobbler in an apron steps out from his shop on Windsor Street, Uxbridge, to see runner number 64, Fred Simpson of Canada, with a maple leaf on his shirt, stride past. A few yards behind is the American Johnny Hayes (number 26), the eventual winner. Note how each runner is accompanied by a cyclist from the Polytechnic Cycle Club.

All the buildings seen here still stand, as does the pub from which the photograph was taken.

Another landmark along the marathon route that still stands is the Jubilee Clock in Harlesden (*below right*), being passed at 5.10pm by the diminutive Italian, Dorando Pietri, followed closely by the race officials' car.

Pietri was by then in second place, two minutes behind the leader, Charles Heffernon of South Africa. But as the frontrunners reached Wormwood Scrubs Heffernon lost ground after foolishly accepting a swig of champagne from a member of the public.

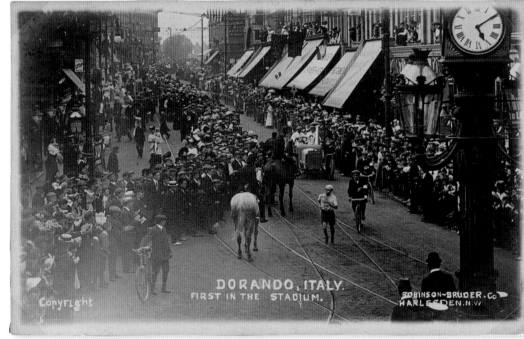

DORANDO, ITALY.
FIRST IN THE STADIUM.

Copyright

ROBINSON-BRUDER.Co
HARLESDEN.N.W

Spectators scan the view from Wormwood Scrubs as Pietri, now in the lead (*above left*), passes the prison and into Du Cane Road, a scene little changed since 1908. Minutes later (*left*) Pietri falls on the track, where he is lifted by Dr Bulger, the medical attendant, while Jack Andrew (holding the megaphone) confers with his fellow officials. A crowd of 80,000, some of whom have paid £5 for entry, gasp in amazement.

'Surely he is done now!' writes *Daily Mail* reporter Arthur Conan Doyle from his seat. But no, Pietri does cross the line, only to be disqualified for having received assistance.

And so history is made.

▲ Viewed in 1928, twenty years after the Olympics, the remaining buildings of the **Franco-British Exhibition** flank what was now officially the **White City Stadium**, with the new Westway (which had yet to extend eastwards) branching off Wood Lane behind the stadium's far corner.

Although saddled with debt and run by a succession of owners, the site continued to stage exhibitions until 1938. But only in December 1926 was the stadium's future assured when it was taken over by the newly formed Greyhound Racing Association. In addition to relaying the tracks, the GRA covered both ends of the stadium and filled in the pool, although, as seen here, its outline could still be made out on the infield for many years.

Meanwhile, seven other White City greyhound stadiums opened elsewhere in Britain, several of them, as in London,

accommodating that other new fangled sport of the 1920s, speedway racing.

Athletics returned too, with White City staging the AAA championships from 1932–70, and in 1934 the British Empire Games, forerunner to the Commonwealth Games. Less successful were attempts to establish rugby league, American football and boxing. Queen's Park Rangers Football Club tried it out during two spells, from 1931–33 and 1962–63, retreating each time to their much homelier ground on the edge of the exhibition site, at Lotfus Road. Bizarrely, White City also hosted Uruguay's game with France during the 1966 World Cup, because Wembley was otherwise booked for greyhound racing.

But by then, with its surrounds now almost totally redeveloped, White City was all but obsolete.

1908

THE GREAT STADIUM SHEPHERD'S BUSH

MEDAL WINNERS					
GREAT BRITAIN	56	GOLD	51 SILVER	38	BRONZE
U.S. OF AMERICA	23	GOLD	12 SILVER	12	BRONZE
SWEDEN	8	GOLD	6 SILVER	11	BRONZE
FRANCE	5	GOLD	5 SILVER	9	BRONZE
GERMANY	3	GOLD	5 SILVER	6	BRONZE
HUNGARY	3	GOLD	4 SILVER	2	BRONZE
CANADA	3	GOLD	3 SILVER	10	BRONZE
NORWAY	2	GOLD	3 SILVER	3	BRONZE
ITALY	2	GOLD	2 SILVER	0	BRONZE
BELGIUM	1	GOLD	5 SILVER	2	BRONZE
AUSTRALASIA	1	GOLD	2 SILVER	2	BRONZE
RUSSIA	1	GOLD	2 SILVER	0	BRONZE
FINLAND	1	GOLD	1 SILVER	3	BRONZE
SOUTH AFRICA	1	GOLD	1 SILVER	0	BRONZE
GREECE	0	GOLD	3 SILVER	0	BRONZE
DENMARK	0	GOLD	2 SILVER	3	BRONZE
BOHEMIA	0	GOLD	0 SILVER	2	BRONZE
NETHERLANDS	0	GOLD	0 SILVER	2	BRONZE
AUSTRIA	0	GOLD	0 SILVER	1	BRONZE

THIS MEMORIAL WAS UNVEILED BY
COMTE JAQUES ROGGE
PRESIDENT OF THE INTERNATIONAL OLYMPIC COMMITTEE
ON THE OCCASION OF THE CENTENARY OF THE
BRITISH OLYMPIC ASSOCIATION
MAY 24TH 2005

▲ On a paved concourse in the centre of the BBC's new **Media Village** lies the inscription, 'This is the site of the finishing line of White City Stadium which hosted the 1908 Olympics'. Yards away the side of an office block bears a further memorial to the 1908 Games (*left*), unveiled by Jacques Rogge, President of the IOC, on the occasion of the BOA's centenary, on May 24 2005.

The 'Great Stadium' itself had been demolished twenty years earlier. The opening of the Crystal Palace stadium had robbed it of athletics after 1972, while diminishing returns on greyhound racing and the building's vast, ageing infrastructure finally became too much for the GRA's coffers to bear. Just days after the final greyhound race was run in September 1984, and with barely a note of protest, the bulldozers moved in on the world's first purpose-built Olympic Stadium.

Today the area and the BBC headquarters retain the name White City, as does the nearby tube station. Otherwise, the only other remembrances of 1908 are the Dorando Marathon, a greyhound race now staged at Wimbledon Stadium, and, tucked behind the BBC's Media Village, **Dorando Close**.

The little Italian did well from his travails. But even so, he surely deserves better than this.

LONDON BOROUGH OF HAMMERSMITH & FULHAM
DORANDO CLOSE W12

◀ 'The important thing in the Olympic Games is not winning but taking part. The essential thing in life is not conquering but fighting well.'

Oft quoted, and forming a central creed of modern day Olympism, these words might easily have been expressed by John Hulley or William Penny Brookes. But of course they were coined by Pierre de Coubertin, and they form one of the most important legacies to have emerged from the London Games of 1908.

Coubertin was first heard to make such a statement during a speech he gave at a government banquet at the Grafton Galleries on Grafton Street, London, on the evening of July 24, within hours of the climax of the marathon. It is therefore tempting to imagine that his inspiration had been the heroics of Dorando Pietri and his fellow runners on that glorious summer's day.

However, as Coubertin acknowledged in his speech, what actually prompted his words was a sermon delivered at St Paul's Cathedral on the previous Sunday, July 19.

So who was the inspirational preacher that day?

In his speech (which appears in French at the end of the 1908 *Official Report*), Coubertin credited the sermon to 'the Bishop of Pennsylvania', an accreditation that remained unchallenged for the next 86 years, until the Swedish historian Ture Widlund revealed otherwise in the Olympic history journal *Citius, Altius, Fortius* in May 1994 (*see Links*). As Widlund discovered, the preacher at St Paul's had been the Bishop of *Central* Pennsylvania, and from this he was then able to identify him positively as **Ethelbert Talbot**.

Talbot (*above left*) had been in London not for the Olympic Games but for the Pan-Anglican Conference at Lambeth Palace, hosted by the Archbishop of Canterbury. Among 78 resolutions passed at this conference, one appeared to chime with the idealistic intentions of the Olympic Games. 'The Conference,' it stated, 'rejoices in the growth of higher ethical perceptions which is evidenced by the increasing willingness to settle difficulties among nations by peaceful methods… and it urges earnestly upon all Christian peoples the duty of … promoting among all races the spirit of brotherly co-operation for the good of all mankind.'

In light of this resolution, it was but a natural step for the bishops to connect with events in west London. Hence the Archdeacon of London organised a service for Olympic athletes and officials at St Paul's on the middle Sunday of the main Games fortnight.

Chosen to preach the sermon that day, Talbot selected as his text 1 Corinthians 9, 24–26:

'Know ye not that they which run in a race run all, but one receiveth the prize? So run, that ye may obtain. And every man that striveth for the mastery is temperate in all things. Now they do it to obtain a corruptible crown; but we, an incorruptible.'

After a week in which there had been so many disputed decisions in the stadium, particularly between the British and the Americans, how the words of St Paul must have pricked the ears of those Olympians gathered in worship.

'We have just been contemplating the great Olympic Games,' said Talbot. 'What does it mean? It means that young men of robust physical life have come from all parts of the world. It does mean… that this era of internationalism as seen in the Stadium has an element of danger. Of course, it is very true… that each athlete strives not only for the sake of sport, but for the sake of his country. Thus a new rivalry is invented. If England be beaten on the river, or America outdistanced on the racing path, or that American has lost the strength which she once possessed. Well, what of it?

'The only safety after all lies in the lesson of the real Olympia – that the Games themselves are better than the race and the prize.

'St Paul tells us how insignificant is the prize. Our prize is not corruptible, but incorruptible, and though only one may wear the laurel wreath, all may share the equal joy of the contest. All encouragement, therefore, be given to the exhilarating – I might also say soul-saving – interest that comes in active and fair and clean athletic sports.'

But if Talbot's sermon struck a chord with Pierre de Coubertin, as Widlund pointed out, several of the athletes were clearly unmoved. The worst disputes to take place during the Games – over the 400 metre race and the marathon – both occurred in the second week.

Coubertin's mood can thus be well imagined when during his speech on the following Friday he echoed Talbot's words. 'The importance of these Olympiads,' declared the Frenchman, 'is not so much to win as to take part… The important thing in life is not the triumph but the struggle. The essential thing is not to have won but to have fought well.'

Over the years he would finesse these words. And as another Olympic historian, David Young (*see Links*), has shown, Coubertin had already voiced similar sentiments earlier in his career, so that the Bishop's sermon may be seen more as a catalyst. Nevertheless, it was in London that this famous creed gained its first public airing.

As for Ethelbert Talbot, he returned to his diocese, which was renamed the Diocese of Bethlehem in 1909, and served as its Bishop until his retirement in 1926. He died in 1928, four years before the Olympic creed that he inspired in London was then formally unveiled by the IOC at the 1932 Olympic Games in Los Angeles.

And now, thanks to Ture Widlund, we know his name.

THE IMPORTANT THING IN THE OLYMPIC GAMES IS NOT WINNING BUT TAKING PART. THE ESSENTIAL THING IN LIFE IS NOT CONQUERING BUT FIGHTING WELL.

BARON de COUBERTIN

Forty years had passed, and two world wars fought. But now the words of Pierre de Coubertin stand sentinel over the opening ceremony of the second London Olympic Games, at Wembley Stadium. On the searingly hot afternoon of July 29 1948, as an expectant crowd of 85,000 spectators did their best to forget the privations of austerity Britain and the wounds of recent conflict, the head of the organising committee, Lord Burghley, echoed the words of Ethelbert Talbot by wishing for two weeks of 'keen but friendly rivalry'.

'That warm flame of hope,' declared Burghley, would lead to 'a better understanding in the world which has burned so low,' and would 'flare up into a very beacon, pointing a way to the goal through the Fellowship of Sport.'

It was then left to a dashing young medical student, John Mark, to ignite that flame, a moment captured also on the cover of this book by the photographer seen here on the right of the balcony's edge.

Chapter Ten

London Olympic Games 1948

One link between 1908 and 1948 was the use of Henley, where old Etonian Dickie Burnell, *The Times'* rowing correspondent, won gold in the double sculls along with Bert Bushnell, a marine engineer and Dunkirk veteran. It was their first race together. This is Burnell's vest, on display at the River and Rowing Museum. Another link is that Burnell's father, Charles, won a gold in 1908, in the eights (*see page 113*).

When London hosted its first Olympic Games of the modern era, in 1908, it did so in response to an emergency, and with only two years' notice. It would be almost the same for the 1948 Olympics, although for different reasons and in different circumstances.

The 1948 Games are remembered as 'the austerity Olympics' because they took place in a war weary nation still littered with bomb sites and constrained by shortages of food, clothing, housing and building materials. And yet, not only were they a great success from an operational and a sporting point of view – unless one measures success by the number of gold medals won by the host nation – but they also gave new life and purpose to the international Olympic movement after years of international conflict and after the political embarrassment of the previous Games, held in Nazi-ruled Berlin in 1936.

The 1948 Games even made a small profit of £29,000, which has led many a critic to ponder why the spirit of austerity cannot be reinstilled in the modern Games.

So how did post war London come to stage its second Olympic Games of the 20th century?

Briefly, as a result of the First World War only the 1916 Games had had to be cancelled. During the Second World War, two Olympiads fell victim. The first, scheduled to take place in Tokyo in 1940, had been hurriedly switched to Helsinki after Japan's invasion of Manchuria in 1938. The Finns reacted much as London did in 1906, with admirable alacrity. They even got as far as building a stadium and printing the posters, before invading Soviet troops finally scuppered the Games in May 1940.

In June 1939, meanwhile, the IOC had awarded the 1944 Games to London, in preference to seven other European and North American cities.

So come the peace, and with the IOC anxious to make sure that the quadrennial sequence would not be broken for a third time in succession, Lord Burghley, the Chairman of the British Olympic Association, member of the IOC and a former Olympic gold medallist, wasted no time and in October 1945 put forward London's name for the 1948 Games. For Burghley the prospect was one to be savoured, a chance for Britain to have something to cheer about. For the majority of the public it was a dim and distant irrelevance.

But whatever anyone thought, five months later it became a hard and fast fact. In an IOC ballot held in March 1946, London beat five cities that had suffered no damage at all during the war, four of them in the USA, plus Lausanne in Switzerland (where the IOC was now based). To the victors the spoils... and a gargantuan task.

A London Olympic Organising Committee (LOOC) duly convened on March 16 1946 under the chairmanship of Lord Burghley. With him sat Britain's other IOC member, Lord Aberdare, who had been a leading figure in the pre war National Fitness Council, and a New Zealand member of the IOC now resident in London, Arthur Porritt, who, like Burghley, had won a medal at the 1924 Games. The Committee duly established an executive committee, and over the next two years gathered under its wing an array of the great and the good of the British political, military and sporting establishments. These included Stanley Rous of the Football Association, the former Olympic rower Jack Beresford and two senior Army officers.

Three main factors would enable LOOC to achieve its goals. Firstly, as might be expected in a nation which had been at war for six years, the Games were to be prepared for and run with military precision. Army and RAF Camps were commandeered as athletes' villages. Army facilities were lined up for specific events. Even the Organising Committee's offices were, for a time, located above the Army and Navy Store in Victoria Street, London.

Secondly, largely thanks to Lord Burghley's powers of persuasion, the BOA won over the Labour Prime Minister, Clement Attlee, who could not promise any funds but could at least mobilise various government departments (despite the often outspoken antipathy of certain civil servants). His was, after all, an administration with a firm belief in state intervention.

Thirdly, the Organising Committee was able to count on the support of possibly the most important figure on the London sporting scene, the recently knighted Sir Arthur Elvin, chairman of Wembley Stadium Ltd, proprietors not only of the stadium but also of the Empire Pool. Elvin had attended the 1936 Olympics and was so confident that the 1948 Games would be good for business that in 1946 he not only offered Wembley's facilities but also persuaded his shareholders that the company should underwrite £100,000 worth of works needed to stage the Games in return for first call on ticket receipts. Elvin went further still by offering an additional £100,000 guarantee against losses, provided that LOOC compensated Wembley for any loss of business incurred as a result of it acting as the main host (that business being essentially greyhound racing).

Elvin may have been shrewd, but he was extraordinarily driven too, becoming personally involved in a host of minor details regarding logistics, ticketing, the printing of programmes and, the single largest piece of construction to take place as a result of the Games, the laying out of the Olympic Way at Wembley.

That this road should incur also the single largest outlay for the Games, of around £120,000, gives an indication of how much LOOC were able to beg and borrow other existing facilities. In fact, apart from the Olympic Way, the only other permanent structures to have been built specifically for the Games were some basic, uncovered stands at the Herne Hill velodrome, costing only a few thousand pounds.

Otherwise, in the spirit of the age, it was entirely a case of making do with whatever was available and mending where necessary. In view of this, it is hardly appropriate to consider the heritage of the 1948 Olympics merely in terms of buildings or places. In fact, Wembley Stadium apart, very few of the venues used for the Games – of which 19 out of 29 survive in one form or another – have made any serious attempt at all to mark or commemorate their involvement in 1948, other than perhaps a brief mention buried somewhere in their histories.

Rather, the real legacy of 1948 is what we call 'intangible heritage'. The Games live on as a story, as a reminder of a time when, just as the nation was down on its uppers, it chose to send out an invitation to the world and put on a seventeen day jamboree. Not surprisingly there were no Germans at this party, and no Russians or Japanese either, or Romanians (although in a spirit of rapprochement the Italians were invited). Even so, the 1948 Games were the largest yet, larger than Berlin in 1936 and more than double the size of the 1908 Games.

In 1908 just over 2,000 athletes from 22 nations had attended, with only 37 women competing and one female changing room being deemed sufficient. In 1948 just over 4,100 athletes attended from 59 countries (out of 70 which had been invited), including a record entry of 390 women. Another new challenge was the need to provide halal food for athletes from countries attending their first Olympic Games; the likes of Iraq, Lebanon and Syria.

Following on from the first tentative attempts to televise the 1936 Games, the London Olympics of 1948 »

OLYMPIC GAMES

Designed by Heros Publicity Studios Ltd.   Printed in Great Britain by McCorquodale & Co. Ltd., London, S.E.1.

29 JULY 1948 14 AUGUST
LONDON

▲ With its strong appeal to patriotic sentiment and to tourism, the official 1948 poster was designed by **Walter Herz**, who had fled to London from Czechoslovakia in 1939. The figure of **Discobolus**, the discus thrower, was a more established London presence, having been excavated from Tivoli in 1790 and displayed in the British Museum since 1805, since when it has often adorned Olympic-related events and exhibitions, as seen elsewhere in this book. A total of 100,000 posters were printed, with originals now fetching over £1,000 at auction.

Pictured at the 1932 Olympics – on a cigarette card issued by the Gallaher tobacco company – Lord Burghley (1905–81) was a leading athlete of the inter-war period. Educated at Eton and Cambridge, he made his Olympic debut at Paris in 1924 in the 110m hurdles, an event for which he trained by positioning matchboxes on each hurdle (rather than champagne glasses, as depicted in the film *Chariots of Fire*, in which he was, in any case, renamed Lord Lindsay). He went on to win a gold medal in the 400m hurdles in 1928 and a silver in the 4 x 400m relay in 1932.

▲ Speaking at the opening of the **Olympic Village** in **Richmond Park** on June 30 1948, **Lord Burghley** was a consummate Olympian; a handsome and charismatic aristocrat, a former holder of both the World 440 yards and the Olympic 400m hurdles records, and, in 1948, chairman of the Organising Committee (the role that Lord Desborough had assumed in 1908 and that Lord Coe would take up for 2012).

By the time he captained Great Britain's Olympic team at the 1932 Games in Los Angeles – where a local gossip-writer marvelled that the blond peer was known to his teammates as plain 'Dave' – Burghley had already entered politics, having been elected as the Conservative MP for Peterborough the previous year. From 1943–45 he served as Governor General of Bermuda.

But perhaps his greatest contribution was as a sports administrator. A passionate advocate of amateurism, Burghley was elected to the IOC in 1933, and, in 1936 became both president of the Amateur Athletic Association and chairman of the British Olympic Association. In 1946 he was also elected president of the International Amateur Athletic Federation.

Had it not been for Burghley's powers of persuasion it has often been said that the 1948 Games might never have happened. Instead, his wildly optimistic prediction that over £1 million in foreign currency would flow in from the Games, did a great deal to swing the doubters in Whitehall.

》were the first to be watched by a significant television audience. That year's FA Cup Final, also at Wembley (in which Manchester United beat Blackpool) had been watched by an unprecedented one million viewers. For the Olympics, the BBC undertook the most ambitious programme of outside broadcasting ever attempted in Britain, paying LOOC £1,000 for the privilege. Indeed some of their efforts can still be seen today as part of the 1948 archive collection on the BBC website.

Also new for London, following on from the failure of the 1908 organisers to launch anything similar, was a series of cultural events accompanying the 1948 Games. The most significant of these was the *Sport in Art Exhibition* held at the Victoria and Albert Museum. Just as Pierre de Coubertin (and William Penny Brookes before him) had envisaged, the Fine Arts Committee invited entries in the fields of painting, graphic art, architecture and sculpture. But although 196 medals and diplomas were eventually handed out to entrants from 27 nations, few of the exhibits stood out. Nor did the public show much interest, particularly once they discovered the entrance fee was two shillings.

Competitions in literature and music were also held, along with a concert at the Royal Albert Hall, in which Sir Malcolm Sargent led the BBC Symphony Orchestra, with soloists including a 20 year old Polish born violinist, Ida Haendel, who had spent part of the war playing lunchtime concerts in British factories.

Haendel was not the only refugee to leave her mark. Within this chapter are the Olympic related works of three Jewish artists whose families had fled to London, while in the next chapter we shall see how, on the same day as the opening ceremony, a German doctor who had escaped just before the war organised the very first Games involving disabled sportsmen, 20 or so miles north of Wembley, at Stoke Mandeville Hospital.

That is not to say that all was sweetness and light in the Britain of 1948. As has often been stated, most recently by historian David Kynaston (*see Links*), while the obvious choice of a runner to set the Olympic flame alight at the opening ceremony was a short, bespectacled middle distance runner called Sydney Wooderson, the Organising Committee chose instead John Mark, a tall, blond, but largely unknown Cambridge athlete. And while a month before the Games a ship called the *Empire Windrush* docked in Tilbury, bringing into Britain the first wave of Jamaican immigrants, on the same weekend as Lord Burghley welcomed the world to Wembley, a series of attacks on black workers took place in Liverpool.

Nor should it be forgotten that while the Lords Burghley, Aberdare and Portal (as president of LOOC) were espousing the virtues of Olympism and athleticism, the corridors of power were bustling with socialist MPs preoccupied with implementing the new National Health Service and on nationalising major industries such as coal mining, the railways, gas and electricity supplies.

Conversely, there were some conservative elements of the press, such as the *Evening Standard* in London, who actively campaigned against the Olympics, in a clear effort to embarrass the Labour government.

There are, in short, a number of contradictory themes underlying the 'Austerity Olympics'. Even from a sporting point of view there is a marked ambivalence. For while ticket sales for some of the early Olympic events were disappointing, that year Britain's football and cricket grounds had been packed to unprecedented levels, as had been the cinemas, amusement parks and seaside resorts. It could even be argued that, far from being a success, based on the final medal count the Olympics offered only further proof of how low British sport had sunk, as measured also by humiliating defeats by Australia in 1948, in cricket, and two years later, by the USA in football, at the World Cup in Brazil.

From our distant viewpoint in the 21st century, the 1948 Games are therefore rich in historical context. On their 50th anniversary in 1998 they were barely celebrated at all. Yet with the coming of the 2012 Games, and the sudden realisation that there were hundreds, if not thousands, of people still alive who had either participated in, or watched the 1948 Games, a plethora of documentaries, articles and books appeared on the 60th anniversary. Of these, the most informative remains that of Janie Hampton, whose 2008 book, *The Austerity Olympics*, has provided genuinely new and illuminating insights.

Above all, in interview after interview, Hampton's work shows that, as stated earlier, the most significant legacy of 1948 is its intangible heritage; that so many of the stories to have emerged reflect the very essence of what we fondly imagine to be our innate qualities as a nation; of 'making do' when times are hard, of celebrating 'the taking part' more than 'the winning', of fair play, and of hospitality and generosity towards visitors.

Certainly, all those qualities were on full display during the 1948 Games. Foreign visitors and reporters commented on them repeatedly. Typical was a letter to the *Picture Post* from a man in Pittsburgh. 'Thanks a million to you fine people of London, for your kindness, hospitality, courtesy and friendliness'. Another correspondent to the magazine, a Swedish journalist, wrote, 'in no country could one have found such friendliness and politeness.'

His only real gripe had been the acute lack of teaspoons in London restaurants.

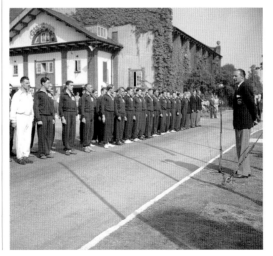

Even though the war had ended three years earlier, British life was still permeated by the culture and discipline of the armed services, in the form of military-style parades, the wearing of uniforms and the dictates of rank.

Seen here in July 1948, the Secretary of State for War, Manny Shinwell, officiates at the raising of the Olympic flag at the Royal Military Academy, Sandhurst, which hosted teams due to compete in the modern pentathlon. In the background is Sandhurst's New College, built in c.1912 and now listed Grade II.

Shortly after this, on July 28, members of the Canadian and British Olympic teams were welcomed to their quarters at RAF Uxbridge by Lieutenant General Sir Frederick Browning. Once again, the building in the background – the camp's cinema, dating from the late 1920s – survives and is Grade II listed.

Note that, unlike today's Olympic Villages, there was strict segregation of the sexes in 1948.

◀ For all their avowed idealism, the organisers of the 1948 Games also had an ulterior motive. As one Foreign Office official noted, 'The government's main interest is to seize the occasion to develop the tourist trade'.

This was hardly a new development. Tourist campaigns had been a feature of several Summer and Winter Olympics during the 1920s and 1930s. But in post war austerity Britain, the need was more acute than ever.

Other departments to play their part in this push included the Ministry of Civil Aviation, the Ministry of Town and Country Planning, and the Board of Trade's Tourist, Catering and Holiday Division.

One of the more ambitious publicity campaigns aimed at the overseas tourist market was that of **British European Airways**, one of the new breed of companies nationalised by the Labour administration under Clement Attlee. Created in 1946 and based partly at the newly opened London Airport at Heathrow, BEA's remit, as its name suggested, was to open up routes from the capital to continental Europe. The airline also played its part during the Olympics by hosting a dinner for athletes billeted at RAF Uxbridge and by treating them to a private flight over London.

Displayed in BEA's offices and at airports all over Europe, this poster, from the Victoria and Albert Museum, illustrates perfectly the government's desire to rebrand Britain as a modern, forward looking nation, even if the reality on the ground was quite different.

Appropriately the name of its artist was **Abram Games**, who perhaps also significantly was a great exponent of the art of air-brushing. The east London son of Jewish immigrants, Games had risen to prominence during the war for producing several hard hitting propaganda posters, all based on his design philosophy of 'maximum meaning, minimum means'.

Games would continue this approach for private clients after the war. But his most widely circulated designs were those he contributed towards the official set of commemorative postage stamps for 1948 (as a result of which he earned the apposite nickname 'Olympic' Games). According to the *Official Report* from 1948, nearly 250 million of these stamps were sold, worth £3 million to the Post Office.

As to how successful were efforts to attract foreign currency, precise visitor figures for the Olympics have never been identified. But as Janie Hampton has shown (*see Links*), the British were not alone at this time in their lack of disposable income. For example, the USA ordered £98,000 worth of advance tickets but ended up selling only £18,000 worth, with the excess being returned for sale on the domestic market.

A lack of cash was seemingly not the only problem. In his otherwise upbeat guide to *The London Olympic Games*, the **Reverend Samuel Evelyn Thomas** (known chiefly for his cartoon compilations during the 1940s), candidly admitted that 'no visitor in his right mind comes to London expecting to be able to wallow in the kind of gay night life so familiar in Paris, New York and other cities.

'That sort of thing is simply not among the attractions of our town, most of which, from an entertainment point of view, go to sleep before midnight.'

Hardly a ringing endorsement, though from all accounts of the period, an honest one at least.

It may be noted, incidentally, that the cover of Thomas' guide (*above*) – which is held in the library of the Bishopsgate Institute – and that of the welcoming poster issued jointly by **London Transport** and the recently nationalised **British Railways** (*above right*) – from the collection of the Victoria and Albert Museum – both prominently feature the five ring symbol of the Olympic

Games. So too does the cover of the *Daily Telegraph's Guide to the Olympic Games*, a copy of which, from the archives of the London Borough of Brent, is reproduced on the right.

In today's highly litigious world the use of this Olympic symbol is closely guarded by the IOC to protect its commercial interests. But even in 1948 a fee for its use in advertising material was charged, albeit a relatively modest one of £250 (worth around £6,750 today). Among those companies known to have taken up this opportunity were Ovaltine (who supplied their products to each of the athletes' camps), Brylcreem, Coca Cola, Gillette, Guinness, Nescafé and Quaker Oats.

There were limits. As the *Official Report* put it, the IOC was keen to ensure that the Games were 'promoted not so much as a commercial venture but in the best interests of sport'. But as these posters and publications suggest, even in 1948 commercial interests were starting to wake up to the potential benefits of association with what we now term 'the Olympic brand'.

▲ In the midst of clothes rationing, **Selfridges** of **Oxford Street** did its best to raise spirits with this Olympian window display during the summer of 1948, centred around the now familar figure of Discobolus.

No doubt on sale inside the store was a selection of brightly coloured **Jacqmar scarves**, including the one seen opposite, designed by the London company's head designer, **Arnold Lever**. Having imported large quantities of silk just before the war, Jacqmar decided to market such scarves, each one yard square, in order to use up offcuts. Apart from their spirited designs, many of which during the war featured unabashed propaganda messages, they had the advantage of costing only half a clothing coupon. This scarf is held by the Victoria and Albert Museum, but there is another Lever design of note – featured in Nicky Albrechtsen and Fola Solanke's book *Scarves* (*see Links*) – on which all the medallists at the 1948 Games are listed. Because Jacqmar's largest market was in the USA, and so many of the medallists were American, Lever designed the scarf on the day of the closing ceremony. It was then printed the following day, and flown out across the Atlantic the day after.

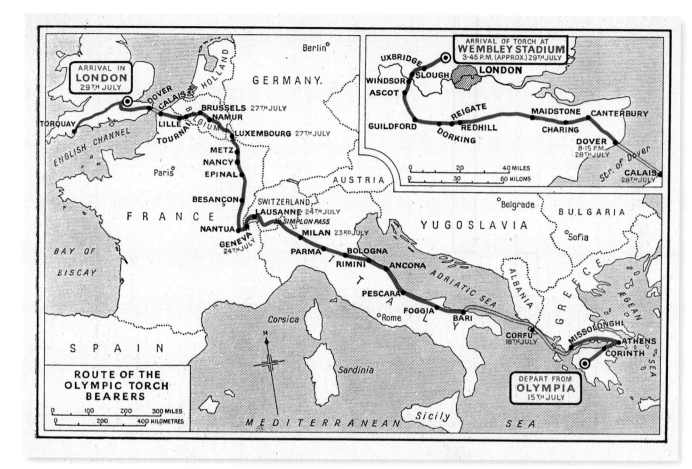

▲ From the *Daily Telegraph Guide,* this was the route of the **torch relay**, as originally planned. One celebrated facet of the ancient Olympics had been that no matter what wars were being fought, a truce would be called to enable the Games to take place. Yet ironically in 1948, Greece was embroiled in a bitter Civil War. As a result, after the flame lighting ceremony at Olympia on July 17 (two days later than the *Telegraph* guide indicated), instead of heading east to Athens, the relay was re-routed directly west to Katacolon, from where a Greek ship took it to Corfu.

A British frigate then transported the flame to Bari, on the east coast of Italy. Thereafter a relay of runners, each one covering two miles, bore the flame to Switzerland – where it paused briefly by Coubertin's tomb in Lausanne – and from there to Calais, where *HMS Bicester* awaited for the final sea crossing to Dover. English runners then carried the flame through Kent, Surrey, and Berkshire.

At Windsor its path met up with the 1908 marathon route, before branching off to Wembley for the opening ceremony on July 29. Finally, after a 2,000 mile journey taking 12 days, the last relay runner, John Mark, lit the torch in the stadium just 30 seconds behind schedule.

On August 1, a second relay started from Wembley to Torquay, where the Olympic sailing was due to start.

As noted earlier, the torch relay was no ancient ritual but one concocted by the Nazis in 1936. Yet its success in 1948 appeared to cleanse it of any negative associations.

'After long years of apparently almost unending national and international strain and stress,' stated the *Official Report*, 'here was a gleam of light...which crossed a continent without hindrance, which caused frontiers to disappear in its presence, which gathered unprecedented crowds... and which lit the path to a brighter future for the youth of the world...'

At a time when Britain's boffins were applying their brains to the turning of swords into ploughshares, the challenge of designing a torch for the Olympic relay was taken on by the Fuel Research Station at the government's Department of Scientific and Industrial Research.

Each torch, stated the brief, had to be light enough to carry for two miles, with enough fuel to burn for 15 minutes (more than runners would need, but allowing for contingencies). Further, the design had to ensure that the flame remain alight in all weathers, and that the torch be cheap to manufacture yet also 'of pleasing appearance and a good example of British craftsmanship'.

Seen here is the scientists' elegant response. Made from aluminium to the designs of the architect **Ralph Lavers**, the torch combined simple classicism with technological practicality. Inside the upper rod were eight tablets of commercially available solid fuel, of a type known as hexamine, laced with a small amount of napthalene to add luminosity. As each tablet burnt away, the next one down would ignite, having been pushed up from below by a simple springloaded mechanism.

In total 1,720 torches were manufactured, free of charge by EMI Factories, of which 1,688 were used.

But how many survive? No one knows, largely because each runner was allowed to keep his torch, and therefore the majority presumably remain in private hands. The one seen here is from the Victoria and Albert Museum. Others are held at the River and Rowing Museum in Henley and by the BOA. But occasionally they come up for auction. In 2008, for example, one was sold at Bonhams for £2,520.

Despite several doubters on the 1948 Organising Committee the Olympic torch relay turned out to be hugely popular with the public. Here at Limpsfield Common in Surrey they gathered at 6.10am on July 29 to see Reuben Mehew of the Cambridge Harriers (*left*) hand over to WW Humphreys of Oxted. Possibly the best turnout was at Chard in Somerset, when on August 2 an estimated 3,000 people turned up to greet the torch... at 3.30am.

▲ With thousands of Britons still homeless after the war and building materials in short supply, the creation of an athletes' village in 1948, as had occurred at the previous Games in 1932 and 1936, was out of the question. Instead, the government agreed to provide accommodation for the 4,100 or so athletes, plus over a thousand officials, at two RAF stations, Uxbridge and West Drayton, and here, at a former army camp in **Richmond Park**. A further 19 schools, colleges and nurses' homes in Middlesex, central and south London were also made available.

Even so, the organisers had to contend with a barrage of obstacles put in their way by civil servants, some of them downright hostile to the Olympics.

Nor were they alone. Covering a 15 acre site close to the Kingston Gate, the Richmond Park camp – shown here shortly before its opening by Lord Burghley (*see page 130*) – had originally been erected for the East Surrey Regiment in 1938, and during the war had served as a convalescent centre for injured servicemen and as barracks for various women's auxiliary services. But as the Army prepared to hand it over to the Olympic Organising Committee it became the focus of angry protests by the Kingston Homeseekers Association, led by a local vicar, who argued forcefully that homeless Londoners should be given priority over foreign athletes.

By today's standards, the Richmond Park Olympic Village was hardly luxurious. In order to house 1,470 competitors – all male – rooms were shared between four to six individuals (*above*). But otherwise it was as well appointed as could be expected in the circumstances. There was a cafeteria, bank and reading room (*top left*) and a hut (*left centre*) containing a tailor, a laundry, plus branches of the newsagent WH Smith, the dry cleaners Burtol, and the Kingston department store, Bentalls.

Mexican athletes enjoy their complimentary drink of Horlicks in one of the Richmond Park dormitories (*right*). Based in Slough, Horlicks was one of several companies to supply their products to the 1948 Games.

Working out who slept where involved great diplomacy. The North Mess area was reserved for five Scandinavian nations, with the South Mess allocated to South and Central American countries. The 207 Italian athletes, meanwhile – representing a nation that only six years earlier had been in the enemy camp – was kept separate in the Small Mess area. But once the Games started others would move in, for example from New Zealand and Afghanistan, while the Swedes, despite the provision of 'Scandinavian vapour baths' (or saunas), decided it was all too basic and booked into hotel rooms instead.

Transport to and from the various venues was provided by buses and by Ministry of Supply station wagons, whose female drivers were billeted just outside the camp.

According to reminiscences recorded by Janie Hampton (*see Links*), one of the biggest problems for athletes at Richmond Park was boredom, whereas RAF Uxbridge, where 1,600 male athletes were billeted, was at least within a populated area. Yet the rooms were certainly less crowded than at other centres, such as Pinner County School, where 94 Indian and Burmese athletes slept in converted classrooms. One of the most multi-cultural gatherings was at Southlands Training College in Wimbledon, where 180 female athletes from 17 countries were accommodated.

After the Olympics the Richmond Park camp remained intact, and in 1956 was used to house refugees from the Suez Crisis. Finally in 1965 the Ministry of Defence decided to clear the site, leaving no trace at all today other than a set of concrete steps leading up a grassy slope.

There is, however, one remnant of the camp elsewhere.

As a schoolboy in 1948 Frank Dobson had worked at Richmond Park, helping his father, who ran a photographic business in Kingston, to develop films taken by the visiting athletes. Later he became a keen member of the **Malden Rifle and Pistol Club** (formed in 1907), and in 1960 competed in the 50m free pistol event at the Rome Olympics. When the Richmond Park huts were put up for sale in 1965 Frank drove there in his company van, bought half of one of the huts, and with the help of fellow members re-erected it a mile to the south, where it remains to this day, hidden away amongst allotments on Alric Avenue in New Malden (*see right*).

Compared with the scale and luxury of the athletes' village constructed for 2012 – destined to become private flats after the Games – this cosy, if creaky shed may not appear to offer much of a legacy. And yet with its rickety timbers and its make-dO-and-mend assortment of fixtures and fittings, and for its sheer uniqueness – no other huts from Richmond are known to have survived – it is in many respects a perfect piece of 1948 Olympic heritage.

Concrete steps close to Dann's Pond – all that remains of the Olympic Village in Richmond Park.

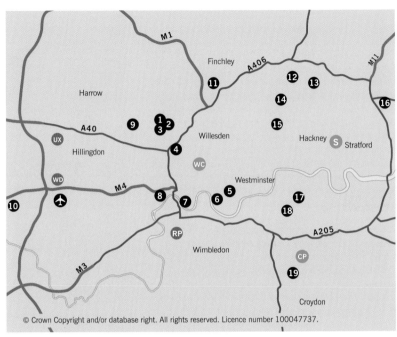

▲ Two days before the Games, and still there are long queues outside the main **Olympic box office** at the **Empire Pool, Wembley**, despite it having been open since the previous November, twelve hours a day, seven days a week.

Part of the problem, it is true, stemmed from initial antipathy towards the Games amongst large sectors of the public. Less of an issue were the ticket prices, which ranged from two shillings up to a guinea (at a time when entry to a London football ground typically cost 1s 6d).

But it was logistical issues that mainly plagued the ticket operation (run entirely by Wembley Stadium Ltd). In effect the Olympics were the equivalent of staging around 20 FA Cup Finals over a period of 17 days, at 29 different venues (*as shown on the accompanying maps*).

The scale of this operation was further complicated by the fact that originally, in the hope of large numbers of tourists, half the tickets had been reserved for overseas visitors, leaving the remaining half to be divided between clubs and associations and the general public. But then from May 1948 the domestic market was flooded by large numbers of returns from overseas, particularly from the United States. Many ended up on the black market.

Even so, the ticketing operation was hardly a failure. Excluding the football preliminaries and the sailing, 1,024,872 tickets were sold, yielding income amounting to just under £550,000; less than the £850,000 expected had every ticket been sold at face value, but at least above the minimum of £500,000 originally budgeted.

Incidentally, behind the queue seen above is the **Palace of Arts**, a survivor from the 1924 Empire Exhibition. During the Games it served as the headquarters of the BBC. Although listed in 1976 it was subsequently purchased by the developers Quintain in 2003, then delisted and demolished the year after. The Empire Pool, on the right, does however survive, as the Wembley Arena.

London locations used in 1948

1. **Empire Stadium, Wembley** athletics, football and hockey finals, equestrianism (stadium rebuilt 2002–07)
2. **Empire Pool** swimming, diving, water polo and boxing finals (now Wembley Arena)
3. **Palace of Engineering** fencing (site now retail units)
4. **Guinness Sports Club, Park Royal** hockey prelims (site now Diageo offices)
5. **Empress Hall, Earl's Court** boxing prelims, wrestling, gymnastics, weightlifting (site now Empress State Building)
6. **Craven Cottage, Fulham FC** football (extant)
7. **Polytechnic Sports Ground, Chiswick** hockey prelims (extant)
8. **Griffin Park, Brentford FC** football (extant)
9. **Lyon's Sports Club, Sudbury** hockey prelims (now David Lloyd Centre and housing)
10. **Windsor Great Park** road cycling
11. **Finchley Lido** water polo prelims (site now Finchley Lido Leisure Centre)
12. **White Hart Lane, Tottenham Hotspur FC** football (extant)
13. **Green Pond Road, Walthamstow Avenue FC** football (site now housing units)
14. **Harringay Arena** basketball (site now Arena Shopping Park)
15. **Arsenal Stadium, Highbury** football (part extant as residential development)
16. **Lynn Road, Ilford FC** football (site now housing units)
17. **Champion Hill, Dulwich Hamlet FC** football (site now modern stadium and retail park)
18. **Herne Hill Velodrome** track cycling (extant)
19. **Selhurst Park, Crystal Palace FC** football (extant)

Other locations: Olympic athletes accommodation: **Uxbridge** (UX), **West Drayton** (WD), **Richmond Park** (RP); **White City Stadium** (WC), **2012 Stadium** (S), **Crystal Palace** (CP)

▲ Sailing enthusiasts gather on the harbour at **Torquay** in **Devon**, in advance of the Olympic regatta.

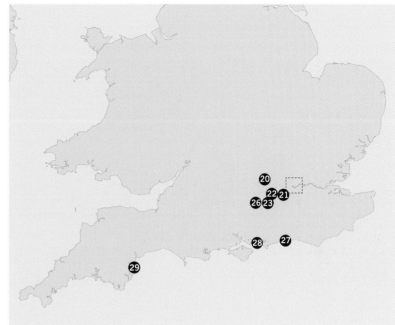

This took place in **Torbay** between August 3–12, and was described in the *Official Report* as the largest international event ever held in the annals of yacht racing. Overall 75 boats in five different classes took part, representing 25 nations. (The Solent, where most of the sailing events had taken place in 1908, had been ruled out because its waters were now too congested.)

Royal Navy personnel from Devonport marked out three courses in Torbay and provided patrol boats to help police the event. During the regatta there would also be visits by the navies of Belgium, France and the USA, thereby adding to the military flavour of the event.

Despite its distance from London, Torbay enjoyed the full Olympic experience, to the extent even of having its own opening ceremony amidst the ruins of Torre Abbey, and its own Olympic flame. This had been made possible by an additional torch relay involving 107 runners between Wembley Stadium and the Devon coast. To add to the sense of carnival, 1,000 pigeons were released, bearing messages to yachting centres all over Britain.

After a series of enthralling races in ideal conditions, with the winners in some classes not being decided until the last few minutes of the final day's racing, the regatta ended with a closing ceremony attended by 10,000 spectators and the spontaneous singing of *Auld Lang Syne*.

As seen on the map (*left*), Torbay was one of eight locations outside London. Once again, the military establishments at Bisley, Sandhurst and Aldershot maintained the Games' links with the armed services, while on the south coast Brighton and Portsmouth hosted preliminary matches in the football tournament.

Just as in 1908 and in 2012, the 1948 Olympics did not belong solely to the capital.

Non London locations used in 1948 (*also used in 1908)

20. **Henley-on-Thames*** rowing, canoeing (course still in use)
21. **Bisley Camp*** shooting, modern pentathlon/shooting (facilities still in use)
22. **Royal Military Academy, Sandhurst, Camberley** modern pentathlon/running (extant)
23. **Aldershot – three venues** (*see also map on page 158*):
    (23) **Central Stadium** three-day eventing/dressage and jumping (still in use)
    (24) **Central Gymnasium** modern pentathlon/fencing (extant, as Fox's Gymnasium)
    (25) **Municipal Pool** modern pentathlon/swimming (extant, as Aldershot Lido)
26. **Tweseldown Racecourse, Church Crookham** three-day eventing/cross-country, modern pentathlon/riding (course still in use)
27. **Goldstone Ground, Brighton & Hove Albion FC** football prelims (now retail park)
28. **Fratton Park, Portsmouth FC** football prelims (extant)
29. **Torbay, Devon** yachting (Royal Torbay Yacht Club and bay still in use)

▲ Although the stadium at the end of the road has been rebuilt, and the route itself is now lined by an assortment of buildings and far fewer trees, one of the best known legacies of the 1948 Games is the **Olympic Way, Wembley**, seen here as men from the Automobile Association erect temporary signs in the vicinity. As the signs stacked up against one of their familiar yellow vans suggest, the AA men would later move on to Earl's Court, Highbury, Craven Cottage and the Harringay Arena.

Costing £120,000 – the largest single expenditure on any building project for the Games, most of it funded

by Wembley Stadium Ltd – Olympic Way bridged a new pedestrian subway leading from Wembley Park Station, which was itself expanded that summer. (The bridge has since been rebuilt and named after Bobby Moore.)

Among the workforce of 123 men employed on the project (*see opposite*) were 44 German prisoners of war, who had yet to be repatriated, three years after VE Day.

Building works at this time were notoriously subject to delays, so the **Mayor of Wembley** and the **Minister of Transport**, **Alfred Barnes** (*right*) were no doubt delighted to declare the job done on July 6, with three weeks to spare.

A packed Wembley on July 31 1948, the third day of the Games. To the right of Olympic Way can be seen the Palace of Engineering, and on the left, the Palace of Industry, both survivors of the 1924 Exhibition. In front of the latter, on the left, is the Empire Pool (now the Wembley Arena).

The British Olympics **143**

Despite paper shortages, and in the hope of healthy sales, the 1948 organisers opted to produce daily programmes at each of the venues for all but six of the Olympic sports, with covers printed in different colours to avoid confusion.

Designed by the McCorquodale company (who also printed the official poster), the event programmes cost one shilling each, rising to 2s for the opening and closing ceremonies.

Numerous copies have survived in archives, while on internet auction sites typical prices range from £5–20, depending on their rarity.

▲ Of the 740 or so men and women who competed in 33 track and field events at Wembley Stadium during the 1948 Olympics, none grabbed more headlines or won more hearts than the Dutch athlete **Fanny Blankers-Koen**.

Seen here in her home-made orange shorts winning the final leg of the 4 x 100 m relay on the last day of the athletics, Saturday August 7, the 'Flying Housewife' – as the 30 year old mother of two was dubbed by the press – already had three gold medals to her name. Apparently she had arrived for the relay only in the nick of time, having popped into the West End to buy a raincoat.

Wet weather, it will be recalled, had blighted attendances at the Great Stadium in 1908. Forty years later, torrential rain on the Monday and Friday of the first week sent thousands of spectators scurrying under the stand roofs. But on most other days the weather held.

Another feature of the 1908 Games had been the number of disputes between athletes and track officials. Happily in 1948 there were almost none. One reason for

this was that, as a result of 1908, all officials were neutral, rather than from the host nation. Another factor was the increased use of technology.

For example, as seen above, 1948 was the first time that photo-finish cameras had been used at an athletics meeting in Britain. In truth much of the technology for this already existed, having first been trialled at the 1912 Olympics in Stockholm, and further improved in both 1932 at Los Angeles and 1936 in Berlin.

But in post war Britain there was only one stadium which had the necessary expertise and that was Wembley, where cameras had been in use since 1945, not for human runners but for greyhounds. Relocating the cameras to new positions on the track was easily done. But it required the aid of various hand-operated lifts and telephones in order to link the judges on the finishing line to the camera room positioned up in the roof of the North Stand.

Once this system was hooked up and tested, the Race Finish Recording Co Ltd promised that its operators could deliver prints to the track officials within 90 seconds of the tape being broken. Fanny Blankers-Koen was to discover just how quick they were.

In the final of the 80m hurdles there appeared to be a dead heat between herself and Britain's Maureen Gardner (a ballet teacher), both being clocked at 11.2 seconds, a new Olympic record. When *God Save Our King* struck up and the crowds started cheering, Blankers-Koen naturally assumed she had come second. However, it transpired that the anthem had been played because King George VI and Queen Elizabeth had entered the stadium at that moment. After it ended, the photo-finish images showed that the Dutchwoman had, after all, won the gold.

If there was any resentment amongst the home crowd it did not show. On the contrary, foreign reports praised the fans' sportsmanship, especially as the British had yet to win a single gold medal in any track or field event, and would still not do so by the time the Games ended.

One reason often cited for this disappointing tally was that, at a time of rationing, the diet of the British athletes appeared inferior to that of some of their rivals, particularly the Americans (who brought with them mountains of beef and topped the medals table) and the second-placed Swedes, who, it was noted caustically, had been neutral during the war. Between them, the USA and Sweden won 40 per cent of all the medals at Wembley.

That said, Britain did notch up six silvers, more than any other nation, while two of its sprinters managed to reach the final of the prestigious men's 100m. As captured on the cover of the following week's *Picture Post* (*right*), the winner on that occasion was **Harrison 'Bones' Dillard**, from the USA. Intriguingly, both the silver medallist in that race, Barney Ewell of the USA, and bronze winner Lloyd LaBeach of Panama, turned professional soon after and went on to compete at the Morpeth Olympic Games (*see Chapter Seven*). Quite a contrast to Wembley.

As for those British athletes who came so close to glory in 1948, who today could recall the names of Maureen Gardner, Dorothy Manley, Audrey Williamson and their fellow silver medallists in the men's 4 x 100m relay, Alastair McCorquodale, John Gregory, Kenneth Jones and John Archer? Or Tom Richards, runner-up in the marathon?

As for the star of that summer, Fanny Blankers-Koen ended her career in 1955, having amassed 16 world records in eight different events. In 1999 she was voted 'Female Athlete of the Century' by the IAAF. In Holland she is commemorated with a statue in Rotterdam and by a stadium in Hengelo. So when she died in 2004, aged 85, not surprisingly many sports historians questioned whether she might also be suitably commemorated at the scene of her greatest triumph. But it has yet to happen.

THE FASTEST MAN
'Bones' Dillard (U.S.A.), winner of the Olympic 100 metres

HULTON'S NATIONAL WEEKLY — OLYMPIC GAMES SPECIAL — AUGUST 14, 1948 — Vol. 40. No. 7 — 4D

If Britain's athletes failed to strike gold in 1948, its boffins certainly made their mark. Watched by Donald Pain from the IAAF, and a Mr C Noakes, this is engineer Henry Rottenburg, a don at King's College, Cambridge, demonstrating a simple device that would transform sprint racing.

An inventive all-rounder with several patents to his name and five Scottish rugby caps, in 1932 Rottenburg helped prepare White City for the return of the AAA Championships, and worked on a number of measuring devices for events such as the long jump and high jump.

Prior to 1948, in order to gain a push off when a race started, sprinters dug toe holes in the track, usually using trowels. Rottenburg's solution could hardly have been simpler.

Made from aluminium, with fixing pins on the underside and footrests lined with sponge, his starting blocks made their full international debut at Wembley in 1948 and soon became standard at all athletics meetings.

▲ This rare colour image of the **opening ceremony** on July 29 1948, with the Olympic flame yet to be lit, vividly illustrates how transformed **Wembley Stadium** had become since that year's FA Cup Final on April 24.

Astonishingly, the bulk of the works took just 17 days, starting only after the usual Saturday evening's greyhound racing finished on July 10. Apart from the building of the torch platform, scoreboard and new dressing rooms at the east end – creating a tunnel that would become one of Wembley's best known features – the original ash terraces were concreted and, on both terraced sections in front of the covered stands, bench seats were added, thereby reducing the capacity from 100,000 to 83,732.

But the greatest feat was the laying of the track. First the greyhound track was dug up to reveal the foundations of the original running track, last used in the 1920s. Next, 800 tons of cinders were laid by the specialist Leicestershire company En-Tout-Cas and levelled and measured to within a tolerance of one in a thousand.

There were fears it would be a slow track. Instead, despite rain on at least two days, ten Olympic records were broken on its distinctive reddish surface.

▶ One of the most abiding stories relating to the 1948 Olympics concerns the fate of the **running track** at Wembley. Although its exact mix was never revealed, we know that it consisted mostly of cinders sourced from domestic coal fires in Leicester. And that it was dug up within days of the closing ceremony on August 14, so that dog racing could recommence as soon as possible.

However no documentation has survived, if it ever existed, to explain why those cinders were subsequently relaid at the sports ground of the **Eton Manor Boys Club** on **Temple Mill Lane**, **Leyton** (just east of Hackney Marshes). No reference to the transaction can be found in the club minutes, now held by the Bishopsgate Institute, and there is only a passing reference in the club magazine, *Chinwag* (when, in January 1949, members were urged to give an hour of their time to help lay it).

Certainly Eton Manor was a prominent organisation. Founded for working class boys in 1909 by an old Etonian, Gerald Wellesley, grandson of the Duke of Wellington, its 32 acre sports ground, known as **The Wilderness**, had been commandeered during the war, resulting in extensive damage to its original cinder track. Lea Valley historian Jim Lewis (*see Links*) has speculated that the person most likely to have put in a bid for the Wembley cinders was Eton Manor's athletics secretary, Les Golding, for many years manager also of the Great Britain athletics team and a runner in the 1948 torch relay. But whoever had the original idea, almost certainly the deal was finalised by Eton Manor's main backer, Arthur Villiers, another Old Etonian, who worked at Barings Bank but had a house adjoining The Wilderness.

With its Olympic track in place, Eton Manor soon became a popular athletics venue (*top right*). In 1951 it became the first in Britain to stage a floodlit meeting, and over the years would see the likes of Roger Bannister, Gordon Pirie and Chris Brasher compete there.

But as its name suggested, The Wilderness was not in an ideal location, and when Villiers decided to refocus his efforts on other philanthropic schemes, in 1967 the sports ground closed, eventually to be absorbed within the Lee Valley Regional Park. Coincidentally, the site now forms part of the 2012 Olympic Park, to be used for temporary swimming pools, wheelchair tennis and hockey.

Various Eton Manor alumni have worked hard to ensure that war memorials from The Wilderness have been saved, and will be reinstated on the site after 2012. But one-time squash and rugby enthusiast Dicky Franklin (*above right*) has kept another reminder of Eton Manor.

Visiting The Wilderness for one last time in 1967 he was suddenly aware that the former Olympic track was about to be covered by tarmac. With only a seven iron golf club to

hand he therefore scooped some of the cinders into a bag and later decanted them into a glass jar.

'Most of the time I keep the jar in a cupboard, a bit like the ashes of a relative,' Franklin explained in 2011. 'I showed it to Seb Coe when he visited the Eton Manor site in 2010, and sometimes I even give a few handfuls away.

'I rescued it because this was the track on which Fanny Blankers-Koen and so many other wonderful athletes performed in 1948 and in later years.

'I just could not bear the thought that this amazing piece of history would be lost for ever.'

▶ As we saw in the previous chapter, the 1908 marathon formed a defining moment in Olympic history. Not only did the route from Windsor to White City establish the official distance for the race at 26 miles and 385 yards, but its dramatic finish, courtesy of Dorando Pietri, would generate more interest than any other event at the Games.

By comparison, even though its climax was almost as compelling, **the 1948 marathon** is much less celebrated.

When it came to planning the route – work on which started as early as March 1946, with Lord Burghley taking a close interest – there were no concessions to history. Even though London's annual Polytechnic Marathon (first run in 1909 as a direct result of the 1908 Games) always started at Windsor Castle, and despite the fact that the 1908 route had passed just south of where Wembley Stadium now stood, an entirely fresh route was agreed.

Firstly, the organisers insisted that only properly surfaced roads were used. Secondly, instead of the 'point-to-point' approach taken in 1908, in 1948, as had been the practice at all Olympic marathons since 1928, the route was designed on an 'out-and-back' basis; that is, it started and finished with a lap around the stadium track.

As this map from the *Daily Telegraph Guide* shows, the route headed north from Wembley to Stanmore, and then made a 15 mile loop through Middlesex, reaching its northernmost point at Radlett in Hertfordshire, before heading south back to Wembley. What the map does not show is that there was a steady 85 metre climb between Wembley and the ten mile mark, and then a dip, followed by another slow climb from Radlett to Stanmore, making it one of the most testing marathon routes yet.

This, plus the heat of the day, Saturday August 7, led to a finish not dissimilar to 1908. This time the tottering hero was a 21 year old Belgian paratrooper, Etienne Gailly, who had led for most of the way, then lost the lead, then regained it, only to enter the stadium in a state described in the *Official Report* as 'practically insensible'. With just 500 yards to go on the track and with 85,000 spectators wondering if a repeat of 1908 was on the cards, the exhausted Gailly was overtaken, first by Delfo Cabrera, an Argentinian fireman running his first ever marathon, and, then by a 38 year Welshman, Tom Richards, a nurse in a London hospital. Still, Gailly at least managed to limp home bravely for the bronze.

Dorando Pietri, meanwhile, had not been forgotten. During the build up to the marathon the now ageing Italian was to be found in London being wined and dined by admirers. Until that is he was unmasked by four men from Pietri's home town, one of whom had been present at the runner's funeral, in 1942. The hoaxer was Italian, but far from being a hero was a barman in Birmingham.

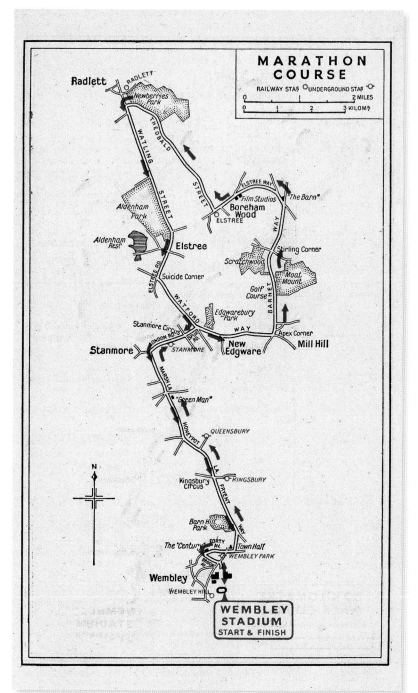

▲ An Olympic flag and a Union Jack flutter from the twin towers of **Wembley Stadium** as, just after 3.00pm on the final day of the athletics programme, **Eusebio Guinez** of Argentina, wearing number 23, leads the field of 41 runners up the gentle incline of the new Olympic Way.

Once again we cannot help but remark on how completely different is the view from this spot today.

Guinez would continue to hold the lead for the first two miles. But just over two and half hours later – by which time all the other athletics finals in the stadium had been decided – he ended up in fifth place, out of 30 finishers.

Compared with today's highly regimented marathons, the 1948 race was managed with a very light touch. Apart from a few police constables to keep order, there were boy scouts to hold up the mile markers and refreshment stations every five kilometres serving tea, coffee, barley water, sugar or fruit. Even the method used to keep officials back at Wembley informed as to the progress of the race was brilliantly simple. Instead of using radios, selected public telephone kiosks along the route were reserved, allowing reports to be filed throughout the afternoon at the cost of only a handful of pennies.

SWIMMING
at the
EMPIRE POOL WEMBLEY
TUESDAY AUGUST 3RD 1948

OFFICIAL PROGRAMME · ONE SHILLING

After track and field, aquatic sports formed the second largest category of competition at the 1948 Games, with 528 participants entering three disciplines: swimming, diving and water polo. Not only was there fierce competition in the main venue, the Empire Pool (*see right*) and the Finchley Lido (*page 153*), but also amongst swimmers vying for training slots in various pools dotted around London. As a result, some Olympic swimmers ended up having to dodge members of the general public as they swam up and down in busy municipal pools.

▲ Nowadays the **Wembley Arena** – as the **Empire Pool and Sports Arena** has been called since 1978 – is known largely as a concert venue. However at the 2012 Olympics it will host badminton, thereby becoming the only venue from 1948 to be involved in London's third Games.

But, as seen here on the eve of the 1948 Olympics, one of the building's original functions was as a competition swimming and diving pool. In that guise, a month after its opening in July 1934, it staged the aquatic events of the Commonwealth Games, followed in 1936 by the ASA National Championships and in 1938 by the European Championships. When not set out for competition, the 50m boom was removed to create a 200 foot long leisure pool, complete with wave machines, a paddling pool, dance bands, cafés and folding doors at the far end, opening out onto a sunbathing terrace and a boating lake (a remnant from the 1924 Empire Exhibition).

Britain at that time was going through a lido craze, but there was no lido or indoor pool on the scale of this one.

Not even overseas. Indeed it was the first indoor pool ever used at an Olympic Games, a fact which caused some concern to swimmers from around the world, accustomed as they were to competing outdoors.

But the very fact that the pool was in use for swimming at all was something of an achievement in 1948.

Designed by the brilliant engineer Sir Owen Williams, the Empire Pool was then, as now, a breathtaking piece of structural design. Located immediately next to Wembley Stadium, on which Williams had collaborated with architect Maxwell Ayrton eleven years earlier, it offered between 5–7,000 seats on either side of the pool, over which a series of reinforced, cantilevered concrete beams, meeting at the centre, created what was then the largest clear span roof yet built, measuring 236' 6".

During the winter the pool was boarded over for ice hockey, skating and various indoor sports, activities that proved so lucrative that after the Second World War the pool remained covered.

An illustration of how costs for the 1948 Games were controlled is that the joists supporting the boxing rink in the Empire Pool were purchased on a 'sale and return' basis. As noted by Janie Hampton (*see Links*), the steelwork was bought from a Sheffield steelworks for £20 7s 6d, and then sold back two weeks later for £14 10s.

Positioning the rink above the pool may not have been ideal from the spectators' point of view, but it did result in amusing scenes when various Hungarian and Argentinian officials dived in the water to celebrate their boxers' victories, fully clothed.

Having to recommission it for the Olympics was no small matter. Wartime blackout paint had to be scraped off the glazing. Ten miles of piping and 70 tons of sand forming the ice rink's refrigeration system had to be removed. The concrete-lined pool, not used since 1939, was found to have a crack caused by an exploding German land mine, so that its 700,000 gallons needed regular topping up during the Games. Officially the water temperature was 23° C, but most swimmers found it shockingly cold. (Today's norm is, by comparison, 28°.)

Just as in the stadium, where the track was dug up to make way for the return of greyhound racing as soon as the Games were over, the water in the Empire Pool did not remain. As the 7,000 spectators filed out after the final swimming event on August 7, workmen moved in to erect a boxing ring over the water, as seen above on August 10 during a bout between Great Britain's Henry Carpenter and Belgium's Alex Bollaert. By the end of the month the water was gone, never to return.

Since its £25m refit in 2006, the Wembley Arena, now Grade II listed, has been restored to much of its original, stunning glory, as seen below. But the swimming pool, although still extant, lies hidden under a new concrete floor. Details of this hidden piece of history can be found in another *Played in Britain* study, *Great Lengths* (*see Links*).

FENCING
at the
Palace of Engineering, Wembley

FRIDAY, JULY 30ᵀᴴ 1948
TO
FRIDAY, AUGUST 13ᵀᴴ 1948

OFFICIAL PROGRAMME · ONE SHILLING

▲ Events at Wembley Stadium and the Empire Pool may have attracted the most attention, but seventeen other venues in London also hosted Olympic events in 1948.

Above is a view of the **fencing** at the **Palace of Engineering**, one of the buildings left over from the 1924 Empire Exhibition (*see aerial view on page 143*). Hailed in 1924 as the world's largest reinforced concrete building, it had actually been designed by Maxwell Ayrton and John William Simpson as a temporary stucture, and had more or less been an empty shell when fitted out for the 1948 Games, to the extent that chemical toilets had to be brought in. This apart, by all accounts it was a popular gathering place for the world's fencers.

The building's rebirth was only temporary, however, and for much of its remaining life the Palace of Engineering remained underused and unappreciated, before being demolished during the 1970s and replaced by a bland office block. This rare glimpse of its interior is therefore a poignant reminder of what was lost.

It was a rather different picture over at **Earl's Court**, where in common with the Empire Pool at Wembley, the **Empress Hall**, the venue chosen for the Olympic boxing preliminaries, the wrestling and the weightlifting, was otherwise a highly successful multi-purpose 7,000 seat venue. Built in 1896 with design input from that great showman, Imre Kiralfy (who would go on to be such an important figure in the 1908 Games), Empress Hall had, since 1935, become famous for ice hockey and ice spectaculars. That it also staged the gymnastics at the 1948 Games, as seen above (with **Alec Wales** from the British team trying out the rings), was, however, purely down to the vagaries of an English summer.

Despite being strongly advised against the idea by the Organising Committee and by the Amateur Gymnastic Association of Great Britain, the sport's international federation and the IOC had insisted that the gymnastics take place in the open air on the pitch at Wembley.

So it seemed entirely predictable that torrential rain on August 8 would all but flood the stadium, requiring hasty arrangements to be made to transfer the entire gymnastic competition to Earl's Court. One other legacy of 1948 was therefore that with the exception of 1960, all subsequent Olympic gymnastics have been staged indoors.

As for the Empress Hall, it was demolished in 1959, to be replaced by the Empress State Building, built originally as a hotel but now offices.

▲ One of the organisational triumphs of the 1948 Games was its use of existing facilities. One of its weaknesses was that, as a result, some competitors faced long journeys across the capital. Away from the main cluster of venues in west London, and excluding football, there were two in north London.

The first was the starkly functional **Harringay Arena**, on **Green Lanes**. Designed by the engineer Oscar Faber, this was a cavernous indoor facility opened in 1936 at the height of London's ice hockey craze. It was also popular for boxing. But in 1948 it housed basketball, a sport barely known to the British, and which on its first day attracted only a few hundred spectators, in a venue seating 10,000. Crowds did subsequently improve, but Harringay should really have hosted boxing instead.

Converted into a food warehouse in 1958, the arena was demolished in 1978, along with the greyhound track next door, and the site is now the Arena Shopping Park.

Above right is **Finchley Lido**, which shared with the Empire Pool some of the earlier rounds in the water polo. Built on **Finchley High Road** in 1931, the Lido staged ten games. For greater visibility when the BBC cameras were in attendance, and for the benefit of spectators, yellow balls were used and each player wore a numbered cap.

Finchley witnessed one of the British contingent's worst moments in 1948. Having won golds in 1900, 1908, 1912 and 1920, the home nation's water polo team were knocked out in round one after failing to beat Egypt.

Contrary to expectations, the British did better in the football, its purely amateur team finishing fourth under coach Matt Busby, who three months earlier had taken his Manchester United team to the Cup Final at Wembley.

Of all the London grounds hosting matches (*see page 140*), the smallest was **Lynn Road**, home of Southern League **Ilford FC**. Visiting the site today, a housing estate built in the 1980s, centred on Dellow Close, it is almost impossible to imagine it hosting matches between Turkey and Yugoslavia, and France v. India. To the crowd's amazement, several of the Indians, including their captain (*right*), played not in boots but in bandaged feet.

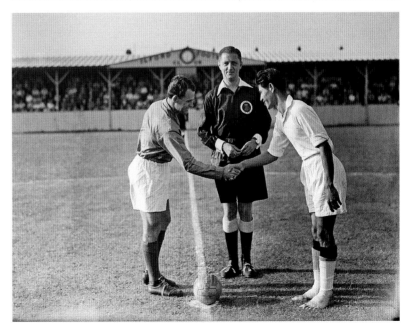

▲ **Herne Hill Velodrome** in south east London occupies a unique place in Britain's Olympic heritage. Firstly, of the six purpose-built sports venues in the capital that hosted finals during the 1948 Games, it is the only one remaining in use for that same sport, having hosted three days of Olympic cycling in August 1948.

Secondly, there survives at Herne Hill a simple, uncovered stand seating a few hundred spectators which, in the words of the *Official Report,* constituted 'the only major construction work of a permanent nature carried out at the instance of the Organising Committee' for the whole 1948 Games. As seen above in 2008, this stand was hardly sophisticated. Nevertheless it formed a useful supplement to the small covered stand (*seen left during the Games*), which dated back to the velodrome's opening in 1891 and which was itself tidied up for the Olympics, and two earlier uncovered stands flanking the main one.

Other works for the Games included a temporary cover over the terracing on the back straight, improvements to the entrance on Burbage Road and repairs to the asphalt track. Photo-finish cameras were also installed, as were twelve telephone boxes for the press. None had lights, however, which did not please reporters when the racing overran one evening. Still, it was the same for the riders. In the absence of any floodlighting, cars had to be parked with their headlights facing the track.

Yet despite these foibles there were remarkably few problems, the only major disappointment being the inability of British favourite Reg Harris to win a gold. But Harris did at least win a silver, in the sprint, and for his lifetime's achievements was later immortalised in bronze at the National Cycling Centre (*see page 176*). Indeed British riders won medals in each of the four events at Herne Hill, (two silvers and two bronzes), plus a silver in the team road race in Windsor Great Park.

Since 1948 Herne Hill has been patched up by a succession of enthusiasts (Olympian Bradley Wiggins included), but also repeatedly threatened with extinction. At last, however, in February 2011 its short term future was assured when the Herne Hill Velodrome Trust gained a 15 year lease, allowing planning for its refurbishment to start in earnest (*see page 187*).

Herne Hill will never match the new 2012 indoor velodrome at Stratford, not least because its 450m track does not conform with the modern 250m standard. But as an historic track which offers potential Olympians a place to learn their craft, it genuinely has no equal in Britain.

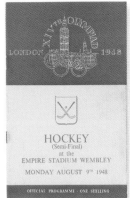

Least advanced of all the London venues used in 1948 were the three that hosted early rounds of the hockey. Seen left, during the USA v. Switzerland match on August 7, is the Guinness sports ground at Park Royal. The brewery buildings behind, designed by Giles Gilbert Scott and opened in 1938, were demolished in 2005, and the sports ground is now the site of Diageo's offices.

By contrast, the lower view, of the Polytechnic sports ground in Chiswick, looking towards Cavendish Road, taken during India's victory over Spain on August 6, has barely changed at all. Of course the Polytechnic, now the University of Westminster, already had a fine Olympic pedigree from its involvement in 1908.

The third hockey venue was the staff ground of the restaurant chain J Lyons and Co, at Sudbury Hill, now a David Lloyd Centre and a housing estate (*see page 181*).

ROWING
at
HENLEY-on-THAMES
SATURDAY AUGUST 7TH 1948

OFFICIAL PROGRAMME · ONE SHILLING

Along with Bisley, Henley-on-Thames welcomed the Olympic Games for the second time in 1948. As in 1908, the IOC was content for the Amateur Rowing Association to oversee the event, but with one subtle difference. In 1908, as noted on page 91, the ARA's strict definition of amateurism ruled out any British rower who earned a living as a 'mechanic, artisan or labourer.' By 1948 that rule had been dropped. Even so, when Bert Bushnell, winner of a gold medal in the double sculls with Dickie Burnell, attempted to enter Henley's exclusive Leander Club, he was denied entry.

▲ 'The most famous and one of the loveliest courses in the world'. So said the *Official Report* of **Henley-on-Thames**, seen here from the south, or Phyllis Court end of the course, as, in the final race on the final day of the 1948 Olympic Regatta, the USA Eights stormed to victory ahead of their British and Norwegian opponents.

In order to stage the Olympic rowing – which drew a record 86 crews from 27 nations – the Henley stewards had to make several changes to a course that only four weeks earlier had hosted the annual Royal Regatta.

Temporary grandstands seating 4,000 spectators were erected on the river bank, together with a 150 seat press box (*bottom right*), built on piles in the water and facing down the length of the course towards the start, near Temple Island (just visible in the distance, with its James Wyatt designed fishing lodge dating from 1771).

Meanwhile the course itself, which normally allowed for only two boats to race alongside each other, had to be widened from 24m to 36m in order accommodate three. As seen above, these three lanes, or stations, were marked

out every 500 metres by large, numbered signs, hung over the water. Another innovation was the installation of electronic timing devices for each station, and of the same type of photo-finish cameras as used at Wembley Stadium, Herne Hill and Windsor Great Park. As it transpired, however, not one of the rowing races required camera evidence to be called upon.

One tradition that did not change was that French, the official language of international rowing, continued to be used. Thus each race commenced with the starter calling out '*Partez!*' Pierre de Coubertin, that great admirer of Henley, would have been delighted. However, he might have been less pleased to see the participation of females in one of nine canoeing events staged at Henley in 1948.

First demonstrated at Paris in 1924, and making its full Olympic debut at Berlin in 1936, canoe racing was still in its infancy in Britain. Nor was Henley accustomed to female participants. All ten of them had to be found hotel rooms in the town, while male competitors were accommodated in schools in Wycombe and Oxfordshire.

One of many Olympic artefacts now held at Henley's River and Rowing Museum, this enamel lapel badge from 1948 – made by Fraisse Demey, a Paris-based maker of medals, badges and decorative arts – was owned by Amy Gentry. A founder member of the Weybridge Ladies Amateur Rowing Club in 1926, Gentry devoted much of her life to the cause of women's rowing, only to die in June 1976, aged 75, just weeks before women were finally allowed to compete in Olympic rowing events, in Montreal. During the Second World War she had worked as the secretary to Barnes Wallis, designer of the 'bouncing bomb'.

▲ While in London the Organising Committee put on its *Sport in Art* exhibition at the Victoria and Albert Museum, at **Henley** there took place the only known attempt by any of the 1948 host communities to celebrate sporting heritage. Indeed Henley's effort, though temporary, may be considered one of the earliest known public exhibitions of this kind ever staged in Britain.

Located in the town's still extant **Drill Hall**, on **Friday Street**, and advertised as the **XIVth Olympiad Rowing Museum**, the display brought together an eclectic range of artefacts belonging to local rowing clubs, Oxford and Cambridge Universities and private collectors.

On the right, by the wall, was exhibited an embroidered Richmond Coat and Badge dating from 1903. (This race was an offshoot of the older Doggett's Coat and Badge race, from which another, plainer scarlet coat was also on display.) The trophy in the foreground was the Eton House IV cup, dating from 1857, while one of the hulls on show was that in which the double Olympian, Sidney Swann, sculled across the English Channel in 1911.

For canoeists attending the Olympics, there was also a 'Rob Roy' canoe, as used by the intrepid John MacGregor on his voyage on the Rivers Nile and Jordan during the 1860s, and a sealskin kayak from Iceland.

Although the exhibition closed after the Olympics, half a century later Henley was to become the site of a permanent museum. Based in an award winning building by David Chipperfield Architects on the banks of the Thames, the River and Rowing Museum was opened by the Queen in 1998 and includes, as we see throughout this book, numerous artefacts from the Olympics. One of them is Bert Bushnell's gold medal from 1948.

'No point in having it nicked from my home,' Bushnell told Janie Hampton (*see Links*). 'I can always go and look at it there. But I know already I won it.'

Alas, Henley will not clock up an Olympic hat-trick, as international rowing regulations dictate that natural rivers may not be used. Instead, Eton College's artificial course at Dorney Lake will be the venue for the rowing and canoe sprints at London's third Games in 2012.

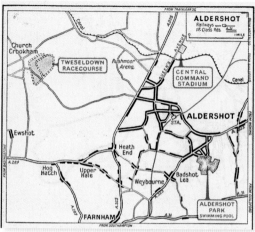

▲ The largest concentration of venues from 1948 that remain in use today is to be found on the borders of Surrey, Berkshire and Hampshire. All six have close associations with military sports and the armed services.

Bisley Camp in Surrey, the home of the National Rifle Association, hosted the shooting, as it had done during the 1908 Olympics, while the five sports that made up the modern pentathlon (as it has been known since 1912, to differentiate it from the ancient pentathlon) were split between the Royal Military Academy in Sandhurst, Tweseldown Racecourse (*see opposite*) and two venues in the Army garrison town of Aldershot.

Shown above on the *Daily Telegraph Guide* map, the swimming element of the modern pentathlon was staged in the **municipal lido** in **Aldershot Park**. Opened in 1930, its irregular shape, still in situ today (*top left*), required a boom to be positioned to create a 50m straight.

On **Queen's Avenue,** the fencing part of the modern pentathlon took place at the **Central Gymnasium** (next to the Central Command Stadium on the map). Seen here during an Inter-Services pentathlon championship in 1958 (*centre left*), **Fox's Gymnasium**, as it is now known, was built in 1894, is still in use by the Army, and has altered remarkably little either internally or externally (*lower left*). It is now Grade II listed, as is the Maida Gymnasium, further south on Queen's Avenue, where a ball for visiting officers in 1948 was hosted by the Mayor.

Overlooked by Fox's Gymnasium is the **Central Command Stadium**. Since modernised and renamed **Aldershot Military Stadium**, this hosted the dressage and elements of the three day eventing. However, as at Aldershot's two other 1948 venues, there is nothing at all on the site to mark its appearance in the Olympic spotlight.

Three miles west of Aldershot is another 1948 Olympic venue still in use. Bought by the Army for manoeuvres in 1854 and opened as a racecourse in 1867, Tweseldown is said to have dismayed foreign riders in 1948 who were rather hoping for lush English countryside rather than an Army training ground. But its undulating landscape, sandy soil and challenging jumps made it ideal as part of the cross-country riding course from Aldershot to Sandhurst in the modern pentathlon, and for the cross-country stage of the eventing.

Five of the late Victorian buildings at Tweseldown are listed Grade II, including the grandstand (*above*) and the offices and stables (*below*). The bronze statue, by Philip Blacker, depicts Philip Scouller (1946–2008) Tweseldown's most successful point-to-point jockey. Scouller was also a leading member of the campaign to save the site, which, in 2012, will be used as a training camp for the Great Britain equestrian team.

◀ In contrast with the praise heaped upon Britain for staging the 1948 Olympics in such testing circumstances, the performances of our 393 competitors in 138 events provided few grounds for self-congratulation. Great Britain's tally totalled just 23 medals, of which six were bronze, fourteen were silver and only three were gold.

At the time this poor showing was largely blamed on general war weariness and poor nutrition as a result of rationing. But in truth, Britain's final ranking of twelfth place in 1948 was not that much worse than the tenth place it had achieved in 1936, even if it was a huge comedown from its table-topping performance in 1908, which amounted to 146 medals, 56 of them gold.

Britain's three golds in 1948 were all won on the water, by Dickie Burnell and Bert Bushnell in the double sculls and Ran Laurie and Jack Wilson in the coxless pairs – both at Henley – and to yachtsmen David Bond and Stewart Morris in the swallow class, at Torbay. (Actually another Englishman, George Raynor, did win a gold, but that was as coach of the winning Swedish team in the football.)

Shown on this page at their actual size are two medals once belonging to cyclist **Dave Ricketts** from Totteridge, a member of the **Polytechnic Harriers Cycling Club**.

At the top is his bronze medal, won in the team pursuit at Herne Hill. Its design, by the Italian artist Giuseppe Cassioli, was the one originally adopted by the IOC for the Games of 1928, and used thereafter in both 1932 and 1936, but with the legend changed to read 'XIVth Olympiad London 1948'.

In the centre is Ricketts' commemorative medal, as presented to every competitor at the Games. This featured on its reverse side a rendition of the Houses of Parliament and, on the obverse side, Sir Bertram Mackennal's charioteer design from 1908.

Incidentally, all the commemorative medals in 1948 were made by the London firm of John Pinches Ltd, and had one of its staff been less honourable he would have earned one too. John Pinches, son of the proprietor, was himself a leading oarsman, and was invited to team up with Dickie Burnell in the double sculls at Henley. Pinches refused, however, believing that an open trial for the position should be held instead. Thus Bert Bushnell took his place, and of course went on to win the gold.

Also belonging to Dave Ricketts was the lapel badge on the left. Once again, every competitor received one, and was expected to wear it for identification purposes, and to carry an identity card. Ricketts' badge and card, as well as his medals, sundry correspondence and cuttings relating to 1948, are now held in the archives of the University of Westminster, and can be viewed on the *Winning Endeavours* website (*see Links*).

We complete our hunt for remnants from the 1948 Olympics at the new **Wembley Stadium**, where a number of artefacts are either on display or, pending the creation of a Wembley museum, held in the stadium archives.

This is the original moulded concrete pedestal and bowl in which the Olympic flame burned. Iconic in its simplicity, its designer unknown, the flame holder still contains the original butane-powered mechanism, which can be seen clearly on the front cover.

From the *Official Report* we learn that propane, as used at Berlin in 1936, would have been more suitable for the flame but was in short supply in post war Britain. Even then the authorities were careful not to use up their precious supply of butane. Thus the flame burned for only 70 or so hours throughout the Games, while during the time that the stadium lay empty only the pilot light remained lit. Failing to spot this faint glimmer, one newspaper reported that Wembley had run out of fuel and that, shockingly, the 'sacred' flame had gone out.

Immediately after the Games the pedestal and bowl were removed, only to reappear some years later on the exposed balcony between the twin towers when tours of the stadium started in 1977. Alongside was displayed a bust of the former Wembley chairman, Sir Arthur Elvin, gazing northwards up the length of the Olympic Way. As noted earlier, without Elvin's backing it is doubtful the Games could ever have taken place in London.

Following the closure of Wembley Stadium in 2000, the flame holder was placed in storage in a warehouse, where it was found a couple of years later in a parlous state by representatives of the newly formed Wembley National Stadium Ltd, who immediately sent it for restoration to Hirst Conservation of Lincolnshire.

Now, happily, it has a place of honour inside the vast lobby of the new stadium's main entrance where, fittingly, it faces at the far end of the lobby, the bust of Sir Arthur (also restored). Above the flame holder is a quote taken from Lord Burghley's speech at the 1948 opening ceremony, as reported on page 127.

▲ Wesley Taylor (*left*) and David Moulds of Wembley National Stadium Ltd, hold up the only **Olympic flag** known to have survived from the main events at Wembley.

This one is thought to have flown from one of the twin towers, and indeed was rediscovered, as the stadium was being cleared before demolition, inside a storeroom within one of the towers (along with other flags, banners and tape recordings of various foreign national anthems).

Rotting and bug infested, the Olympic flag has since been carefully restored by experts at the London company of Plowden and Smith.

As stated in the *Official Report* for 1948, strict protocol governed the display of flags. Nowhere were any national flags allowed to be larger than the main Olympic flags. Nor were any to be flown on higher poles.

Amongst other material relating to the 1948 Games now held in the Wembley Stadium archives are daily programmes, books of unused tickets, a starting pistol and correspondence between Sir Arthur Elvin and the Organising Committee, showing just how closely he watched over every detail, and also how confident he remained that the Games would not operate at a loss.

▲ Finally we come to perhaps the most venerated items of Britain's Olympic heritage from 1948, the two **Rolls of Honour**, seen here on the day of their unveiling by **Lord Burghley** at **Wembley Stadium** on April 14 1950. One photograph taken a few moments earlier (reproduced in the *Official Report*) shows the plaque on the left draped with an Olympic flag, perhaps the very one seen opposite.

The Rolls of Honour, listing the names of all 135 individuals and teams winning gold medals and the nations they represented, were mounted, as seen, on either side of the huge gates that marked the entry to the Royal Box.

Above, where the four buglers stand, was the terrace on which in later years the Olympic flame holder and the bust of Sir Arthur Elvin would be displayed.

So many major events took place at Wembley other than the 1948 Games – the 1966 World Cup, FA Cup finals, Rugby League finals and so on – that in time the two Olympic plaques became merely part of the Wembley furniture. Yet just once in a while one would see older men and women point up to this or that name, recalling memories of those extraordinary few weeks, when austerity Britain forgot its woes and welcomed the world.

American sprinter Harrison Dillard, known to his teammates as 'Bones', leads the Olympic Roll of Honour, now on display at the new Wembley Stadium.

Taking down the plaques from the old stadium in 2002 proved a major challenge. Exposed as they were on north facing walls, their condition had deteriorated considerably. Moreover, weighing 18 tons with their stone surrounds, each plaque consisted of nearly 250 embossed ceramic tiles.

Diamond cutters were used to cut out the plaques in one piece. They were then lifted by crane onto a flat bed truck. In case of damage, silicone impressions were made.

From Wembley the plaques were transported to a storage yard in Liverpool, and after that to Hirst Conservation of Lincolnshire, where they were painstakingly restored before being returned to the new stadium in 2011.

The plaques' designer, incidentally, was sculptor Hugh L Powell, while the tiles were glazed and fired by JF Walford.

▲ Having spent some £60,000 on the restoration of the two **Olympic Rolls of Honour**, Wembley National Stadium Ltd faced difficult choices as to where they might be displayed. They were too heavy to mount on any of the new stadium's existing load bearing walls, and in any case too delicate to risk being displayed in an upright position. At the same time it was imperative to place them in a sheltered spot where visitors to the stadium could see and appreciate them. Hence their current resting place, set at a slight angle, surrounded by protective barriers, on a covered concourse by the stadium's souvenir store.

The two plaques, flame holder and of course Olympic Way stand out as the three most tangible examples of Wembley's Olympic heritage. As we hope to have shown in this chapter, they and all the other remnants elsewhere enable us to piece together a strong sense of the Games' character and their place in the national story. Self evidently, austerity Britain had concerns that went far beyond those of considering an Olympic legacy. All the more reason, therefore, for us not only to make do with what fragmentary heritage survives, but also to ensure that it stays mended for future generations.

Chapter Eleven

Stoke Mandeville Games

Just as the Greek village of Olympia is known around the world for the Games that once took place in its vicinity, so the Buckinghamshire village of Stoke Mandeville is famous for its hospital and as the birthplace of the Paralympics (even though the hospital is just outside the village, on the edge of Aylesbury). Mentioned in the Domesday Book, the manor of Stoke acquired its current name during the mid 13th century, when it was held by a Geoffrey de Mandeville.

Of all the seismic shifts in social and cultural attitudes that shaped the history of sport in the 20th century, the most significant were those that contributed to the steady dismantling of barriers to universal participation; most notably those that affected class, gender and race.

But well into the second half of the century there persisted one other barrier that would prove just as resistant to change; the belief that people with physical disabilities should not be involved in competitive sport.

That in the early 21st century this is no longer the case, and that the Paralympics now form an inseparable and celebrated part of every modern Summer and Winter Olympic Games, is a development of which the Olympic movement can be justifiably proud.

It is, moreover, a development that, in common with so much of Olympic history, can be traced back to a British institution.

As we have already noted, Chipping Campden, Much Wenlock and Liverpool can each claim a special place in the back story of the modern Olympic Games. To this list we must now add Stoke Mandeville in Buckinghamshire, the undisputed birthplace of the Paralympics.

And it all started, modestly enough, with a bus.

On July 29 1948, the same day that the opening ceremony of the Olympic Games was taking place at Wembley Stadium, the Spinal Injuries Unit at Stoke Mandeville Hospital took formal delivery of a specially adapted single decker bus – a joint gift from the British Legion and London Transport – complete with its own wheelchair ramp.

To mark the presentation, the hospital hosted an archery competition between two teams of wheelchair-bound patients, one representing Stoke Mandeville Hospital, the other from the Star and Garter Home for ex-servicemen in Richmond, London.

Responsible for organising this contest, and for scheduling it quite deliberately on the same day as the opening ceremony at Wembley, was the director of the Spinal Injuries Unit, Dr Ludwig Guttmann.

As Robert Dover was to the Cotswold Olimpicks, William Penny Brookes to the Wenlock Olympian Games, and Pierre de Coubertin to the IOC, so Dr Guttmann was to the Paralympics. He was its instigator, its inspiration and, in its formative years, its driving force.

Guttmann was not the first person to recognise how individuals with disabilities might gain from sporting activity. In Britain alone, a team of deaf footballers had been formed in Glasgow as early as 1871. During the First World War, an organisation for blind ex-servicemen in London, called St Dunstan's, offered swimming, rowing, race walking, cycling and football as part of its socialisation and rehabilitation programmes. The formation of the British Society of One-Armed Golfers, in 1932, further demonstrated that physical disability need be no bar to sporting activity.

Patently the main impetus for developments at Stoke Mandeville was the Second World War. Although the number of casualties amongst British servicemen was not as high as it had been during the 1914–18 war, the number of survivors with disabilities was considerable. Unlike the previous conflict, this number included many civilian casualties, particularly victims of aerial bombing.

At the same time, advances in medicine meant that many of those who had suffered the trauma of sudden disability were able to live longer and more active lives than had previously been the case. For example, the availability of 'sulfa drugs' – or antibacterial sulfonamides, as developed during the 1930s by the German pharmaceutical company Bayer – helped save the lives of tens of thousands of people who might otherwise have died from streptococci, a common cause of blood and skin infection in patients immobilised after suffering from acute spinal injury. Before such drugs became available, most sufferers tended to be written off by the medical profession and, on average, given two years to live. Even so, those who were now able to survive longer could expect to lead only very limited lives, with few prospects of remedial treatment.

Guttmann's part in reversing this trend commenced in 1943. Born in Silesia in July 1899, he began his medical training in the city of Breslau (or Wroclaw as it was renamed after reverting to Polish rule in 1945), where he specialised in neurology and neurosurgery, and developed a further specialism in the rehabilitation and physiotherapy of people suffering from spinal injuries.

In common with all Jewish citizens under the Third Reich, Guttmann's professional and personal life became increasingly hampered by Nazi edicts. Already barred from treating non-Jewish patients, in November 1938 the destruction of the main synagogue in Breslau finally persuaded him to escape with his wife and two children.

Thanks to his international contacts within the Society for the Protection of Science and Learning, Guttmann managed to obtain the necessary visa for Britain, and in early 1939 he and his family were able to settle in Oxford, where he became a research fellow at the Nuffield Department of Neurosurgery at the Radcliffe Infirmary. There he managed to avoid the fate of many other German refugees, interned as aliens during the war, and even served as an air raid warden.

But it was his radical ideas in relation to the treatment of spinal injuries that really got him noticed. This led in 1941 to Guttmann being asked by Dr George Riddoch of the London Hospital to report on various case studies. Contrary to accepted practice, and leading on from tentative trials carried out in Boston by Dr Donald Munro, Guttmann argued that instead of being kept immobile, patients should be encouraged to move, and to develop as much independence as possible.

Encouraged by what he saw, in late 1943 Riddoch asked Guttmann to leave the Nuffield and, under the jurisdiction of the Ministries of Health and of Pensions, to set up a specialist unit dedicated solely to spinal injuries. To have selected a German for such a role was, at the time, a highly sensitive matter, not least because so many of his patients were servicemen returning from the battlefields of Europe. But it was a challenge that Guttmann relished.

Two sites were considered, at Basingstoke in Hampshire and the preferred option, Stoke Mandeville, conveniently situated next to the Great Central Railway line linking London with Aylesbury and the East Midlands. There had been a hospital there since the 1830s, when the parishes of Aylesbury and Stoke Mandeville had combined to set up an isolation hospital for sufferers from cholera. In fact, it had maintained that role, catering for such diseases as scarlet fever, and had a range of recently constructed buildings designed by the local architectural firm of Collcutt & Hamp.

Come the outbreak of war in September 1939, however, in common with so many British hospitals these facilities were taken over by the War Office, and supplemented by an additional range of basic, prefabricated timber huts, each with room for 26 beds.

Guttmann took up his new post in early 1944, and with a small budget, two nurses and eight orderlies, set about converting one of these huts, Ward X, into the new Spinal Injuries Unit. As Susan Goodman shows in her book on Stoke Mandeville (see Links), Guttmann stated that the Unit's basic aim 'was to provide a comprehensive ≫

Heavy wheelchairs with poor manoeuvrability severely limited the options for early pioneers of disabled sport, seen above at Stoke Mandeville in the late 1940s. But if anyone could push for progress it was Ludwig Guttmann (*left*). To many patients he was affectionately known as 'Poppa'. Even his name translated as 'good man'. Yet to achieve all that he did, not only with patients but also in dealing with sceptics within the medical and sporting professions, Guttmann often had to show his tougher side.

On the left, from the first issue of *The Cord*, the Journal of the Paraplegic Branch of the British Legion, is the adapted bus being delivered to Stoke Mandeville in July 1948.

Major Sir Brunel Cohen, who had lost both his legs at the Battle of Ypres during the First World War, made the presentation.

» paraplegia and tetraplegia service to rescue these men, women and children from the human scrapheap and return most of them, in spite of permanent, profound disability – by clinical measures and psychological adjustment – to a life worth living, as useful and respected citizens in the community'.

This is where sport came in. Many of the patients were young, and had been physically active before their trauma. Most came from the armed forces, where games and team spirit, and obeying orders, were part of the culture. Guttmann's caring but firm attitude, therefore, suited the hospital's ethos perfectly. Demanding complete control of his unit, he never shrank from yelling at patients who were not doing as they were told.

As 1944 drew to an end – by which time the unit had admitted men evacuated directly from the Normandy beaches – Guttmann, his staff and selected patients were already experimenting with various games designed to supplement the physiotherapy and occupational therapy classes, such as in woodwork, that were routinely on offer. Not all of these experiments were successful. For example, when Army instructor Thomas Hill and a group of patients tried out a form of wheelchair polo they found the chairs too unwieldy and that players kept toppling over. Rather more successful as a team game were trials with basketball, together with individual games such as skittles, snooker and darts.

But it was archery that would form the competition on that historic day in July 1948. Stoke Mandeville was at that time under the control of the Ministry of Pensions, whose minister, Hilary Marquand, the MP for Cardiff East, attended as guest of honour. (Not until 1951 would control of the hospital pass to the new National Health Service, itself launched also in July 1948.)

As noted earlier, patients from the Star and Garter in Richmond formed the opposition, in a tournament that involved fourteen men and two women, most of whom had sustained their injuries in the course of military duties. For the record, the visitors won. But more important was that Guttmann and his team had demonstrated to an outside world otherwise engaged with the Olympic Games, that being in a wheelchair need not stop an individual from taking part in competitive sport. These early archers proved that people with spinal injuries could and would compete in sport if only given the appropriate training and support.

Under the headline 'Games for Paralysed', *The Times* of July 30 described the event as a 'most surprising' and 'unusual display of toxophily'. The 'two teams of spinal-paralysis patients... shot their arrows with remarkable and consistent accuracy, while seated in their self-propelled chairs'. Other sports to be found at the hospital were listed as darts, billiards, snooker, polo, skittles, badminton and netball, all of which, Dr Guttmann was quoted as saying, could be played at a competitive level by individuals in wheelchairs.

As well he proved. Spurred on by the response from the press and the patients, Guttmann and his team resolved to turn the competition into an annual event for all-comers. From sixteen entrants in 1948, the roster for the second Games in July 1949 attracted 60 individuals, most of whom had spent at least part of their rehabilitation at Stoke Mandeville, but who now represented seven units and care homes spread around the country.

Two sports were added to the 1949 programme; netball, and 'dartchery', in which arrows were fired at a target more akin to a dart board (*see opposite*).

Guttmann, who had been naturalised as a British citizen at the end of the war, called this 1949 event the

WITH MY BOW AND ARROW

As reported by the *Bucks Advertiser* on August 6 1948 (*top right*) – the day that Fanny Blankers-Koen won the third of her four gold medals at Wembley Stadium – the first organised competition at Stoke Mandeville was confined to archery.

A year later, in its edition of July 29 1949 (*right*) the *Advertiser* returned to the hospital and, picking up on Guttmann's speech, delivered its own prescient headline.

"Olympic Games" Of Disabled Men Is Born At Stoke

INCIDENTS IN A CINEMA

Court Confirms Prison Sentence

"Horrible and despicable," was how Mr. A. H. Hulton described a series of offences against young girls that have brought a six-months prison sentence on 64-years-old Harold Andrew MacJerie, Chalfont St. Peter house

WHEELCHAIR ATHLETES

A FORERUNNER to what its organiser hopes will be the equivalent of the Olympic Games for disabled men and women of the whole world was held at Stoke Mandeville Ministry of Pensions Hospital on Wednesday.

Last year the two spinal units, the Star and Garter Home at Richmond and the Stoke Mande-ville unit took part in an archery

putting up a fine show among nine burly men.

The medals, and a shield for the netball were designed and made by patients in the precision

Grand Festival of Paraplegic Sport. But in his speech he made it clear that he harboured wider ambitions. With his customary brio, he looked forward, he announced, to the Stoke Mandeville Games becoming famous throughout the world as the 'paraplegic equivalent to the Olympic Games'.

Stoke Mandeville goes international

Guttmann was as good as his word. At the 1952 Stoke Mandeville Games a Dutch team from the Military Rehabilitation Centre at Aardenburg became the first contestants from overseas. Fourteen nations competed in 1954. By the Games' eleventh year, in July 1959, the number of entrants had risen to 360 from 20 teams, while the number of sports had increased to eleven, including athletics, fencing, snooker, table tennis, weightlifting and swimming in the hospital's new purpose-built pool.

The event was now spread over three days and went under various names. Formally it was the Stoke Mandeville Games. Informally it was also known as the 'Paraplegic Olympics' and even, in the summer 1951 issue of *The Cord*, the British Legion magazine for paraplegics, as the 'Paralympiad'.

Throughout the decade, Guttmann worked tirelessly to raise money for Stoke Mandeville, so that the Games no longer had to take place on spare patches of tarmac around the hospital site. His courting of celebrity athletes also ensured wider press coverage. Roger Bannister, famous for his four minute mile in 1954 but soon to be making his name also as a neurologist, gave out the prizes at the 1955 Games. He was followed in 1956 by the New Zealand surgeon Arthur Porritt, who had won a bronze in the 100 metres at the 1924 Olympic Games, but rather more significantly was a member of the IOC.

At that time the IOC made an annual award, known after its donor as the Sir Thomas Fearnley Cup, to an amateur sports club or association that had made a particular contribution to the Olympic movement. The trophy's award to the Stoke Mandeville Games in 1956 represented a significant landmark in Guttmann's long term ambitions.

Three years later these were further advanced by the formation of an International Stoke Mandeville Games Committee, made up of representatives from Great Britain, Belgium, France, the Netherlands and Italy.

The ISMGC's aim was to establish a four year cycle to echo that of the Olympics, with Games held annually at Stoke Mandeville for three years, interspersed with larger Games on the fourth year, held elsewhere.

So it was that, assisted by lobbying from the World Veterans Association, the Italian authorities agreed to »

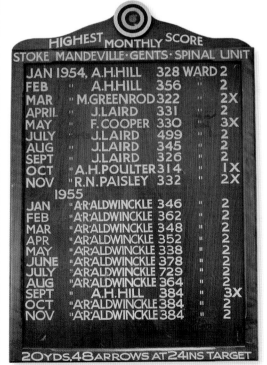

Dartchery practice at Stoke Mandeville during the 1950s, on the field where the athletics track is now sited. Note the evolving design of wheelchairs and wheel configurations.

Few artefacts and none of the original buildings from this period have survived, so this recently discovered honours board from the inter-ward dartchery contest (*left*) is of special interest.

HIGHEST MONTHLY SCORE
STOKE MANDEVILLE · GENTS · SPINAL UNIT

JAN 1954, A.H.HILL	328 WARD	2
FEB " A.H.HILL	356	" 2
MAR " M.GREENROD	322	" 2X
APRIL " J.LAIRD	331	" 2
MAY " F.COOPER	330	" 3X
JULY " J.LAIRD	499	" 2
AUG " J.LAIRD	345	" 2
SEPT " J.LAIRD	326	" 2
OCT " A.H.POULTER	314	" 1X
NOV " R.N.PAISLEY	332	" 2X
1955		
JAN " A·R·ALDWINCKLE	346	" 2
FEB " A·R·ALDWINCKLE	362	" 2
MAR " A·R·ALDWINCKLE	348	" 2
APR " A·R·ALDWINCKLE	352	" 2
MAY " A·R·ALDWINCKLE	338	" 2
JUNE " A·R·ALDWINCKLE	378	" 2
JULY " A·R·ALDWINCKLE	729	" 2
AUG " A·R·ALDWINCKLE	364	" 2
SEPT " A.H.HILL	384	" 3X
OCT " A·R·ALDWINCKLE	384	" 2
NOV " A·R·ALDWINCKLE	384	" 2

20YDS. 48 ARROWS AT 24 INS TARGET

Whether annually at Stoke Mandeville (*above*), or overseas every four years, as in Tokyo in 1964 (*right*), the Stoke Mandeville Games grew every year. Twenty three nations were represented at Rome in 1960, rising to 41 in Tokyo, four years later. At that stage only paraplegics competed, as indicated on the programme cover and by the logo of the newly formed International Sports Organization for the Disabled (ISOD). This has since been renamed the International Paralympic Committee and is based in Germany. However Stoke Mandeville remains the home of the International Wheelchair and Amputee Sports Federation.

» the ISMGC's proposal to stage what were effectively the world's first Paralympics, in form if not in name, in September 1960, a week after the Rome Olympics.

At that early stage the IOC had yet to give the initiative its blessing. Hence, wherever the Games were staged in the world, their official title remained the 'Stoke Mandeville Games'. Incongruous though this might now seem, it was hardly different from naming the Olympic Games after Olympia. The retention of the Stoke Mandeville name also reflected Guttmann's influence.

Nevertheless, informally the Games were equally referred to as the 'Wheelchair Olympics', or as the 'Paraplegic Games'. It was also during this period that the term 'paralympic' gained currency. Having been coined, it is believed, during the 1950s, it made its first international appearance at Tokyo in 1964, on handmade signs welcoming competitors at the airport.

THE THIRTEENTH INTERNATIONAL STOKE MANDEVILLE GAMES FOR THE PARALYSED

8th-12th November, 1964   TOKYO

The early Games did not always take place in the same city, or even the same country, as that year's Summer Olympics. After Rome in 1960 and Tokyo in 1964, Mexico City in 1968 felt unable to oblige, so the Games were staged in Tel Aviv instead. Four years later, while the main Olympics were staged in Munich, the Stoke Mandeville Games took place 200 miles away in Heidelberg. Similarly in 1976, while the Summer Olympics were in Montreal, the Stoke Mandeville Games were in Toronto. Arnhem in Holland played host in 1980 (instead of Moscow), while in 1984 the event was split between New York (rather than Los Angeles) and Stoke Mandeville itself.

Finally in Seoul in 1988, for the first time the IOC's Olympics and the Stoke Mandeville Games were held not only in the same city, but also in predominantly the same venues, a practice that has continued ever since, and has, since 2001, become a requirement for all host cities.

The Seoul Games in 1988 were also the first at which the title 'Paralympics' was officially endorsed.

Meanwhile, in 1976 a winter programme for disabled athletes was started in Örnsköldsvik, Sweden, and this too established a four year cycle that has run in parallel with the Winter Olympic Games ever since.

One other development worth noting from this period was the gradual broadening of disabled sport's reach. Until the 1976 Stoke Mandeville Games in Toronto, only entrants in wheelchairs competed. Since then, six categories have emerged: for individuals in wheelchairs, for amputees, for the visually impaired, for those with cerebral palsy, for those with intellectual disabilities, and a final category known collectively, if somewhat awkwardly, as *les autres*, or 'the others', to include those with disabilities (such as dwarfism, multiple sclerosis and congenital deformities) that do not fall within the other five categories.

Stoke Mandeville develops

Mirroring the success of the movement overseas were developments back at Stoke Mandeville, where annual Games, both national and international, continued to be staged. In 1961 Guttmann helped to form the British Sports Association for the Disabled. Also during the 1960s the unit at Stoke Mandeville was officially recognised as the National Spinal Injuries Unit. Whereas in the 1940s its staff had treated mainly ex-servicemen and women, increasingly they were dealing with civilians injured on the sports field or in road accidents.

As for Guttmann, having been knighted in 1966, he finally retired as the Centre's director in 1967, although his workaholic tendencies meant that he devoted much of his time to negotiations with the Ministry of Health concerning the planning, funding and construction of the world's first purpose-built sports centre for disabled athletes at Stoke Mandeville. By this time the hospital, originally, it will be recalled, an isolation unit built in a rural setting, had found itself absorbed within the expanding outer districts of Aylesbury.

Construction of the new £350,000 sports centre, located on the former playing fields between the main hospital and the railway line, started in 1968, funded by public subscriptions and grants from central and local government. At its heart was a multi-purpose indoor sports hall, hardly different from any other of its time except for the fact that it was designed to be fully accessible for people in wheelchairs. Nowadays such accessibility forms a legal requirement under the Disability Discrimination Act, first passed in 1995. In the late 1960s, however, this was an area in which architects, particularly those operating in the field of sport and leisure, had little experience.

The centre's main hall accommodated archery, badminton, basketball and volleyball. Other spaces within the centre were designed for fencing, table tennis, snooker and weight lifting. There was also a 25m six lane swimming pool and a two lane tenpin bowling alley.

Named the Stoke Mandeville Sports Stadium for the Paralysed and Other Disabled, the facility was officially opened by Queen Elizabeth on August 2 1969. The timing was significant, for it marked the 21st anniversary of that first archery competition in July 1948.

Over the ensuing years, a number of additions and improvements were made to the centre. Various fundraisers and donors contributed to the costs, most famously the disc jockey Jimmy Savile, who also volunteered as a porter at the hospital. Less high profile events arranged by staff, patients and friends included a fish and chip supper with music from paraplegic band The Paratones, and several bring-and-buy sales organised by the Jewish Ladies Guild.

In 1971 a 400 metre athletics track was laid on the former playing field next to the main centre. This was joined in September 1974 by the Lady Guttmann Indoor Bowls Centre. Having supported her husband's work and the cause of disabled sport throughout their years together in Britain, Else Guttmann had died the previous year, in December 1973, having never regained consciousness following a car crash in 1972.

Guttmann himself lived on in a bungalow in nearby Aylesbury until his death at the age of 80 in March 1980, after which the complex was renamed the Ludwig Guttmann Sports Centre for the Disabled – Stoke Mandeville.

As the number of athletes and the range of sports increased throughout the 1960s, the demand grew for modern, purpose-built facilities at Stoke Mandeville. Seen above is basketball action from the 1964 National Games, with two of the original wartime huts in the background. None survive. On the left, Ludwig Guttmann studies an early model of his pet project.

The 1984 Games and beyond

In the two previous chapters we learnt how London twice stepped into the breach when it came to hosting the Olympic Games of 1908 and 1948. In 1984 it was Stoke Mandeville's turn to help out at short notice.

As noted earlier, the Summer Olympics that year were held in Los Angeles, but owing to various funding and political obstacles the disability groups in the USA that were affiliated to the International Stoke Mandeville Games Federation decided to stage their games in New York and Champaign, Illinois, instead. »

▲ In order to celebrate the opening of the new **Stoke Mandeville Sports Stadium for the Paralysed and Other Disabled** in 1969, a series of postcards was commissioned during the early 1970s. Since that time all the buildings have been substantially remodelled, so images such as these form a vital part of what is now a growing archive documenting the history and evolution of disabled sport in Britain since 1948.

Not least, once again, we see how wheelchair design continued to evolve during this period, not only to make life easier for everyday use, but also to improve sporting performance. For example, modern day bowlers at Stoke Mandeville, several of whom play for the local club alongside able-bodied members, can now use lightweight wheelchairs designed specifically for bowling, with roller-like main wheels balanced by smaller plastic wheels at the rear, and with a tilting footplate that makes it easier for the bowler to lean forward to play.

Note the presence in their official blazers of Ludwig Guttmann and his wife Else (*above*), this being shortly before the road accident that would bring a tragic end to their long and successful partnership.

» Those in New York, involving athletes in four categories of disabled sport, went ahead in June 1984. President Ronald Reagan opened the Games, and over thirteen days a total of 80,000 spectators watched some 1,800 athletes from 45 countries in action. For the first time the major television networks were also on hand.

However, preparations by the co-hosts in Illinois met with funding problems, and so, with just four months to go, it was decided to stage the wheelchair events at the spiritual home of the sport, Stoke Mandeville.

In terms of sports facilities, the site was already well equipped. Accommodating 1,100 athletes and a further 500 officials from 41 countries was an altogether trickier challenge. There was a small residential block next to the main centre, opened in 1981 and later renamed rather grandly the 'Olympic Village'. But for the bulk of the accommodation the organisers had to emulate their 1948 counterparts by making the best use of whatever they could find. Extra beds for athletes were thus found in the hospital, at a local agricultural college and RAF Halton, while Ryecote College in Thame and other nearby schools took in most of the visiting officials.

On July 22, three weeks after the New York Games had ended, Terry Willet of the British team carried the Olympic torch into the Stoke Mandeville stadium, using a special attachment to fix it to his wheelchair, before Prince Charles declared the Games open. The event was watched by an estimated 3,000 spectators, the largest crowd yet to have gathered at the Stoke Mandeville track.

What followed over the next ten days was a far cry from the early days at Stoke Mandeville. Ten sports were featured: archery, athletics, basketball, fencing, bowls, powerlifting, shooting, snooker, swimming and table tennis. There was also a marathon, starting at Chalfont St Peter and ending in the stadium.

But if the 1984 Games represented a high point in the story of Stoke Mandeville, it was also a watershed. As we noted earlier, from Seoul in 1988 onwards all subsequent Paralympics would take place in one city, immediately after the IOC's Summer Olympics. This meant that Stoke Mandeville would never again host the Paralympics. The event had outgrown its roots.

This growth was reflected also in the changing nature of the administration of disabled sport. Because of the various difficulties faced by the organisers in the run up to the 1984 Games, in 1982 it was decided that for future Paralympics a more co-ordinated approach would be needed at international level. Hence the International Stoke Mandeville Games Federation merged with three other international federations to form a single body called the International Coordinating Committee of »

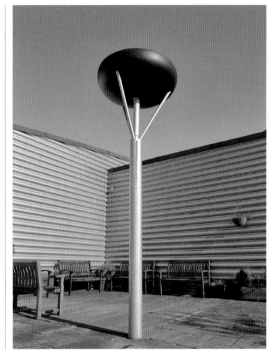

Wherever you turn at Stoke Mandeville there are reminders of the site's history, with virtually every building sporting one plaque or another detailing when that particular facility was opened and how it was funded.

Positioned outside the Indoor Bowls Centre (*left*) is the tall, slender torch which Terry Willet lit to signal the start of the 1984 Paralympics.

Not far from this, the Olympic Lodge (*below left*) is used extensively to accommodate wheelchair athletes and amputees attending events and training programmes at Stoke Mandeville.

And of course one is never far from a reminder of the man who started it all. Just outside the hospital is a residential road named in honour of Ludwig Guttmann. His portrait may also be seen hanging in the reception.

'If I ever did one good thing in my medical career,' Guttmann is quoted underneath, 'it was to introduce sport into the rehabilitation of disabled people.'

Commissioned and funded by the Poppa Guttmann Project (*see Links*) this is a clay model of a bronze statue to be unveiled outside the Stoke Mandeville Stadium in June 2012 and then sited permanently by the entrance to the National Spinal Injuries Centre.

Sculpted by the artist Jacko, it is designed so that people in wheelchairs can position their shoulder under Poppa's outstretched arm, a gesture that Guttmann often adopted when comforting and encouraging his patients.

›› World Organizations for the Disabled (ICC). In 1989 this became the International Paralympic Committee (IPC), with its base in Bonn.

Not that Stoke Mandeville has been left behind. In April 2003 Prince Charles returned to re-open the facility after a major three year refurbishment and expansion of the site that cost £10.2 million, half funded by the National Lottery, with the rest coming from Aylesbury Vale District Council and charitable donations.

Renamed the Stoke Mandeville Stadium and with a new track and fitness centre added to the existing bowls centre, swimming pool and sports hall, it is in regular use by all sectors of the community, disabled and able-bodied. Thus while Paralympians are training in one part of the site, elsewhere there may well be hospital staff using the gym and schoolchildren in the pool. However, the needs of disabled athletes remain paramount and the centre as a whole is run by a charity, Wheelpower.

Also on the site, based in the Olympic Lodge, is the International Wheelchair and Amputee Sports Federation. This body was formed in 2004 following the merger of the International Stoke Mandeville Wheelchair Sports Federation, formed by Guttmann in 1952, with the International Sports Organisation for the Disabled, which Guttmann helped establish in 1961.

Meanwhile, in the sport centre's main reception is a Roll of Honour. Only four names are so far inscribed, although no doubt in time this number will increase.

Ludwig Guttmann, naturally, heads the list. He is followed by Cardiff-born Tanni Grey-Thompson. Born with spina bifida, she won sixteen Paralympic medals between 1988 and 2004. Then there is Carol 'Caz' Walton, ten time Paralympic medallist in five sports.

The final name is that of Philip Craven. Confined to a wheelchair at the age of sixteen after a mountaineering accident, Craven went on to represent Britain in basketball at five Paralympics and, since 2001, has served as president of the International Paralympic Committee. As well as filling the role once filled by Guttmann, Craven is one of the most senior and respected British representatives in the higher echelons of the Olympic movement, serving as a member of the IOC since 2003.

As for the 2012 Paralympics, Stoke Mandeville is too small to host any events, but it will serve as a training centre for the British Paralympic team. Its contribution to the Olympic story has also been recognised by the name 'Mandeville' being given to one of the official mascots.

One other benefit of the 2012 Paralympics being staged in London is that a number of organisations have started the important task of cataloguing and conserving the various archives and collections relating to Stoke Mandeville and the early Paralympic movement. These parties include Stoke Mandeville Hospital, Wheelpower, the Buckinghamshire County Archives, the Wellcome Trust Library (which holds several boxes of Guttmann's own archive) and the Guttmann family itself.

The Special Olympics and definitions of Olympism

That the IOC eventually widened its embrace to take in competitors with physical disabilities is yet another part of the Olympic story that emanates from Britain.

Yet even though its origins lie elsewhere, one other Olympic event deserves mention.

Established in the United States during the 1960s, the Special Olympics is an event for people with learning disabilities, another category of individuals that the early leaders of the Olympic movement would never have considered able to compete at international level.

During its formative years the event's organisers, led by Eunice Kennedy Shriver, lobbied hard to secure recognition. They succeeded, and as a result the Special Olympics is the only event outside the jurisdiction of the IOC to be officially sanctioned to use the 'Olympic' tag.

As chronicled by Susan Barton (*see Links*), the first international version of these Special Olympics was held in 1968, with quadrennial games being staged since 1975, and a parallel winter programme running from 1977.

Supporting this movement in Britain, Special Olympics UK was formed in 1978, and as well as sending teams to the international games, has organised national events since 1982, with Leicester the most recent host, in 2009.

That summer, on their way to Leicester, runners participating in the Special Olympic's torch relay, known as the Flame of Hope, called in at the Wenlock Olympian Games, where they were greeted by local officials and special guests, including three British Olympians, Tommy Godwin, Ann Packer and Robbie Brightwell.

Of all the celebrations held to mark the build up to the 2012 Games, surely none has managed to bring together in one place so many of the old and new manifestations of modern-day Olympism. The Special Olympics demonstrate, as do the Paralympics, that modern Olympism has evolved, and that the Olympic ideal can be interpreted by outside organisations in ways that need not clash with the primary aims of the IOC.

How this story will develop in the 21st century we cannot say. But as the efforts of Ludwig Guttmann and his staff at Stoke Mandeville so ably demonstrated, Olympism must always adapt to the needs, ambitions and sensibilities of those who see sport as a force for good and for personal development, whoever and wherever they may be.

▲ The **Stoke Mandeville Stadium** may no longer be a Paralympic venue, but it is used by some 500,000 people annually (of which around 20 per cent are disabled), and hosts regular national and international events.

Above is the sports hall, in use for the **Women's European Wheelchair Basketball Championships** in August 2009, and, above right, the outdoor track, shown during a **'Mini Games'** staged for young hopefuls by **Disability Sport Events**, a division of the English Federation of Disability Sport, in May 2009.

Both images were taken by **Graham Bool**, who played basketball for Britain at three Paralympics, in 1972, 1976 and 1980, before becoming a professional photographer, in which guise he covered every Paralympics from Barcelona in 1992 to Beijing in 2008. Much admired by all in the Paralympic movement, Bool, who had contracted polio as a child, died in 2010, at the age of 62.

The family name will live on in photographic circles, however, for the image of the **Inter Spinal Unit swimming competition** at Stoke Mandeville in April 2011 was taken by Roger Bool, who continues his father's pioneering work by documenting disability sport across Britain.

Mandeville the mascot makes an appearance outside the London 2012 outlet at London's St Pancras International station.

Chapter Twelve

British Olympians

Olympian hopefuls riding at the National Cycling Centre in Manchester can hardly miss this bronze statue created by James Butler, or fail to be inspired by its subject. Reg Harris (1920–92) was expected to win three gold medals at the 1948 Olympics. But the Bury-born racer suffered a serious road accident three months beforehand, then broke his elbow. Yet still he managed two silvers. Then in 1974 Harris reclaimed the British title... at the age of 54.

As this book has sought to demonstrate, over the last four centuries Britain has contributed to the wider Olympic story in a number of ways and from an assortment of locations. Our Olympic heritage is rich, and unique. But it is also fragmented.

We have shown how artefacts and documents from various Olympic Games have been scattered amongst a range of archives and collections. We have seen how few Olympic-related buildings survive from 1908, and how several of those that survive from 1948 display no evidence at all of their Olympic connections.

There is, however, one area in which the British have, at least in recent years, shown demonstrable enthusiasm for celebrating our Olympic heritage, and that is in the commemoration of individual sportsmen and women.

Compared with other nations, the British have traditionally shown a marked reluctance to name places, buildings, parks or streets after individuals, at least other than senior members of the military, aristocracy and royalty. Whereas the Paris Metro has numerous stations named after individuals, such as Victor Hugo, Alexandre Dumas and Pablo Picasso, the London Underground has just one, Victoria, and only then because it serves the mainline railway terminus of the same name.

Similarly in sport. Whereas stadiums named after individuals are common overseas – Madrid's Bernabeu Stadium being one of the best known – in Britain they remained rare throughout most of the 20th century, and confined mostly to smaller club grounds, such as The Stoop (named after Harlequins player Adrian Stoop). Naming sections of grounds after individuals was also once unusual, the Grace Gates at Lord's cricket ground, named after WG Grace in 1922, being an early 20th century exception. Even Lord's – which takes its name from the leaseholder of the original site, Thomas Lord – was named for business reasons rather than as a tribute.

That said, since the latter years of the 20th century this reluctance to name stadiums, grandstands and sports centres after individuals has receded. During the same period we have also witnessed a rise in the number of streets, plaques, statues and memorials commemorating popular heroes from the sporting world.

Partly this trend can be attributed to the growing democratisation of heritage, a trend that has seen not only sportsmen and women but also actors, comedians and musicians commemorated in various forms; for example, the John Lennon Airport in Liverpool, dedicated in 2001. The trend may also be viewed as a sign of how sport itself has become increasingly aware of its heritage and more confident of its role in our national story.

Nor can we overlook the potential of sporting commemorations to act as magnets for tourism.

But whatever the cause or effect, we are certainly witnessing an increase, and one that has been particularly evident in relation to the celebration of British Olympians.

There is, it must be stated, no official body responsible for overseeing these dedications. As with other aspects of Britain's Olympic heritage the approach has been piecemeal, with bodies such as English Heritage (in its blue plaque scheme for London), local authorities, sports clubs, educational institutions and voluntary groups all proceeding on a case-by-case basis.

Inevitably some choices have prompted debate. Is it appropriate to name a building after someone who is still alive? Do certain types of commemoration amount to tokenism? Yet these caveats notwithstanding, the commemoration of Britain's Olympians does matter, if mainly for what it tells us about ourselves and our times.

For unlike, say, high-earning professional footballers or tennis aces, whom we follow all year round but who often appear remote, an Olympian may come to the fore meaningfully only once every four years. The rest of the time they could be our neighbours or fellow members of our local sports club. There is also a sense that those picked out for commemoration have been chosen not merely for their medals, but for their wider contribution to society, for their impact as role models, and even, it has to be acknowledged, for their personalities. Modesty and affability are great assets in a British Olympian.

The individuals featured in this chapter are of all ages, colours and creeds. They include a lawyer and a railwayman, a politician and a salesman, a missionary and a swimming pool attendant.

But whoever they are, or were, the consequences of them being commemorated are real enough. They become, in the process, part of our national heritage, of that centuries old link we referred to at the start of this book, between Britannia and Olympia.

▲ This endearing if somewhat crude example of Edwardian cut-and-paste is one of the earliest known celebrations of Olympians to have been issued in Britain. It is also an early example of a British company seeking to exploit the Olympics for commercial gain.

Held by the National Archives, the collage was put together after the **1908 Games** by **Gamage's**, a store on London's Holborn which branded itself as the 'People's Popular Emporium' and was well known for its range of sporting goods. Gold medallists from all nations are represented and numbered – a key to their identity featured underneath – with the British athletes given no particular prominence. This, and the portrayal of the Irish 'harp' flag may have owed less to Gamage's sense of fairness than to their hopes for healthy international sales, mail order being a large part of their business.

Also represented are some of the public's favourite characters from the 1908 Games, such as William Knightsmith, the London toastmaster, and the female Danish gymnasts, whose displays had formed such a talking point (amongst male spectators at least).

The Stadium itself is represented rather less accurately, with the far stand bearing the slogan 'Gamage For Sport Outfits', a slogan that of course did not appear in reality.

We need to look elsewhere for commemorations of those 1908 Olympians who competed away from the Stadium. One such was **Dorothea Lambert Chambers**, who won a gold in the women's lawn tennis singles, but who was rather better known for winning the Wimbledon title on seven occasions. This English Heritage blue plaque (*right*) was unveiled at her former home at **7 North Common Road, Ealing**, in west London, in July 2005.

ENGLISH HERITAGE
DOROTHEA
LAMBERT
CHAMBERS
1878-1960
Lawn Tennis
Champion
lived here
1887-1907

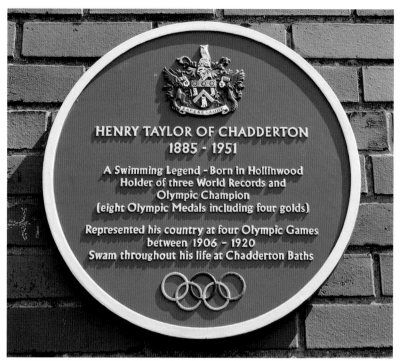

HENRY TAYLOR OF CHADDERTON
1885 - 1951

A Swimming Legend - Born in Hollinwood
Holder of three World Records and
Olympic Champion
(eight Olympic Medals including four golds)

Represented his country at four Olympic Games
between 1906 - 1920
Swam throughout his life at Chadderton Baths

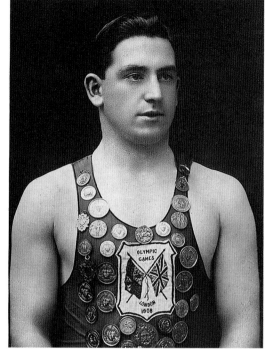

▲ When **Henry Taylor** from Chadderton, near Oldham, paraded his honours in 1908, and was carried shoulder-high after winning a third gold medal in the Great Stadium (*as seen left*) – a British record for a single Games matched only by the cyclist Chris Hoy a century later – he cannot have imagined how low he would one day sink.

The son of a coalminer, as a child Taylor swam in the Hollinwood Canal, and continued to do so during his breaks once he started work in an Oldham cotton mill. Eventually he began serious training at Chadderton Baths, going on to break three world records and win a string of medals at the Games in 1906, 1908, 1912 and 1920. In between the last two he served in the Royal Navy, legend having it that during the Battle of Jutland in 1916 he saved many lives by swimming in the freezing waters, assisting crewmen whose ships had been sunk. True or not, his later attempt to become a publican failed, and he was forced to eke out a living as an attendant at Chadderton Baths and eventually, to sell all his medals.

In 2002 the plaque seen here was erected at Chadderton Baths; a salutary reminder of how, in the days before professionalism was finally sanctioned, for working class sportsmen, Olympian acclaim offered only a fleeting reward. Taylor died penniless, and alone, in 1951.

▶ Surpassed only by the achievements of Steve Redgrave and Matthew Pinsent, Britain's greatest Olympic rower during the inter-war period was **Jack Beresford**, seen here at his fifth and final Olympiad, at Berlin in 1936 where, much to the annoyance of Adolf Hitler in the stands, he won the double sculls for Britain with Dick Southwood.

Beresford was the son of Julius Wiszniewski from Danzig (present day Gdansk), a furniture manufacturer in London's east end who, as Julius Beresford, rowed for Great Britain at the Stockholm Olympics in 1912. Initially Jack favoured rugby, but after being wounded in battle in 1918 he joined his father's club, the Thames Rowing Club, based in Putney, and went to work in the family business.

His first Olympic medal was a silver in the sculls at Antwerp in 1920. He then went on to win medals in the next four Olympic Games before retiring from competition and, like so many Olympians, becoming a member of various sporting bodies, the British Olympic Council included. It was in this last capacity that he was involved in the organisation of the 1948 Games.

On the far right is the blue plaque unveiled by English Heritage in 2005 at **19 Grove Park Road, Chiswick**, the house in which Beresford lived for much of his early life.

Another Olympic rower honoured with a plaque is **William Duthie Kinnear** (1880–1974). Born in Aberdeenshire, 'Wally', as he was known, moved to London in 1902 to work in Debenhams department store, where workmates introduced to him rowing. Kinnear then collected titles at Henley in 1910 and 1911, before winning a gold in the single sculls at Stockholm in 1912.

The plaque in his honour (*right*) is displayed on the boathouse of the **Kensington Rowing Club**, on **Lower Mall, Hammersmith**, where he was a member for 69 years, and where artefacts from his Olympic triumph are still treasured, a century after the event.

Known to her family as Biddy but to the sporting public as Kitty, **Kathleen Godfree** combined an impressive record in grand slam tournaments with a haul of five Olympic medals. She brought home three from Antwerp in 1920 – a gold in the women's doubles, a silver in the mixed doubles and a bronze in the singles – to which she added a silver in the doubles and a bronze in the singles at Paris in 1924. The English Heritage blue plaque shown here was unveiled at her home at **55 York Avenue, East Sheen**, in south west London, in 2006.

The third English Heritage blue plaque on this page commemorates **Philip Noel-Baker**, a runner who gained greater renown for his later work in politics and foreign affairs than for his prowess on the track.

As Philip Baker – he added the Noel after his marriage in 1915 – he ran for Great Britain in the 1912 Olympics,

and at the 1920 Games in Antwerp won silver in the 1500 metres. Thereafter he focused on politics, including a spell as a Labour MP, and on campaigning for disarmament, while continuing to work for various sporting bodies, particularly during the 1948 Olympics and as the founder of the International Council for Sport and Physical Recreation. In 1959, he was awarded the Nobel Peace Prize, a fitting tribute to a man who embodied Coubertin's idealistic vision of the Olympic spirit. The plaque seen here is located at his London home, at **16 South Eaton Place** in Westminster.

The son of a Lithuanian migrant and the younger brother of Olympic athlete Solly Abrahams, Harold Abrahams won the 100m at Paris in 1924, before pursuing a career in the law, as a broadcaster and in athletics administration. The blue plaque at 2 Hodford Road, Golders Green, in London, was unveiled in 2007.

▲ Two of Britain's most celebrated Olympians of the inter-war years were the runners **Harold Abrahams** (*above left*) and **Eric Liddell**, seen here being feted at his graduation ceremony at Edinburgh University in July 1924, shortly after his return from the Paris Olympics.

Both Abrahams' and Liddell's triumphs at those Games were famously celebrated in Hugh Hudson's 1981 Oscar-winning film *Chariots of Fire*. Although the film exercised considerable artistic licence in its portrayal of certain events and characters, it did at least serve to stimulate interest in Olympic history and in the careers of these two remarkable men; Abrahams, who was Jewish, and Liddell, a devout Christian.

Born in China into a family of missionaries in 1902, Liddell's athletic prowess had first been spotted as a schoolboy at Eltham College in Mottingham, London. He continued to develop at Edinburgh University, whilst also playing rugby for Scotland and preaching in his spare time. At the 1924 Olympics he won a bronze in the 200m, but more impressively took the gold in the 400m, an event he chose to enter only because the heats for his preferred distance, 100m, were being held on a Sunday.

Liddell gave up competitive athletics in 1925 to concentrate on missionary work. This took him back to China, where he was interned by the Japanese in 1943 and where he died, in Weihsien Camp, in July 1945.

In addition to *Chariots of Fire*, Liddell's memory has been honoured by the naming of a sports centre after him at **Eltham College**, where there is a bronze sculpture by Emma Power (*right*). The **University of Edinburgh** has an identical bronze, together with a display of his Olympic medals, including the one seen above right. Also in Edinburgh is the Eric Liddell Centre, run by a Christian charity whose website features numerous photographs and artefacts from his short, but inspirational life.

▲ **Tommy Green** (1894–1975) was an unlikely Olympic champion. As a child he suffered from rickets. During the First World War he was gassed once and wounded three times. After the war he worked at the Eastleigh Railway Works in Hampshire, and did not take up sport until the age of 32. But he soon made up for it.

Competing for the south London club Belgrave Harriers as a long distance race walker, Green chalked up triumphs in various inter-city races, including the London-to-Brighton and the Nottingham-to-Birmingham. But chiefly he is remembered for becoming the oldest individual ever to win an Olympic gold in race walking when, in the unrelenting heat of a Californian summer, he came from behind to win the 50km race at Los Angeles in 1932. He was then 38 years old.

After that Green became a publican back in Eastleigh, but remained active in race walking and other sports. After his death a road in Eastleigh was named after him (*right*) and appropriately too, given his chosen event.

Street names on housing estates are often themed, but it is rare to find a sporting theme, as at the Wood End estate, built in the 1980s on part of the Sudbury Hill sports ground of J Lyons & Co, where nine hockey ties were staged in the 1948 Games.

Running through the estate is Lilian Board Way. Brought up in nearby Ealing, Board died tragically of cancer only two years after winning a silver medal in the 400m at the 1968 Olympics.

Other athletes named at Wood End are Chris Brasher (a gold medallist in 1956 and founder of the London Marathon), Roger Bannister (of four minute mile fame), David Hemery (a medallist in 1968 and 1972) and Mary Peters (who won gold in 1972).

Also commemorated are footballers Stanley Matthews, Alf Ramsey and Eddie Hapgood, cricketers Harold Larwood and Alec Bedser, and broadcaster Peter Dimmock; an eclectic if somewhat random mix, given that, Board apart, none had any links with the area.

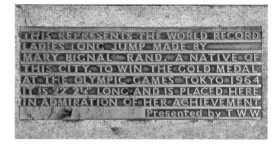

In contrast to the seemingly arbitrary naming of streets on a west London estate, this commemoration of an Olympian feat in the **Market Place** at **Wells**, in **Somerset**, is both appropriate and extraordinarily inspiring.

Born and raised in Wells, at the 1964 Games in Tokyo **Mary Rand** became the first female British athlete to win an Olympic gold medal in a track and field event. Aged 24 at the time and instantly dubbed 'the Golden Girl', Rand also won a silver medal in the pentathlon and a bronze in the 4 x 100m relay. But it was her final leap in the long jump that earned her the most plaudits. It measured 6.76 metres, but, unsure what this meant in feet and inches, Rand had to grab a programme to work out that she had in fact broken the world record.

In imperial units her effort amounted to 22 feet and 2¼ inches. As later reported in *The Sunday Times,* when that same distance was measured out on the floor of Buckingham Palace during Rand's visit, shortly after the 1964 Games, the then four year old Prince Andrew was reported to have exclaimed, 'Nobody could jump that far!'

Rand's success brought other rewards. In an age when live television broadcasts were beaming the Olympics into an increasing number of British homes, she was voted BBC Sports Personality of the Year in 1964, and the following year awarded an MBE.

And if ever there was an award for the simplest and most effective method of marking a great sporting achievement, this one would surely be a contender.

▶ While Britain may not have the right climate to stage the event, it has enjoyed some success at the Winter Olympics. Sculpted by Stanley Taub, this bronze figure of the balletic, Birmingham-born **John Curry** was unveiled at the **National Ice Centre** in **Nottingham** in 2001, seven years after the skater's death from AIDS at the age of 44.

Curry took up skating at the age of seven. Obliged to work in a supermarket and as a receptionist in order to pay for his training, in 1976 he eventually won an Olympic gold at Innsbruck, along with the British, European, and World titles. Made an OBE and voted the BBC's Sports Personality of the Year, also in 1976, Curry was Britain's first openly gay Olympian.

One reason for the National Ice Centre being in Nottingham is that the city was the base of two other Olympians, **Jayne Torvill** (born 1957) and **Christopher Dean** (born 1958), who together captured the world's imagination at the 1984 Winter Olympics in Sarajevo with their interpretation of Ravel's *Bolero* – a performance that not only won the gold but also received the highest score possible for artistic impression. That same year they too were awarded OBEs and voted the BBC's Sports Personalities of the Year.

Nottingham has since honoured the duo by naming streets after them, and Bolero, in the suburb of Wollaton. When the National Ice Centre opened in 2000, the area in front of it was also renamed Bolero Square. Fittingly, Torvill and Dean were the first skaters on the ice.

Built in 1967 on the edge of Wormwood Scrubs, half a mile from White City, the West London Stadium was renamed the Linford Christie Outdoor Sports Centre in 1993. This was to mark the gold winning run of Christie – a member of the Thames Valley Harriers, who are based at the stadium – in the men's 100m race at Barcelona the previous year.

Only two British sprinters had achieved this before; Harold Abrahams in 1924 and Alan Wells in 1980. Aged 32 at the time, Christie was also the oldest male gold medallist recorded at this distance.

In 1993 he was voted BBC Sports Personality of the Year, and in 1998 awarded an OBE. However, a year later Christie tested positive for nandrolone, and even though a British Athletics Federation enquiry later cleared him, he received a lifetime ban from the British Olympic Association. Thus, while young athletes train at the stadium bearing his name, Christie himself has been all but ostracised from the preparations for 2012.

▲ With four gold medals and one silver to his name from the 2004 and 2008 Olympics, Scotland's most successful Olympian of all time, track cyclist **Sir Chris Hoy** – voted BBC Sports Personality of the Year in 2008 and knighted the year after – was given the **Edinburgh Award** in 2009.

Following on from previous winners, novelists Ian Rankin and JK Rowling, part of this award involved the making a mould of his handprints to be displayed in the quadrangle outside Edinburgh's City Chambers.

For Hoy, who grew up in the city, studied at the University and is a member of the City of Edinburgh Racing Club, the award meant a great deal. But it was only one of several. Also in 2009, over in Glasgow, work started on the Sir Chris Hoy Velodrome, destined for action during the 2014 Commonwealth Games, while in same year Hoy became the first sportsman to have a British Airways plane, a Boeing 767, named after him.

From planes to trains, one of Hoy's co-riders in the team sprint at Beijing, **Jamie Staff**, was himself honoured in 2009 (*above left*), when a high speed Javelin train bearing his name was unveiled by Southeastern, the rail operator based in his home county of Kent. Eleven other trains in the fleet were named after Olympians, including Daley Thompson, Duncan Goodhew, Steve Blackley, Ben Ainslie, Katherine Grainger, Dames Tanni Grey-Thompson and Kelly Holmes, and Rebecca Adlington.

▲ Born in Mansfield in 1989, Rebecca Adlington personifies the acclaim, but also the pressures heaped upon modern Olympians. She was first taken to her local pool – built by the Miners Welfare Fund in 1934 and originally called the **Sherwood Colliery Baths** – at the age of four. From there she graduated to the Nova Centurion Swimming Club in Nottingham, before grabbing the headlines as a 19 year old at the Beijing Olympics in 2008.

By winning both the 400 and 800 metres freestyle she became Britain's first female swimmer to win gold since 1960, and the first British swimmer to win more than one gold at an Olympics since Henry Taylor in 1908.

Feted upon her return to Mansfield with an open-top bus parade and a civic reception, almost overnight Adlington became a national figure, in demand for public appearances, endorsements and by the media. Amongst several honours to come her way, in 2009 she was awarded an OBE, before in February 2010, after a £5 million refurbishment, the Sherwood Baths were re-named in her honour.

By any standards these achievements would be deemed impressive. Yet amidst a constant round of commitments, Adlington has chosen to remain entirely focused; a celebrity, but one with a strict training regime that, for the time being at least, must come first.

It is not easy, being a modern Olympian.

Last but not least, the most prominent British Olympian of the modern era is Sir Steve Redgrave, whose commanding statue, sculpted by Neale Andrew, was unveiled by the Queen in 2002. Located in Higginson Park and funded by public subscription, the statue looks out over the stretch of the Thames where, as a member of Marlow Rowing Club, Redgrave honed his skills.

Redgrave's medal haul, from five consecutive Olympics between 1984 and 2000, numbers one bronze and five golds.

To this we must add an MBE, a CBE, BBC Sports Personality of the Year in 2000 and a knighthood in 2001. He is also a vice president of the BOA, for whom he played an active role in the bid for the London Games of 2012.

Meanwhile, a second statue of Redgrave is to be found at the River and Rowing Museum, Henley, where he is depicted alongside his rowing partner Matthew Pinsent (himself knighted in 2004). The pair also have a rowing lake named after them in Oxfordshire.

No doubt Redgrave will achieve more in years to come, on dry land if not on the water. For as the stories of such individuals as Lord Burghley and Lord Coe remind us, once an Olympian, always an Olympian.

Chapter Thirteen

Legacy

Now some two thousand years old, the familiar figure of Discobolus – one of the British Museum's most distinctive treasures – helps to spread knowledge of the ancient Olympics as part of an exhibition staged in Shanghai, shortly before the 2008 Olympics in Bejing. But can Britain do more on its own doorstep to increase awareness of our unique contribution to the Olympic story?

Compared with London's previous Olympic Games in 1908 and 1948, for which, as we have seen, no provisions were made concerning any form of meaningful legacy, the organisers of the Games of the 30th Olympiad have placed a great deal of emphasis on ensuring that the benefits to east London and to Britain as a whole extend well beyond 2012.

But as academics, politicians and media commentators have argued, since 'legacy' in the Olympic context emerged as a concept in the latter decades of the 20th century – becoming in the process embedded within the IOC's requirements for bidding cities – the term has been invested with numerous meanings. Much has depended on the place, the time and the priorities of those charged with its delivery.

As far as London is concerned, of the various initiatives concerning legacy provision for 2012, undoubtedly the most significant is the setting up in May 2009 of the Olympic Park Legacy Company (OPLC), whose task it is to oversee the post-Games development of the 250 acre site that, from mid 2013, will become officially known as the Queen Elizabeth Olympic Park.

Given the current uncertainties facing the national economy and inevitable shifts in future political and social priorities, it is of course hard to predict exactly how closely the OPLC will be able to achieve all its goals. The proposed use of the Olympic Stadium by a professional football club, for example, raises issues that, in this country at least, have never been faced before (most notably the question of how fans will adapt to viewing matches in a venue designed primarily for athletics).

On the other hand, by its very existence and by its retention of statutory powers the OPLC holds out the promise that the planning opportunities lost after 1908, as a result of the piecemeal break up of the Franco-British Exhibition site, and also after 1924, following the Empire Exhibition at Wembley, are less likely to be repeated.

Meanwhile, a second body, the Legacy Trust UK, has allocated £40 million towards four national and twelve regional grassroots programmes in the fields of sport, culture and education, again to ensure that the benefits of staging the Games are not confined to 2012, or to the London area alone.

Amidst these and other initiatives – too many to list in

total – it is however important to bring into the equation one further issue, that of heritage, and more specifically to ask how an appreciation of Britain's wider Olympic heritage might form part of the legacy of the 2012 Games.

This book, we hope, will help to inform that debate.

Collections and archives

Above all, the approach of London 2012 has brought into focus how scattered our national stock of Olympic-related collections and archives are across a range of institutions and locations. In addition it has raised concerns that, for a variety of reasons, not all the relevant archives are as accessible to researchers as might otherwise be desirable.

Whilst interest in the Olympics remains at its current heightened level, these concerns need to be addressed in order to ensure that the study of Britain's Olympic history will continue to attract the attention of scholars and academics beyond 2012.

One example of how disparate public collections have been brought together in an accessible format is the *Winning Endeavours* website, launched in March 2011 by Archives for London, the British Library and the London Metropolitan Archives, with funding from the Heritage Lottery Fund. This contains some 1,700 items from 25 repositories in London and the south east. Regrettably however, without further funding the site is not expected to remain live after December 2012.

Also meriting support beyond 2012 and, lest we forget, the 2014 Commonwealth Games in Glasgow, is the work of the Sports Heritage Network, whose now well established programme of touring exhibitions, entitled *Our Sporting Life*, has done so much to extend knowledge of Britain's Olympic and sporting heritage.

The same hope extends to the ongoing efforts of various parties to catalogue and make available archives relating to the Stoke Mandeville Games and the formative years of the Paralympics.

In relation to the archiving of the 2012 Games, the following initiatives are worthy of note.

Firstly, there is the Olympic Games Knowledge Management programme, administered by the International Olympic Committee. Launched during the preparations for the 2000 Olympics in Sydney, this requires that all raw data and documentation relating to the bidding process and to the organisation and management of every Summer and Winter Games is lodged with the IOC, for the benefit of future bid cities.

This 'Transfer of Knowledge' process, as it is known, also allows for the cities concerned to lodge extracts from that material in a locally accessible archive.

In a parallel initiative, as part of its wider programme called UK Web Archive (which incidentally includes the *Played in Britain* website), the British Library has, since April 2010, undertaken the task of archiving as much written and web-based material relating to the 2012 Games as possible. This archiving will include historical works, critical commentaries, personal blogs and testimonies, such as those published by the University of East London on its *East London Lives 2012* website.

A third initiative is *The Record*, a project run by the National Archives and the Museums, Libraries and Archives Council, which seeks to collect Olympic material from various government and institutional sources and make it publicly accessible through a web portal.

In short, the 2012 Olympics are destined to become the most comprehensively archived Games in history.

An Olympic 'Hall of Sport' or museum

Echoing the dispersion of Olympic-related archives is the spread of artefacts relating to Olympic history. Many of these artefacts have a particular relevance to their locality, for example those pertaining to rowing at the River and Rowing Museum in Henley and to the Wenlock Olympian Games at Much Wenlock. The question is, should a nation whose capital is about to stage its third Olympic Games have a museum of its own, or at least a form of post-Games visitor centre with some historical content?

Apart from the main IOC Museum in Lausanne, opened in 1993, there are now Olympic museums, or museums with a strong Olympic theme, in around 75 cities. These include the former host cities of Amsterdam, Helsinki, Seoul, Barcelona and Atlanta, but also non-host cities such as Thessaloniki, Cologne, Wellington and Xiamen.

As far as London 2012 is concerned, plans for a 'Hall of Sport' within an 'Olympic Institute' were mooted as part of the legacy proposals back in November 2004. We earnestly support any deliberations that might bring those plans to fruition. Whatever the eventual building is called, there should be a permanent Olympic presence within the Queen Elizabeth Olympic Park.

Such a presence, as well as providing a link between the events of 2012 and the site itself, would not only complement the capital's more specialised sports museums at Twickenham, Lord's and Wimbledon, but could also offer temporary exhibition space for Olympic-

related holdings held elsewhere. The collection of the BOA especially deserves to be seen by a wider audience.

In addition, despite the misgivings that many sports historians have concerning the concept, some form of Hall of Fame in such a centre might supplement the commemorations featured in the previous chapter.

On which subject, we note that at the time of writing one of the names proposed for one of the five residential districts being built within the Queen Elizabeth Olympic Park is 'Redgravia'. Splendid though this would be, a visitor centre with historical content could add balance by celebrating many of our earlier, lesser known Olympians.

To conclude, just as a puppy is not just for Christmas, so the Olympics should not be of interest only once every four years, or only when they come to these shores.

Nor should we forget our history. Britannia's engagement with Olympia started not with 2012, nor even with 1948 or 1908. It goes all the way back to 1612 and to the works of Shakespeare.

That is the full measure of our Olympic heritage. That is why heritage should form such an integral part of how the legacy of 2012 is passed on to future generations.

Whatever historians may argue, Britain's Olympic heritage is often best served by the actions of our Olympians – men such as Tommy Godwin, seen here in 2011 at the Herne Hill Velodrome, with the vest that he wore and the two bronze medals he won on this same track in 1948. Aged 90, Godwin has never ceased to be an Olympian in thought or deed, always willing to attend events and support the cause. But as someone who ran a cycle shop in Birmingham for many years after retiring from the track, Godwin also argues that without facilities there can be no future Olympians, which is why he, and many others, believe that one of the best possible legacies from 2012 will be the securing of Herne Hill's future.

At the launch of the Herne Hill Velodrome Trust in February 2011, the MP for the Herne Hill area, former Olympics Minister Tessa Jowell, said, 'It is incredibly important to honour Olympic history when you are about to be an Olympic city.'

Of course we should be judged as a nation by our medal tally in 2012. But we must also be judged on how we guard our heritage, and put it to good use for the future Tommy Godwins of this world.

Links

Where no publisher listed assume self-published by organisation or author

Abbreviations:
BOA British Olympic Association
IJHS International Journal of the History of Sport
IOC International Olympic Committee
IRSS International Review for the Sociology of Sport
UP University Press

The Olympic Games and sport general
Anthony D *Minds, Bodies and Souls: An anthology of the Olympic Heritage Network* BOA (1995–99)
Anthony D *Minds, Bodies and Souls: An A-Z* BOA (1995–99)
Anthony D Minds, *Bodies and Souls: An Archaeology* BOA (1995–99)
Coubertin P de *Olympism: Selected Writings* IOC (2000)
Findling J & Pelle K (eds) *Historical Dictionary of the Olympic Movement* Greenwood Press (1996)
Findling J & Pelle K (eds) *Encyclopedia of the Modern Olympic Movement* Greenwood Press (2004)
Girginov V (ed) *The Olympics: a critical reader* Routledge (2010)
Girginov V & Parry J *The Olympic Games Explained* Routledge (2005)
Gold J & Gold M (eds) *Olympic Cities: city agendas, planning and the World's Games, 1896–2012* Routledge (2007)
Hill C *Olympic Politics* Manchester UP (1996)
Hobsbawm E & Ranger T (eds) *The Invention of Tradition* Cambridge UP (1983)
Holt R *Sport and the British: A Modern History* Oxford UP (1989)
Lovesey P *The Official Centenary History of the Amateur Athletic Association* Guinness Superlatives (1979)
MacAloon J *This Great Symbol: Pierre de Coubertin and the Origins of the Modern Olympic Games* University of Chicago Press (1981)
Martin D & Gynn R *The Olympic Marathon* Human Kinetics (2000)
Segrave J & Chu D (eds) *The Olympic Games in Transition* Human Kinetics (1988)
Timmers M *A Century of Olympic Posters* V & A Museum (2008)
Toohey K & Veal AJ *The Olympic Games: a social science perspective* CAB International Publications (2000)
Wallechinsky D *The Complete Book of the Olympics* Aurum (2008)
Wimmer M *Olympic Buildings* Edition Leipzig (1976)
Young D *The Modern Olympics: A Struggle for Revival* Johns Hopkins UP (1996)

Chapter 1. Introduction
Cochrane A, Peck J & Tickell A *Manchester plays the games: exploring the local politics of globalisation* Urban Studies 33 (1996)
National Archives, London: AT 60/102: Proposed 1984 Olympic Games in London Docklands; AT 60/156: Proposed hosting of the 1988 Olympic Games in Britain; AT 60/161: London bid for 1988 Olympic Games: development of facilities; INF 12/1261: Manchester's Olympic bid to the International Olympic Committee to host the Olympic Games in the year 2000

Chapter 2. Olympia and Britannia
Berenger Lt Col Baron de *Helps and Hints: How to Protect Life and Property* T Hurst (1835)
Chandler R *Travels in Asia Minor, and Greece: or, An Account of a Tour made at the Expense of the Society of the Dilettanti* (3rd edition) Joseph Booker & R Priestley (1817)
Coubertin P *The Olympic Games of 1896* The Century Magazine (November 1896)
Credland A *Charles Random, Baron de Berenger, inventor, marksman and proprietor of the Stadium* Arms & Armour, vol 3 (2006)
D'Ewes S *College Life in the Time of James the First: as illustrated by an unpublished diary of Sir Symonds D'Ewes, Baronet* Kessinger (2009)
Glanfield J *Earls Court and Olympia* Sutton (2003)
Herodotus *The Histories* Penguin (2003)
Homer *The Iliad* Penguin (1992)
Kyrieleis H *The German excavations at Olympia: an introduction* in Phillips DJ and Pritchard D (eds) *Sport and Festival in the Ancient Greek World* Classical Press of Wales (2003)
Lancaster O *Classical Landscape with Figures* John Murray (1947)
Pausanias *Description of Greece* Loeb (1989)
Pindar *The Odes* Penguin (1969)
Pollard J *The Story of Archaeology in 50 Great Discoveries* Quercus (2007)
Shakespeare W *The Complete Works* Oxford UP (2005)
Swaddling J *The Ancient Olympic Games* British Museum Press (2004)
Spivey N *The Ancient Olympics* Oxford UP (2004)
www.britishmuseum.org

Chapter 3. Cotswold Olimpick Games
Bearman CJ *The end of the Cotswold games* Transactions of the Bristol & Gloucestershire Archaeological Society, 114, 131–41, 1996
Brand J *Observations on Popular Antiquities Chiefly Illustrating the Origin of our Vulgar Customs, Ceremonies and Superstitions* Chatto & Windus (1888)
Brome R *A Jovial Crew or, The Merry Beggars* JY for ED & NE(1652)
Burns F *Robert Dover's Cotswold Olympick Games 'Annalia Dubrensia' (1636)* Robert Dover's Games Society (2004)
Burns F *Heigh for Cotswold! A history of Robert Dover's Olimpick Games* (2nd edition) Robert Dover's Games Society (2000)
Burns F *Robert Dover and the Cotswold Olimpick Games* Stuart Press (2000)

Burns F *Robert Dover's Cotswold Olimpicks: the 20th century from the Festival of Britain to the Millennium* Robert Dover's Games Society (2000)

Graves R *The Spiritual Quixote: or, The Summer's Ramble of Mr Geoffry Wildgoose: a comic romance* J Dodsley (1773)

Griffin E *England's Revelry: A History of Popular Sports and Pastimes, 1660–1800* Oxford UP (2005)

Haddon C *The First Ever English Olimpick Games* Hodder & Stoughton (2004)

Somerville W *The Chace, a poem, to which is added Hobbinol, or The Rural Games: a burlesque poem* G Hawkins (1749)

Stubbes P *The Anatomie of Abuses* JR Jones (1583)

Underdown D *Revel, Riot and Rebellion: Popular Politics and Culture in England 1603–1660* Oxford UP (1986)

Verey D & Brooks A *Pevsner Architectural Guides: Gloucestershire* Yale UP (1999)

Walbancke M *Annalia Dubrenisa upon the yeerely celebration of Mr Robert Dover's Olimpick Games upon Cotswold-Hills* (1636)

Whitfield C *A History of Chipping Campden and Captain Robert Dover's Olimpick Games* Shakespeare Head Press (1958)

Williams J *The Curious Mystery of the Cotswold Olympic Games: did Shakespeare know Dover, and does it matter?* Sport in History, Vol 29, No 2 (June 2009)

www.chippingcampdenhistory.org.uk

www.olimpickgames.co.uk

Chapter 4. Wenlock Olympian Games

Beale C *Born out of Wenlock, William Penny Brookes and the British origins of the modern Olympics* DB Publishing (2011)

Bellamy V *A History of Much Wenlock* Shropshire Books (2001)

Furbank M, Cromarty H, McDomald G & Cannon C *William Penny Brookes and the Olympic Connection* Wenlock Olympian Society (2007)

Gaydon AT *Athletics* in Pugh RB (ed) *A History of Shropshire* Institute of Historical Research (1973)

Mullins S *British Olympians: Willam Penny Brookes and the Wenlock Games* Birmingham Olympic Council / BOA (1986)

Newman J *Pevsner Architectural Guides: Shropshire* Yale (2006)

Norrey M *Much Wenlock Windmill* Ellingham Press (2010)

Opinions of Eminent Men on the Importance of Physical Education and Out-Door Gatherings for Healthful Recreation and Athletic Exercises Shropshire Archives (1864)

Shropshire Archives, Shrewsbury: 665/3/1223: Shropshire Olympian Society; 665/4/369: Shrewsbury Show, 1860; 665/4/507: Shrewsbury Show, 1876; DA 5/909/2/2: Shrewsbury Olympics Society, 1890; SA 359: books and documents, 17th, 18th & 19th centuries; 7577/29/14: Scrapbook of Oswestry ephemera

Wenlock Olympian Society minute book and programmes

www.muchwenlock2012.com

www.wenlock-olympian-society.org.uk

www.wpbf.co.uk

Chapter 5. Liverpool Olympic Festivals

Anthony D *Organic Olympism or Olympic Orgy: the routes of modern Olympism and the mystery of John Hulley* Journal of Olympic History (Winter 2001)

Melly E *Memoirs to Charles Melly* Curtis & Beamish (1889)

Phillips R *The Liverpool Olympic Festivals of the 1860s* North of England Athletic Association (nd)

Physick R *Played in Liverpool: charting the heritage of a city at play* English Heritage (2007)

Rees R *The Olympic festivals of mid-Victorian Britain* Olympic Review (1977)

Rees R *The Development of Physical Recreation in Liverpool in the 19th Century* MA Thesis, Liverpool University (1968)

Ruhl J & Keuser A *The History of the Liverpool Olympics in 19th Century England* Deutsche Sportochschule Köln (1989)

www.johnhulleymemorialfund.co.uk

www.liverpoolmonuments.co.uk

www.noeaa-athletics.org.uk

Chapter 6. National Olympian Games

Anthony D *The National Olympian Triumvirate: the third man* Journal of Olympic History (2001)

Cherry B & Pevsner N *Pevsner Architectural Guides: London 4: North* Yale UP (1998)

Foster A *Pevsner Architectural Guides: Birmingham* Yale UP (2005)

National Olympian Association programme 1866 London Metropolitan Archives 26/1

Ravenstein E & Hulley J *A Handbook of Gymnastics and Athletics* (1867)

Ravenstein E & Hulley J *The Gymnasium and its fittings: being an illustrated description of gymnastic apparatus, covered and open-air gymnasia* (1867)

www.kingscrosscentral.com/gg_history

Chapter 7. Morpeth Olympic Games

A Portrait of Morpeth Through the Ages Castlecross Productions / Northern Heritage

Coubertin P *The Olympic Games of 1896* The Century Magazine (November 1896)

Metcalfe A *Leisure and Recreation in a Victorian Mining Community: The Social Economy of Leisure in North-East England, 1820–1914* Routledge (2006)

Moffatt F *Turnpike Road to Tartan Track: a history of professional footrunning on Tyneside 1850 to 1970* (1979)

Pearson L *Played in Tyne and Wear: charting the heritage of people at play* English Heritage (2010)

Tweddle AH *Town Trail for Morpethians: Nos. 3 & 5* Northumberland County Library Service (2008)

Northumberland Collections Service, Woodhorn: NRO 04677, 01565 & 2639/D/27: Morpeth Olympic Games programmes; NRO 02865: Morpeth Olympic Games, newspaper extracts

Chapter 8. Coubertin and the British

Anthony D *Coubertin, Britain and the British: a chronology* Journal of Olympic History (1997)

Coubertin P de & Philemon TJ *The Olympic Games in 1896* Grevel (1897)

Coubertin P de *Une Campaigne de vingt-et-un ans (1887–1908)* Librairie de l'Education Physique, Paris (1909)

Coubertin P de *Olympic Memoirs* Bureau International de Pedagogie Sportive (1932) with later translations in English, IOC (1979, 1997)

Gillmeister H ed *From Bonn to Athens – Single and Return; the Diary of John Pius Boland, Olympic Champion Athens 1896* Academia Verlag (2008)

Hughes T *Tom Brown's School Days* Macmillan (1869)

Loland S *Coubertin's ideology of Olympism from the perspective of the history of ideas* Olympika (1995)

Mandell R *The First Modern Olympics* Souvenir Press (1976)

Smith M *Olympics in Athens 1896: The Invention of the Modern Olympic Games* Profile (2004)

Taine H *Notes on England* Henry Holt (1885)

Weiler I *The predecessors of the Olympic movement, and Pierre de Coubertin* European Review (2004)

www.coubertin.ch

www.coubertin-awards.org.uk

Chapter 9. London Olympic Games 1908

Baker K *The 1908 Olympics* SportsBooks (2008)

Bryant J *The Marathon Makers* John Blake (2008)

Cook T *The Fourth Olympiad, being the Official Report of the Olympic Games in 1908* British Olympic Council (1908)

Farey H *Marathon Measurement: Myths and Mysteries* Track Stats Vol 45, No 4 (2007)

Grant P *The 1908 Olympic Games in Brent* Wembley History Society/Brent Archives Report (March/April 2008)

Hawthorn FH & Price R *The Soulless Stadium, A Memoir of London's White City* 3-2 Books (2001)

Jenkins R *The First London Olympics 1908* Piatkus (2008)

Kent G *Olympic Follies: The Madness and Mayhem of the 1908 London Games* JR Books (2008)

Knight D *The Exhibitions, Great White City 1908–1978* Barnard & Westwood (1978)

McKelvie R *The Queen's Club Story 1886–1986* Stanley Paul (1986)

Mallon B & Buchanan I *The 1908 Olympic Games: results for all competitors in all events, with commentary* McFarland (2000)

Polley M *From Windsor Castle to White City: the 1908 Olympic Marathon Route* London Journal (2009)

Widlund T *Ethelbert Talbot – His Life and Place in Olympic History* Citius, Altius, Fortius, Vol 2, No 2 (May 1994)

Wilcock R *The 1908 Olympic Games, the Great Stadium and the Marathon – a pictorial record* Society of Olympic Collectors (2008)

Olympic Games of London, 1908 – a complete record The Sporting Life (1908)

National Archives, London: *British Olympic Council minutes*, Copy 1: Copyright Office, Entry forms etc

www.oursportinglife.co.uk

Chapter 10. London Olympic Games 1948

Albrechtsen N & Solanke F *Scarves* Thames & Hudson (2011)

Baker N *The Games that almost weren't: London 1948* in *Critical Reflections on Olympic Ideology* (Centre for Olympic Studies) 1994

Barker P *London 1948* Journal of Olympic History (2006)

Bass H *Glorious Wembley* Guinness Superlatives (1982)

Gordon I & Inglis S *Great Lengths* English Heritage (2009)

Hampton J *The Austerity Olympics: When the Games Came to London in 1948* Aurum (2008)

Kynaston D *Austerity Britain 1945-51* Bloomsbury (2007)

The Official Report of the Organising Committee for the XIV Olympiad Organising Committee for the XIV Olympiad (1948)

Lewis J *From Eton Manor to the Olympics: More Lea Valley Secrets Revealed* Libri (2010)

National Archives, London: T 226/64: Accommodation for competitors and officials at the Olympic Games held in London 1948 T 272/108: Olympic Games Committee 1948; T59/133: Olympic Games: accommodation for competitors and officials; MEPO 2/8026: Olympic Games, 1948 ADM 1/20735: Relay of Olympic Torch from Greece; WO 163/338: Committee on the 1948 Olympic Games

Watt T & Palmer K *Wembley – the Greatest Stage* Simon & Schuster (1998)

Wembley 1923–73 – The Official Wembley Story of Fifty Years Kelly & Kelly (1973)

www.hrr.co.uk

www.savethevelodrome.com

Chapter 11. Stoke Mandeville Games

Bailey S *Athlete First: a history of the Paralympic movement* John Wiley (2008)

Barton S *A Sporting Chance: The History of Special Olympics Great Britain* Special Olympics Great Britain (2008)

Brittan I *The Paralympic Games Explained* Routledge (2010)

Gold JR & Gold MM *Access for all: the rise of the Paralympics within the Olympic movement* Journal of the Royal Society for the Promotion of Health Vol 127, No 3 (2007)

Goodman S *Spirit of Stoke Mandeville* Collins (1986)

Guttmann L *Textbook of Sport for the Disabled* HM+M (1976)

Howe P *The Cultural Politics of the Paralympic Movement* Routledge (2008)

Scruton J *Stoke Mandeville: Road to the Paralympics* Peterhouse Press (1998)

Thomas N & Smith A *Disability, Sport and Society: an introduction* Routledge (2009)

www.paralympic.org

www.poppaguttmanncelebration.org

www.wheelpower.org.uk

Chapter 12. British Olympians

Buchanan I *British Olympians: A Hundred Years of Gold Medallists* Guinness (1991)

http://regharris.co.uk
www.chrishoy.com
www.ericliddell.org
www.english-heritage.org.uk/discover/blue-plaques
www.jamiestaff.com
www.linfordchristie.co.uk
www.matthewpinsent.com
www.olympic.org/athletes
www.rebeccaadlington.co.uk
www.rrm.co.uk
www.steveredgrave.com
www.times-olympics.co.uk
www.torvillanddean.com

Chapter 13. Legacy

The Legacy of the Olympic Games: 1984-2000 IOC Olympic Studies Centre, Autonomous University of Barcelona (November 2002)

www.legacycompany.co.uk
www.legacytrustuk.org
www.uel.ac.uk/ell2012

Newspapers & journals

Architects' Journal, Bell's Life, Bicycling Times, Bucks Advertiser and Aylesbury News, The Builder, Daily Express, Daily Mail, Daily Mirror, Daily News, Derby Mercury, Eddowe's Journal, The Independent, Illustrated London News, Journal of the Institute of Electrical Engineers, Journal of Olympic History, Kingston Guardian, Liverpool Courier, Liverpool Daily Post, Liverpool Mercury, London Review, Morning Post, Morpeth Herald, North Wales Chronicle, Northern Daily Times, The Observer, The Penny Illustrated Paper, Picture Post, Popular Science, The Porcupine, Richmond and Twickenham Times, Shrewsbury Chronicle, Shropshire News, The Sporting Life, Surrey Comet, The Times, The Times Online Digital Archive 1785–1985, Wellington Journal and Shrewsbury News, Western Mail

General websites

www.english-heritage.org.uk
www.bl.uk/sportandsociety
www.gamesmonitor.org.uk
www.insidethegames.biz
www.isoh.org
www.la84foundation.org
www.london2012.com
www.olympic.org
www.oxforddnb.com
www.societyofolympiccollectors.org
www.visionofbritain.org.uk
www.winningendeavours.org

Played in Manchester
Simon Inglis (2004)

Played in Birmingham
Steve Beauchampé and
Simon Inglis (2006)

Played in Liverpool
Ray Physick (2007)

Played in Glasgow
Ged O'Brien (2010)

Played in Tyne and Wear
Lynn Pearson (2010)

Engineering Archie
Simon Inglis (2005)

Liquid Assets
Janet Smith (2005)

Great Lengths
Dr Ian Gordon and
Simon Inglis (2009)

Uppies and Downies
Hugh Hornby (2008)

Played at the Pub
Arthur Taylor (2009)

Future titles

Played in London – charting the heritage of the capital at play
Simon Inglis (2012)
Bowled Over – the bowling greens of Britain Hugh Hornby (2012)
For more information **www.playedinbritain.co.uk**

Credits

games, from the Festival of Britain to the Millennium Robert Dover's Games Society (2000): 31a; Parry NA *The Liverpool Gymnasium* University of Manchester unpublished dissertation (1974): 57

Acknowledgements

The author would like to thank all the individuals and organisations who have helped with the research and production of this book.

At the University of Southampton my thanks go to past and present colleagues who have supported my research, including Gill Clarke, Melanie Nind, Adrian Smith, Joan Tumblety, Candice Williams, Gary Evans, Hazel Brown, Ian Hamilton, Iain Lindsey, Richard Humphrey, John Schulz, Julie Price and Bill Brooks. My students also deserve special thanks for being willing to explore the more obscure byways of Olympic history with me. Anita White and Jennifer Hargreaves also provided support and encouragement.

I have been assisted by the staff of many libraries and archives, and to these custodians of Britain's Olympic heritage and history I extend my thanks: Philippa Bassett (University of Birmingham), Elaine Penn (University of Westminster), Sue Wood (Woodhorn Museum and Northumberland Archives), Mary McKenzie (Shropshire Archives), Raya McGeorge (Fishmonger's Company), Dr Alison Graham (Stoke Mandeville Hospital) and the staff at the British Library, the British Library Newspaper Library, the British Olympic Association, the London Metropolitan Archives, the National Archives, Hampshire Record Office and the public libraries of Hampshire County Council and the London Borough of Richmond. A number of clubs and organisations have been generous with their time and resources. Particular thanks go to Helen Cromarty and Chris Cannon of the Wenlock Olympian Society, who always made me welcome; to the Robert Dover's Games Society, and especially the late Dr Francis Burns, and to Martin McElhatton of WheelPower.

Other historians and individuals who have helped with advice and comments include Don Anthony, Peter Lovesey, Philip Barker and Bob Wilcock (International Society of Olympic Historians), Jimmy Pigden (Auriol Kensington Rowing Club), Prof Alan Davison and Fred Moffatt (Morpeth), Kerry Taylor, David Day, Tom Hunt, Julie Anderson, Frank Galligan, Lynn Pearson, Dilwyn Porter and Alys Key. Thanks also to the British Society of Sports Historians.

It was a pleasure to become a double Olympian during the research for this book, as I ran in both the Wenlock Olympian Games and the Cotswold Olimpicks. Thanks to all the volunteers who work so hard to keep these unique festivals alive.

At English Heritage, my thanks go to Rachel Howard, John Hudson, Robin Taylor, Clare Blick, Mark Fenton, the photography team and to the staff at the National Monuments Record.

In addition, on behalf of English Heritage and the Played in Britain editorial team I would like to thank Major Bob Kelly (Aldershot Military Museum), Simon Welsh (Army Sports Control Board), Stefan Dickers (Bishopsgate Institute), Malcolm Barres-Baker (Brent Archives Service), Judith Swaddling and Anaïs Aguerre (British Museum), Jan Paterson, Amy Terriere and Alice Constance (British Olympic Foundation), Matt Shipton (City University London), Dr Jonathan Oates (Ealing Local History Centre), Fred Spencer (Eton Manor Association), the LOCOG press office, Frank Dobson (and fellow members of Malden Rifle and Pistol Club), Sharon Smith (Missouri History Museum), Mike Mackenzie (Poppa Guttmann Celebration Project), Michael Davison (Friends of Richmond Park), Hettie Ward (River and Rowing Museum), Charlie Addiman (Rosslyn Park RFC), Rusty McLean (Rugby School), Matthew Storey (Victoria and Albert Museum), Villiers Park Educational Trust, Wes Taylor (Wembley Stadium) and also the Rt Rev Paul V Marshall, Rev Canon George C Loeffler and Kat Lehman (Episcopal Diocese of Bethlehem, Pennsylvania).

The following individuals have been of great help: Martyn Day, Dr Ian Gordon, Victoria Herriott, Tim Lever, Eva Loeffler, Jack Murray, Mike Norrey and Stuart Smith.

Finally, I would also like to extend my personal gratitude to my parents, Jean and Brian Polley, for their encouragement and for Dad's inexhaustible knowledge of transport history, and to my brothers, Richard and David. Thanks also to Carole and David Martin and to Rachel and Clive Foster.

At Played in Britain, my thanks go to Simon Inglis, the series editor, who has gone far beyond the call of duty in preparing this book for publication, to Jackie Spreckley for her dogged research and production work, and to Doug Cheeseman for making the book look so good.

Finally, my thanks to James and Ed, who enjoyed going to watch those 'weird Olympics' at Much Wenlock and Chipping Campden. Catherine has been there every step of the way: thanks for everything.

Index

▲ The statue of **Sir John Betjeman** peers up into the magnificent glazed vaults of **St Pancras International Station**, a now treasured Victorian building the poet helped to save during a lifetime of service to the cause of heritage, and which is now temporarily crowned by the familiar five ring emblem of the Olympic Games.

How appropriate that these rings should look down over the platform where rail travellers now alight from Paris, the home of Pierre de Coubertin, founder of the modern Games and also, as it happens, the man credited with first adopting the symbol, in 1913. And also, that just a stone's throw from St Pancras, there stands the German Gymnasium, one of the venues where the first National Olympian Games took place, in 1866.

Researching this book has been a marathon journey, one that has taken me around the country in search of the diverse organisations, events and people that have contributed to Britain's Olympic history and heritage.

It is a story that started in 1612. As I approach the finishing line, I for one cannot wait for the next chapter to unfold at London 2012.

Martin Polley, June 2011